The Brookwood Killers

The Brookwood Killers

Military Murderers of WWII

Paul Johnson

FRONTLINE BOOKS

First published in Great Britain in 2022 by
Frontline Books
An imprint of
Pen & Sword Books Ltd
Yorkshire – Philadelphia

Copyright © Paul Johnson 2022

ISBN 978 1 39901 182 2

Typeset by Mac Style
Printed and bound in the UK by CPI Group (UK) Ltd,
Croydon, CR0 4YY.

MIX
Paper from
responsible sources
FSC
www.fsc.org   FSC® C013604

Pen & Sword Books Limited incorporates the imprints of Atlas,
Archaeology, Aviation, Discovery, Family History, Fiction, History,
Maritime, Military, Military Classics, Politics, Select, Transport,
True Crime, Air World, Frontline Publishing, Leo Cooper, Remember
When, Seaforth Publishing, The Praetorian Press, Wharncliffe
Local History, Wharncliffe Transport, Wharncliffe True Crime
and White Owl.

For a complete list of Pen & Sword titles please contact

PEN & SWORD BOOKS LIMITED
47 Church Street, Barnsley, South Yorkshire, S70 2AS, England
E-mail: enquiries@pen-and-sword.co.uk
Website: www.pen-and-sword.co.uk

Or

PEN AND SWORD BOOKS
1950 Lawrence Rd, Havertown, PA 19083, USA
E-mail: Uspen-and-sword@casematepublishers.com
Website: www.penandswordbooks.com

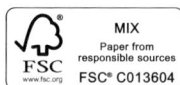

Contents

Acknowledgements   vii

Introduction   viii

Chapter 1   Crime in Wartime, 1939–45   1

Chapter 2   Execution and Commemoration   5

Chapter 3   The Brookwood Memorial, 1939–45   10

Chapter 4   Scrgeant Ernest Charles Digby – The Baby Killer   12

Chapter 5   Gunner Ernest James Harman Kemp – The
                 Cabbage Patch Murder   29

Chapter 6   Corporal Hassan Naameh Medlish – A General
                 Court Martial   39

Chapter 7   Private Cyril Johnson – A Question of Proof   51

Chapter 8   Lance Corporal Walter Clayton – The Morecambe
                 Beach Strangler   60

Chapter 9   Private David Miller Jennings – A Murder in the
                 NAFFI   68

Chapter 10   Private Arthur Peach – The Killing of Kitty Lyon   78

Chapter 11   Lance Corporal Frederick James Austin – I Didn't
                 Know it was Loaded!   86

Chapter 12   Private Theodore John William Schurch – I Have
                 Played My Game and Lost Fairly   99

Chapter 13   Private Terence Casey – A Case of Mistaken
                 Identity?   111

Chapter 14 Private John Gordon Davidson – A Skilful
Interrogation 121

Chapter 15 Corporal Dudley George Rayner – Guilty, Sir! 133

Chapter 16 Private Arthur Thompson – Death at the Nags
Head Inn 141

Chapter 17 Bombardier Joseph Howard Grossley – It was the
Germans! 152

Chapter 18 Private August Sangret – The Wigwam Murder 165

Chapter 19 Private Charles Eugene Gauthier – A Light of
Love 177

Chapter 20 Private Horace Beresford Gordon – Got Any Gum
Chum? 186

Chapter 21 Private Mervin Clare McEwan – The Tattooed
Killer 197

Chapter 22 Private Charles Arthur Raymond – A Voluble and
Incessant Talker 204

Chapter 23 Gunner Kenneth Charles Sydney Prior –
A Disgraceful Death 218

Chapter 24 The Third Man – Killer and Victim 223

Conclusion 231
Sources and Bibliography 232
Index 234

Acknowledgements

My grateful thanks go to the following people, without whose assistance this publication may not have been possible: Doug Banks – Colourising History, Stephen Chambers, Miranda Chumbley, Martin Mace, Suzanne Make, Eve Martin, Robin Matthewman, Jim Maynard, Rebecca Mileham, Winston Ramsay – *After the Battle* magazine, Anneliese Rimmer, Andy Saunders, Kristi Shore, Jim Smithson and Tim Struyf.

Introduction

Firstly, this is a candid book. It does not flinch from the unpleasant, the shameful or the crude and some content may offend modern sensitivities. The combination of true crime and military history may seem an odd mix but, nonetheless, we cannot begin to understand the history of our nation, and its allies, if we do not study all the varying aspects of conflict, including those that some may suggest should be left 'to sleep'. The objective here is simply to supply the reader with the details wherein, during a time when many nations were involved in worldwide conflict, a small minority of the Commonwealth armed forces committed what is considered to be the most heinous of crimes, that of murder, rape and treachery, and whose names are recorded in perpetuity by the Commonwealth War Graves Commission (CWGC). It does not seek to retry the assailants, nor judge their victims, accusers or executioners, yet it may raise an eyebrow regarding the behaviours and attitudes of the period and question the decisions around the ongoing recognition of those members of the armed forces who have been convicted of a serious civil crime.

During the Second World War a large proportion of British and Commonwealth soldiers behaved in an honest and exemplary fashion throughout their period of service. Civil and military courts dealt with frequent examples of criminal acts committed by military personnel, a majority of which were misdemeanours and were dispensed with swiftly, resulting in relatively light penalties. However, there were those whose shocking crimes would lead to the gallows. All of these were driven by a variation of motives, relating to their circumstances and their background. Some because of their environment, culture and experience, some for whom killing may have been a simple solution, and others purely for sadistic pleasure. Lust, jealousy, greed, fear, hate and revenge are deemed to be the most common motives for murder, but they may not always be words you would consider when entering the gates of a Commonwealth military cemetery. The expectation perhaps, particularly for those thousands of people who tour the former battlefields of the world, is that such a visit is the culmination of a journey where, invariably, we seek to pay homage to those who have lost their lives whilst in the service of their country, usually through combat, accident or illness. Often, a more poignant aspect to any such visit, we find ourselves standing before one of the magnificent sprawling memorials, maintained by the CWGC, the panels of which contain the names of those who, having paid the ultimate sacrifice, have no known grave, or whose last resting place cannot be properly maintained. But this is not always the case.

The Brookwood Military Cemetery, located in deepest Surrey, is the largest Commonwealth war cemetery in the United Kingdom, and is beautifully maintained by CWGC. Within its grounds stand 2 splendid memorials dedicated to over 4,000 men and women who, during both the First and Second World Wars, and for varying reasons, have no known grave or whose burial site cannot be preserved. But also listed on their panels are the names of those whose last resting place is very much known and, in most cases, lay within the shores of the United Kingdom. These are the executed, those who were found guilty of a hideous crime and whose bodies lay within the confines of their place of execution. Apart from one individual, their crime is that of murder or rape and in some cases involves the killing of another member of the armed forces. Sadly, incidents such at this occur with great regularity throughout both wars and this area of research has many distressing factors with which some would rather not be associated. Therefore, these assailants and, more importantly, their victims can often be ignored and overlooked. If we are to record the names of the antagonist in such grandeur, then do we not owe it to the victims, even though there may be strong motives for their demise, to bring their stories to the fore?

The scars of these crimes still run deep and during the preparation of this publication, I have endeavoured to contact as many relatives as possible who are linked to the individuals named within the text. This is to ensure that the feelings of the living are given every consideration. In a vast majority of cases, those associated with the victims wish for their story to be aired and, equally, those with a connection to the assailants fully appreciate that this is not an exercise in humiliation, but an attempt to understand the circumstances, the actions and the outcome of a crime in which their relation was involved and how those individuals, by virtue of a national charter, have their names inscribed upon one of the most well-known military memorials in the country.

The cases of the Brookwood Killers are violent, disturbing and often brutal in their content. They are not war crimes, but crimes committed in a time of war, for which the offenders, having been apprehended, tried and executed, have their names recorded and maintained in perpetuity. Something that may not always apply in the case of the victims.

Remember them.

Chapter 1

Crime in Wartime, 1939–45

During the period 1939–45, daily life for the general population of the United Kingdom was often difficult, and crime was afforded the opportunity to flourish. The blackout, air raids, rationing and the influx of Commonwealth and foreign service personnel were just a few of the factors that resulted in reported crimes rising by some 57 per cent across the six years of the Second World War in England and Wales alone. The war also brought with it a vast host of restrictions and rules, which a minority of people chose to break or evade. Whilst the regulating of many different aspects of life offered huge opportunities to fraudsters,

Dances were popular social events with both civilians and service personnel. They were also an ideal haunt for criminals and a hunting ground for rapists and murderers. (*Author's Collection*)

forgers and thieves and helped create a burgeoning black market, there was also a variety of other criminal opportunities, some of which were exclusive to military personnel. The trading of military equipment at a time of great need, or the supplying of arms and ammunition, despite some considerable efforts at imposing stringent controls, remained a significant problem for the British government. The widespread storage and availability of contemporary weapons, combined with those retained from the First World War by both the military and civilian populations, gave rise to increased acts of violence often with fatal consequences.

With cities and towns across the nation plunged into darkness almost every night, a perfect opportunity was provided for some individuals to murder, rape and mutilate. These conditions assisted both men and women in perpetrating crimes, such as robbery, burglary and theft, and social venues, such as dance halls, public houses and cinemas, thrived as civilians and service personnel flocked to escape the grind of daily life, providing assailants with the perfect opportunity to seek out potential victims. The ability to carry arms, particularly knives, combined with an incendiary mix of alcohol, passion and estrangement often became the driving force behind many crimes. Detection was made all the more difficult for a weakened and heavily stretched police force faced with the continual movement of military personnel, the relocation of civilians desperate to escape heavily bombed towns and cities, and the occasional failure of military authorities to fully cooperate with their investigations.

On Sunday, 3 September 1939, the day Britain declared war on Germany, Parliament immediately passed the National Service (Armed Forces) Act, imposing conscription upon all males aged between 18 and 41, which helped greatly to increase the number of men on active service during the first year of the war. Further to this, in December 1941, Parliament passed a second National Service Act, which widened the scope of conscription still further by making all unmarried women and all childless widows between the ages of 20 and 30 liable to call-up. Men were also now required to perform some form of National Service up to the age of 60, which included military service for those under 51. The main reason for this was that there were simply not enough men volunteering for police and civilian defence work, or women for the auxiliary units of the armed forces.

Conscription, however, generated a good deal of disgruntlement amongst drafted civilians as they began a period of basic preparation for military life that included a regime of physical fitness education, discipline and classroom instruction. The combination of strict attitudes that were typical of the service culture of the period, the disappointment of those who were perhaps expecting to be immediately posted to an overseas combat zone and the stationing to dreary wartime locations within the UK, as well as being forcibly separated from loved ones, was to bring about a high level of absence amongst service personnel. Desertion was a commonplace occurrence and was treated, initially, as a minor infraction. Punishments such as confinement to barracks or loss of pay usually deterred those for whom it was a first offence. More persistent offenders saw an incremental rise in the penalties imposed on them, up to and including long-term imprisonment. A minority, with little intention of performing military service under any circumstances, often turned to crime to support their absence and, on occasions, were responsible for the death of civilians and military personnel in their efforts to evade capture. There were those too who were clearly not suited to, or incapable of, meeting with the demands of military service. This was outlined in Parliament when it was demonstrated that between July 1942 and January 1943 of the 203,377 men who joined the British army over 8,000 were recommended for discharge or posting to the Pioneer Corps on psychoneurotic grounds. This was not good news for this arm of the service, as some of its members would soon be committing horrifying crimes that would shock the nation.

Offenders from the British and Commonwealth forces, whilst subject to the conventions of the civil justice system, were frequently eagerly defended in their actions by the military. Often, men who were placed on bail failed to return to the courtrooms on the basis that they had been 'posted overseas'. This is something, when it occurred, that was highly criticised by the judiciary. Equally, it was not uncommon to find charges of murder against a serving member of the military become one of manslaughter, thus negating the death penalty, and their sentences, on occasions, were then shortened in order that they could 'serve the nation'. Not a particularly satisfactory outcome for their victim.

Of the soldiers featured in this book, which is not exhaustive, almost a third were Canadian. It was felt that the treatment of Canadian soldiers in British courts was far harsher than that which they would face at home. Major Maurice Forget, of the Canadian Judge Advocate General's Office, in an extract from the editorial of a Canadian newspaper, drew attention to this, following an execution, and highlighted the plight of Canadian soldiers who faced trials in British courts:

'British Law for Canucks'
We cannot claim to be familiar with all the details of this case or with the legal technicalities involved, but there certainly seems to have been a determination on the part of the British government to apply the full rigour of the law to this Canadian soldier, regardless of the jury's recommendation and regardless of the protest by the Canadian government. We do not know the reasons for this attitude, but it bodes no good for Canadian troops who may get into trouble overseas.

Following the German capitulation in 1945, the population of Britain saw an end to the dangers of air raids and enemy action. The American and other foreign Allied forces departed, and many British servicemen were demobilised. Life began to return to normal but some criminal-friendly wartime conditions lingered. Rationing did not end until 1954, so the black market thrived for a few more years and crime, as always, carried on.

For the Imperial War Graves Commission, later the Commonwealth War Graves Commission, the mammoth task of identifying, classifying and concentrating the war dead for a second time got underway across the globe. Grave Registration Units provided basic details of the individuals, such as name, service number, rank, regiment, unit and date of death, and every effort was made to identify those whose lives had been lost during the period between 3 September 1939 and 31 December 1947. Amongst these were those whose graves had been lost, could not be maintained for geographical or political reasons, or lay in unconsecrated ground. For these, it was decided, their name would be added to an appropriate memorial, such as Brookwood, where they could be maintained in perpetuity and do so today.

Chapter 2

Execution and Commemoration

Throughout the Second World War there were many examples of murder committed by members of the British, Commonwealth and Allied forces. In cases, within the UK, where the assailant was sentenced to death by a civil court, the execution would usually take place in the prison where they had been held during their trial. Wandsworth Prison was most commonly used but executions took place in other provincial prisons such as Bristol, Birmingham, Leeds and Liverpool. Of those listed on the Brookwood Memorial all bar two were hanged for their crime. The majority of these were carried out by Albert Pierrepoint, the well-known English executioner, following guidelines laid down by the Home Office. The principal Home Office executioners and assistants in the United Kingdom during the Second World War were:

- Thomas Pierrepoint, 1906–46
- Thomas Phillips, 1918–41
- Stanley William Cross, 1932–41
- Albert Pierrepoint, 1932–56
- Herbert Morris, 1939–46
- Henry Critchell, 1940–8
- Alexander Riley, 1940–6
- Henry (Harry) Kirk, 1941–50
- Stephen Wade, 1941–55
- Henry Bernard Allen, 1941–64

The hangman and his assistant were required to be at the prison by 4.00 p.m. on the day prior to the execution. Once there, they would be told the height and weight of the prisoner and then look at the prisoner through what was known as the 'Judas hole' in the cell door, to assess their physical features. At a duly appointed time on the day of the execution the hangman, who was in full charge of the proceedings, along with his assistant and two prison officers would enter the condemned man's cell.

The executioners, left to right: Albert Pierrepoint, Steve Wade and Henry 'Harry' Allen.

The prisoner's arms would be secured behind his back with a leather strap, and all five then walked through a second door, which led to the execution chamber. The prisoner was marched to a marked spot on the trapdoor whereupon the hangman placed a white hood over his head and a noose around his neck, whilst the assistant fastened his legs together with a leather strap. The metal eye through which the rope was looped was placed under the left jawbone. The hangman would then step back behind a painted white line, push a large lever, releasing the trapdoor. As the prisoner dropped, the position of the metal eye forced his head back and broke his spine. The neck was broken in almost the same position in each hanging and is known as the 'Hangman's fracture'. It is estimated that from entering the condemned man's cell to opening the trapdoor, on average, took a maximum of 12 seconds.

The Home Office instructions state that the body must be left hanging for one hour before being pulled back up through the trapdoor. The hangman and his assistant were then usually responsible for taking the body down and preparing it for autopsy. They then tidied the gallows, packed away the equipment and were required to sign the Official Secrets Act so as not to divulge any details of the execution to the public or the press. Only then were they free to leave the prison.

The Home Office provided strict instructions regarding burying the bodies of executed prisoners.

1. All the clothing, with the exception of the shirt or similar garment, will be removed from the body which will be placed in a coffin made of half inch wood, deal or pine.
2. The sides and ends of the coffin will be well perforated with large holes.

3. Lime will not be used.
4. The original size of the plot of ground will be 9' × 4', and the grave will be from 8' to 10' in depth.
5. When the coffin has been covered with 1' of earth, charcoal to the depth of 3 inches will be thrown onto the grave, which will then be filled in. The top coffin will be not less then 4' below the ground surface.
6. Arrangements will be made for the gravesites to be reused in sequence, in such wise that no grave shall be used over again until seven years have elapsed. When a grave is reopened the charcoal and the foot of earth above the last coffin will not be disturbed.
7. A register of graves will be kept, containing the name of each convict buried, the date of burial, the sight of the grave, and the position of the coffin in the grave.

Eligibility of Commemoration

The policy for the eligibility of commemoration by the CWGC regarding those who were deserters or judicially executed currently states:

Servicepeople Judicially Executed
We commemorate all serving military personnel who were executed during the First or Second World War:

- following a General Court Martial; or
- after being found guilty of a civil crime.

Deserters
We may commemorate a person considered to be a deserter if there is evidence to show:

- their death occurred whilst in service with another branch of the armed forces or whilst serving with the Merchant Navy and they meet the eligibility criteria for commemoration for that other branch.
- the circumstances of their death provide substantial doubt about their intention to desert; or there are other circumstances to warrant exception e.g., burial having been permitted in good faith by a cemetery authority in a service plot.

The policy for the eligibility seems quite clear, but a question arises concerning how an individual, having been found guilty of murder by a civil court, was discharged from military service prior to their execution, in order that eligibility is denied, and it appears to be a rather haphazard affair. There does not seem to be any clear directive on this point, despite the voluminous contents of the various manuals of military law and guidance on what actions should be taken when it came to the arrest, trial and execution of a member of the armed forces. Both the Royal Air Force and Royal Navy, in the main, opted for a member of their service to be dressed in civilian clothes prior to their execution, in order that the King's uniform was not disgraced. The likes of Gordon Cummins, the Blitz Ripper, Sidney Delasalle, who murdered his instructor, Arthur Heys, who raped and strangled a young WAAF, and Charles Koopman, who murdered an old girlfriend and her child, were all members of the Royal Air Force when their crimes took place but were all executed as civilians, and thus their names are not recorded by the CWGC, despite the fact they were 'serving military personnel' up until the point of execution.

Therefore, their final resting place, located within the prison grounds where their demise took place, does not fall under the care of the CWGC and they are not remembered in perpetuity on any national memorial for which the commission is responsible.

The army, however, under the direction of the War Office, appears to lack any definite structure on the subject. Whilst child killers such as Harold Hill were executed as civilians, the likes of Sergeant Ernest Charles Digby, having been found guilty of a similar crime, remained in uniform and, as a result, were eligible for inclusion in the records of the CWGC war dead. The War Office appears to have concerned itself more with the return of military uniforms and equipment and, consequently, failed to supply any form of civilian dress for those who were due execution. This apparent minor transgression appears to have had a significant impact upon the act of commemoration and, as a result, one of the nation's greatest memorials contains the names of convicted criminals. With regard to the victim, unless they were a serving member of the armed forces, the majority lay in unmarked graves and there is no formal recognition for them. I hope this publication goes some little way to addressing that fact.

In contrast to the British and Commonwealth forces, the US government policy was far more straightforward in relation to cases of convicted murderers and rapists. The body of any member of the American forces who had been killed in either a combat or non-combat role could be returned home or buried within the confines of one of the American military cemeteries that are so carefully tended by the American Battle Monuments Commission, but this was rarely the case for those who were executed. These individuals were simply put to death and buried within their place of execution where, perhaps, they would have remained, had the US government not decided upon one final act of dishonour. In 1949, their bodies were collectively exhumed from their final resting place and buried, anonymously, in a separate plot of an American military cemetery in France, known as Plot E. Their remains, placed with their backs towards the honoured dead of the First World War, are simply marked with a small stone plaque, no larger than a credit card, bearing a grave number. Access to the plot is both difficult and strictly controlled and visitors are highly discouraged. Some, perhaps, would argue that this is the most appropriate way to treat those who have disgraced both their country and their uniform, and is a dignified outcome for the victims of their crimes, even though they too may have an unmarked and isolated resting place.

Chapter 3

The Brookwood Memorial, 1939–45

The following content can be used to form a walking tour around the Brookwood Memorial. The details of each case are listed in panel order, as opposed to chronological or alphabetical order. This is not an exhaustive list, and the reader may be encouraged to study the following cases and explore the events in more finite detail.

Following the end of the Second World War it was determined that where the graves of members of the land forces were unmarked, or could not be maintained, they would be commemorated by means of a memorial relating to a particular campaign such as the Battle of Normandy, a theatre of war such as North Africa or Burma or within certain predetermined dates as with the Dunkirk Memorial. For some, this would be the Brookwood Memorial, designed by Ralph Hobday and unveiled by Queen Elizabeth II on Saturday, 25 October 1958. The panels of the memorial commemorate 3,500 men and women of the land forces of the Commonwealth who have no known grave, the circumstances of their death being such that they could not be appropriately commemorated on any other memorials in the various theatres of war. Some died in smaller campaigns, such as Norway in 1940. Others were lost during raids on enemy occupied territory in Europe such as Dieppe and St Nazaire, or whilst acting as special agents working with Allied underground movements. There are also those men and women of the land forces who died at sea or were killed in flying accidents.

However, the final resting place of a small number is, in fact, known but given that their bodies lie in unconsecrated ground, their names are recorded here. These individuals are those who suffered the fate of a judicial hanging or being shot by a military firing squad. They are the executed and these are their stories.

Chapter 4

Sergeant Ernest Charles Digby –
The Baby Killer

Panel 2. Column 3
Service Number: 1072347
Unit: 200 Battery, 188th Field Regiment, Royal Artillery
Executed: Thursday, 16 March 1944, aged 35

It could be argued that, on occasions, the victim of a murder may have brought about their own demise, but not at 3 weeks old. Dawn Digby was born at 9.30 a.m. on Thursday, 21 October 1943 in Milborne Port, Somerset. Just twenty-five days later, she would die and her tiny body, transported in an attaché case, brutally disposed of in a disused rabbit hole at the edge of a military camp in the heart of Oxfordshire. She had not been the victim of a vile kidnapper or paedophile but had lost her life to one of the people she was most dependent upon, her father, a serving soldier whose job was to defend her in the darkest hours of wartime Britain. Worse still, her death, although quickly discovered, opened the door to a dark tale of deceit and bigamy and revealed that not only had there been another recent child victim, but there had been complicity in its worst form, from the child's mother.

The Assailants

Ernest Charles Digby was born on Saturday, 25 July 1908 in Edmonton, London, the youngest son of Albert Edward and Alice Elizabeth Digby (née Wilson) and one of eight children in total. His father was a nursery gardener and the family lived for a while in Balfour Road. His childhood years, impoverished as many people's were, appear to be quite average for the period, living with his siblings and attending the Raynham Road elementary school in Edmonton. On the completion of his education at

Panel	Column	Rank	Forename(s)	Surname	Age	Date Executed
2	3	Sergeant	Ernest Charles	DIGBY	35	16/03/1944
3	2	Gunner	Ernest James Harman	KEMP	20	06/06/1944
3	3	Gunner	Kenneth Charles Sydney	PRIOR	36	21/12/1941
5	1	Corporal	Hassan Naameh	MEDLISH	19	12/07/1943
10	1	Private	Cyril	JOHNSON	20	15/04/1942
11	1	Lance Corporal	Walter	CLAYTON	22	07/08/1946
12	1	Private	David Miller	JENNINGS	21	24/07/1941
12	1	Private	Arthur	PEACH	23	30/01/1942
16	1	Lance Corporal	Frederick James	AUSTIN	29	30/04/1942
17	1	Driver	Mohamed Musallam	SOULEIMAN	32	24/09/1943
17	3	Private	Theodore John William	SCHURCH	27	04/01/1946
18	2	Private	Terence	CASEY	22	19/11/1943
19	1	Private	John Gordon	DAVIDSON	19	12/07/1944
20	3	Corporal	Dudley George	RAYNER	20	31/03/1943
21	2	Private	Arthur	THOMPSON	34	31/01/1945
23	2	Bombardier	Joseph Howard	GROSSLEY	37	05/09/1945
23	3	Private	August	SANGRET	29	29/04/1943
24	2	Private	Charles Eugene	GAUTHIER	24	24/09/1943
25	1	Private	Horace Beresford	GORDON	25	09/01/1945
25	1	Private	Mervin Clare	McEWAN	35	30/11/1944
25	1	Private	Charles Arthur	RAYMOND	23	10/07/1943

the age of 14, he gained employment as a capstan operator in a local engineering business until June 1927 when he opted to join the army, serving with the Royal Artillery for three years. At this time the country was in the grip of an economic depression but by late 1931 had begun to see a slow recovery from the crisis. On Saturday, 3 October 1931, at Edmonton Registry Office, Ernest married his sweetheart, 20-year-old Violet Amy Gwendoline Thurley. The couple moved into a house in Victoria Road, and it was here that their three sons were initially raised, John (b. 1933), Gordon (b. 1935) and Alan (b. 1937). In 1938, the family moved to a larger home in Hoe Lane, Enfield, and it was here they heard the announcement of the outbreak of war. Ernest was quickly recalled from the Reserve, and after an initial period stationed at Ascot, Surrey, he was posted to the coastal town of Scarborough, Yorkshire, to help form the 39th Signal Training Regiment. Whilst stationed here his family would join him and it would not be long before the hard-working and trustworthy soldier was promoted to sergeant. He remained with this unit when it moved to Bretton Park, Wakefield, and here his troubles began.

Olga Davy Hill, described as a pretty brunette, was born in Scarborough, Yorkshire, on Monday, 11 May 1914, the daughter of Robert and Elsie Charlotte Hill, the second of five children. Her father was a prominent auctioneer and estate agent and the family lived a comfortable life at Garton House, Cromwell Parade. She was educated at Scarborough Council Central School, and after leaving formal education at the age of 14, lived at home with her parents, not entering any form of employment until she was 20 years old. In June 1934, she began work at Field's, a bakers and confectioners situated in St Thomas Street, Scarborough, where she remained until September 1940. It was at this time, with coastal towns appearing to be very vulnerable to attack from both the air and sea, that her father took up employment in Wakefield. Olga moved with her parents and took a job as a manageress with Charles Hagenbach, a confectionery and grocercy business in the town. In all the time she was in employment, Olga was described as a very satisfactory employee and there does not seem to have been any complaint about her behaviour.

One evening in November 1940, Ernest Digby attended a sergeants' dance in the village hall at Bretton, where he met Olga Davy Hill. The couple seemed to really like one another and an intimate relationship quickly developed, even though Digby's family was living with him. Some animosity developed between husband and wife and in January 1941, Violet Digby returned to London with the couple's children, most likely having become aware of what was going on. By now, Olga knew that Ernest was married and had a family, but they continued their affair. He rented a flat with her and they began to live as man and wife. In May 1941, Olga's parents moved to a house in Sherriff Road, West Hampstead, London, and she left Hagenbach's employment claiming she was moving with them, which was not true. What appeared to be a very close relationship with her parents now began to grow distant, and she would write to them intermittently. At one time she explained that she and 'Dig', as she called him, were married, even though they were not. Indeed, this was their plan, but Violet Digby had flatly refused to give Ernest a divorce.

As the war progressed, Digby started to move around the country. By the end of 1941 he was stationed at Sittingbourne, Kent. Olga found lodgings in the area and the couple seemed to have become settled in their relationship, despite the continued upheaval of movement and the growing financial strains he faced in maintaining both her and his family. However, it was not too long before their troubles really began, when Olga discovered she was pregnant.

A Child is Born

According to Digby, his unit moved to the coastal town of Broadstairs, where the couple rented a room together, but the unit was soon relocated to St Nicholas at Wade a few miles away. Olga remained in Broadstairs and, desperate to rid themselves of a further financial burden, the couple made several attempts to abort the baby, however their efforts failed and on Monday, 18 May 1942 the sound of a new-born infant could be heard at a house in Northdown Road. Olga had given birth to the couple's first child, Doreen Digby. One perhaps wonders why he chose to register the birth, given that he may already have had a plan for her disposal, and that fact that Olga made it clear she had no intention of acknowledging the child's existence.

When Doreen was just a fortnight old, Digby told Olga that he was going to have her adopted. She claimed they took a day trip to Margate, where he left her in the street and took Doreen away. Olga always maintained that

Digby was only gone for about 15 minutes, and she had never seen the baby since that day, nor did she know who had adopted her. Digby, however, had a different story to tell. He stated that on Monday, 1 June 1942, they took Doreen for a walk between Broadstairs and St Nicholas at Wade with the intention of finding lodgings for his bigamous wife and abandoning the baby. They were 'in a daze as to what to do' and he recalled having the baby with them when they left Broadstairs but by the time they reached St Nicholas at Wade, she was not there, and he could not recall why. He had taken a room at the home of a lady named Mrs West but soon after Olga moved in, his unit relocated again. This time to the village of Ripple, a little further down the Kent coast. Again, he found lodgings for Olga but by October 1942 both the unit and the couple had returned to Broadstairs.

Dawn Digby – A Plan

On the 27 December 1942, Digby was posted to another unit, No. 200 Battery, 188th Field Regiment, which formed part of the 38th (Welsh) Infantry Division. Then, the worst possible news occurred in January 1943, Olga was pregnant for a second time. Again, the couple made unsuccessful attempts to rid themselves of the foetus but eventually opted to 'let things run their course', which was a deadly turning point both for Digby and the unborn child. Although Olga knew that 'Dig' was already married, they wanted to give the baby a name and, so, on Tuesday, 23 March 1943, Ernest Charles Digby married Olga Davy Hill by a special licence at Canterbury Registry Office. However, more bad news awaited the couple. His unit was posted to Cardigan in Wales, and she was faced with returning to her parents' home, the last place she wanted to be, as she knew that a great many questions would be asked and that is something she wanted to avoid. Although his unit were only stationed in Cardigan for a short period, Digby managed to form a relationship with a local woman named Elizabeth Jones, and appears to have had no concern for his wife, children or expectant bigamous spouse. But before long, the unit was on the move again, leaving the Welsh countryside and moving to the English coastal town of Milborne Port in Somerset.

By this time, Olga was desperate to escape her parents' home and be with 'Dig' and wrote a telling letter to him in the weeks before she gave birth to Dawn. It reads:

The North London home from where Olga Davy Hill wrote her chilling letters to her bigamous husband, Sergeant Ernest Digby.

My dear Dig,

I sure am pleased you have left Wales again, and do hope you will have a better time at Sherborne. Oh, I feel all right in health I guess but I am worried and fed up with the whole thing. My dear I sure am looking forward to a few weeks with you, with good health and no troubles, this year has been one long worry for me. Owens's girlfriend hit it off okay with everyone, she is a fine healthy happy girl and rather nice looking, if you meet her, I am sure you would agree, I daresay you will meet her one day.

No darling I did not start roaming in my sleep, I get very little sleep these days, yes, my tummy does have a dance most nights. Oh, the hospital was not too bad this time, I did not get hurt much, though I fainted right out the trouble was the doctor asked me for the date of the raid when I lost the other, and somehow, I gave out and was a few minutes in coming round, they did not ask me anymore then (lucky was it not). However, I am going on okay and it will be a straight case, though they say if I myself do not pull up I am heading for a nervous breakdown, instead of gaining weight I am fast losing it, as for the child well it is full of life. By the way Dig, Ma and Pa are expecting you having me a place with you now before it comes off, as you told Pa in your letter that you would try if you moved from

Wales. I dare not tell them that in your other letter you said I could come to you after it was all over and not before.

It's no good Dig dear, I cannot get it in a home, nor can I find a place to go to now or after I come out of hospital, it should come of three weeks the coming Saturday, 23 October. Pa does not know this yet and when he does if you won't have me he will insist I take a furnished flat in another week's time at all cost about 35 shillings per week and gas coal food etc extra. Please Dig you get me a place down there, if you do not care to get me a room take a furnished cottage or flat anything will do, I will manage even on one room in someone's house, do not tell them what is wrong I can do without a doctor etc. If you can not get up for me, I will travel down alone, I do not mind but please do help me out it's no good up here.

They gave me a list of things I have to take in the hospital that alone will cost £3 to get them, I shall also have another set of books to get as before, and I do not want them, then there is a pram, cot etc, which they are always on to me about and about a £6 fee which a hospital want before or while I am in, I have had to send the income tax people 10 shillings and now I only have about 6 shillings left, what am I to do, no wonder my nerves are bad.

Don't you agree dear if you take a place and we have to pay more to be in a place alone it will be cheaper than all this, and we won't have to get the books, also soon as I am up, we can take a room, if not just take me a bed sitting room, and we will manage somehow. Will you write back as early as you can and tell me what you will do for me, I cannot stick this worry and the row there will be if you won't have me Dig. Wish I could join you this weekend, but I guess you won't be able to fix anything as quick as that will you. By the way Dig have you sent any money up this last two weeks, because if you have, I have not had any letters with any.

After all that trouble how are you sweetheart, it sure is good to know that you do not love me any less in spite of all the trouble I give you dear, it is no more your fault than mine, I guess in future we will take more care, it is worth it dear, I only wish I could join you this weekend, but I guess you won't be able to fix anything as quick as that will you. By the way Dig have you sent any money up this last two weeks, cause if you have, I have not had any letters with any, I have about six shillings now and then am broke. Guess that's all today darling, write me for Wednesday if you can, and do have me now dear. All my love.

Yours ever and only

Olga

Digby's response was chilling. It reads:

My darling wife,

I am hoping this finds you still in good feelings. Your letters are certainly full of trouble and woe are they not. You sure are fed up with things by the sound of things but keep your wits about you darling. I have tried to get a place for you Olga but so far unsuccessfully. Do this sweetheart. You will have to stay up there and have it. As soon as you leave hospital, I shall have found a place by then. **You need not get the cards for it** [National Identity Card and Ration Card]. I am hoping to have you down here for a few weeks sweetheart. You need it. I expect you are restless these days.

Fancy you fainting Olga, you must be pretty weak, I could kick myself darling, causing you all this bother, when you could have been enjoying yourself. That darn thing must be taking all your strength. I wish you could join me darling, it would save a lot of bother at home. I guess we could manage all okay but this is considered a safe place and rooms are hard to get at the present. You know I will help you out if I can sweetheart. **The pram and cot idea is out, you will not need them**. The fee can be forwarded on later that is quite okay. You must stick it out darling. I want you so much. You know that.

It does not matter how much trouble you cause, I still love you in the darn lot. If I did not, I should have finished a long time ago. I am enclosing 15 shillings Olga, and I shall be writing again tomorrow.

All my love to you darling I love you miss you. Good night sweet wife, fondest love.

Yours always

Dig

Of all the letters that were written by Olga, it is the one dated Thursday, 7 October 1943 that is perhaps the most revealing. Again written from her parents' London home, it reads:

> My dear husband,
> I really am sorry for all that has gone on this week, but it is none of my doing dear.
> **I alone know to what lengths you have gone in the past for me, and I tell you now darling no person living will get one word out of me.** So long as I live, I am yours only and you mine. At the moment we are in a tight corner I cannot think what will come out of it all.
> As you know Pa is on the path and there are some things he must not find out at any cost. He has today wrote to your commanding officer, I could not stop it or I would, I sure am worried as to the result and what will come out, I guess he will be sending for you dear and showing you the letter.
> Dig if you cannot get any sort of place how about asking for 48 hours now and coming up maybe you could find a place here, though I doubt it. Ma and I have tried and tried. Time is going dear and anytime after the 23rd of this month it may come off.
> Whatever you do mind Pa finds nothing out.
> All my love darling roll on the day I see you again.
> Your loving wife
Olga
xxxxx

The Crime

With his unit now stationed on the outskirts of Milborne Port, Digby obtained a billet at Bazzleways Cottages, next door to the Gibbs family. At lunchtime on Monda,y 11 October 1943, he called at their home and asked Edith Gibbs if she could accommodate him and his wife. He told her that Olga was already in the town, and he appeared to be rather annoyed at the fact that she had simply turned up. Edith suggested that they try somewhere else first. Digby went away and returned later with the heavily pregnant Olga, claiming that they were unable to find anywhere to stay. It was pouring with rain at the time and Edith, taking pity on the desperate-looking young woman, agreed to rent them a bedroom and a sitting room for 15s. per week. The following day, she asked Olga if arrangements had been made to have the baby in Sherbourne Hospital, and was told that nothing had been planned, as she did not like hospitals. Olga asked her if she could have the baby at home and, following a discussion with her husband, it was agreed that the baby would be born there, and Edith would do all she could to help. Olga then went on to explain that the baby was going to live with her sister in Peterborough and, once the child was 10 days old, she would take it to her mother's home in London where she would meet her sister and hand it over. On the same day Digby's father died from cardiac failure in North Middlesex Hospital. He requested leave to attend the funeral but it appears he had not been in contact with his parents for seven years prior to this, and only spent one night at the home of his legal wife on the day of the funeral. Perhaps an indication of his nature.

At this time, the district nurse in Milborne Port was 44-year-old Dorothy Marshall. She met Olga Hill for the first time on Tuesday, 19 October 1943, when Olga told her that she had given birth previously but that the baby had been killed in the Blitz and asked her not to tell Edith Gibbs. Dorothy described how she had been called to the house on Thursday, 21 October as Olga was in an advanced stage of labour. She left the cottage to fetch her midwife's bag and on her return a baby girl, weighing 7lb, had been born. The nurse visited mother and child twice a day over the next five days, and once a day after that. They both seemed perfectly healthy, and she was not surprised when Olga told her she was not feeding the baby herself but using a bottle, explaining that she did not want the baby to get used to being breast fed as she was planning on going back to work and the baby was going to live with her sister

Digby began a ten-day leave period on Friday, 12 November and Olga asked him if he was going to take the baby to London the following day. He said he would leave it until the following Monday and Edith recalled Olga saying that she 'might as well get rid of the child first so as not to spoil his whole leave'. That weekend, the couple hatched a plan to dispose of the baby, in the same way they had rid themselves of Doreen. On the morning of Monday, 15 November, Edith Gibbs carefully packed a small suitcase for Dawn in preparation for the trip to London with her parents. She recalled how tearful Olga was as she made the baby ready, and how Digby explained that there may be some 'funny scenes' with Olga's parents, which is why she was upset. Dawn was also crying and Edith recalled how sad the whole situation seemed. Equally, she was surprised at how Olga was somewhat dismissive when she offered her the use of a pram, when she suggested packing some additional nappies and the fact that the baby was unwashed and still dressed in a wet nightie.

Edith did the best she could to get the baby ready and the couple left the cottage with her and two suitcases at around 11.00 a.m., ostensibly to catch the train for London. At around 9.00 p.m. that evening, they returned, and Olga handed Edith a packet of chocolate biscuits, which she said had been given to her by her mother for the children. When asked if she had seen her sister, Olga replied that she had not been there and they had left the baby with her mother, as they were only there for around half an hour.

In reality, the couple had set off on foot heading towards the railway station, which was just over a mile away. Just after a bend in the road, they turned off along a track towards the hamlet of Henstridge Bowden known as Old Bowden Way. The track leads to some woods, and here they took a narrow path into the dark and dank wood itself, called Everlanes Covert. Olga claimed that they were some 150yd apart and when Dig caught up with her, he did not have the baby, and she didn't

Everlanes Covert, near the hamlet of Henstridge Bowden, the location where Sergeant Ernest Digby murdered his 25-day-old daughter. The arrow shows the approximate location.

ask where it was. He was, however, carrying the attaché case loaned to him by a member of his unit, Trooper Alan Arthur Haynes. The couple carried on along the pathway and made their way to the station, where they caught the 12.30 train to Yeovil. After leaving the cases at the lost luggage office, they spent the rest of day and early evening in the town, even going to the cinema.

At some point during their journey, Dawn suffered a blow to her tiny head. This, it was later revealed, was most likely from the corner of the expanding suitcase Digby had been carrying. Initially, he would claim that he could not remember anything until the following day. However, in a revised statement he said that on their return to Milborne Port, it was dark, and he was worried about the baby. Leaving Olga by a gateway, he went back to the woods where he found Dawn was missing from the place he had left her. He claimed she had rolled down a bank, and he found her face down, dead. He picked her up and carried her back to the cottage in the attaché case. In a final statement, Digby claimed he had tripped and fallen, dropping the baby who received a blow to her head. 'In a daze', he did not know what to do, so he had placed the body in the attaché case. Whichever version you choose to believe, the fact is that Digby either left the child in the woods to die, or, more likely, carried her body in the case to Yeovil and left her in the lost luggage office, whilst he and Olga entertained themselves for the rest of the day.

The couple stayed in the cottage all the following day and Dorothy Marshall visited to see how the baby was doing. Digby told the nurse that Dawn had gone to live in London with his sister-in-law, and was asked for the address where the baby could be found, so that Dorothy could inform the local authorities. On Wednesday, 17 November, the couple informed Edith that they were going into Wincanton to have the birth certificate amended, as it had the wrong date on it. In their absence, Edith searched their bedroom looking for the attaché case but could not find it. The couple were only gone for about an hour and returned early claiming that the trains were not convenient so they put off the trip. Edith, now very suspicious of the couple's actions and odd explanations, took it upon herself to investigate further. On Thursday, 18 November, after they had again left the house to go to Wincanton, she went into their bedroom and pulled out the expanding suitcase from under their bed, which had been used as a cot for the baby. After carefully opening it, she was shocked to find that not only did it contain the clothing she had given Olga for the baby, but the bottle of milk she had prepared was also still there, unconsumed. She recalled too, how there was a strong smell of disinfectant as she looked through the clothing. The attaché case was present and had a webbing strap around it. Edith could not bring herself to go any further, but she knew there was something terribly wrong. Had she gone deeper into that case she would have found the dead body of the baby. The following day, Digby returned to his unit at Witney, where his Commanding Officer, Lieutenant Arthur William Platt, said that he carried out his duties in a normal and proper manner and there was nothing unusual about his behaviour.

On Saturday, 20 November 1943, Dorothy Marshall visited Olga for the last time and insisted that she give her the address where Dawn was staying. Olga gave her parents' address and told Dorothy that the baby was only there temporarily, after which she was going to live in Peterborough with her sister. After the nurse left, Olga said that she must write to her mother, warning her that a welfare officer would be calling about the baby. The letter was later produced in court and, virtually childlike in its content, is chilling in the fact it contained no warning to her parents and was written whilst her child, having been dead for five days, lay in a case nearby. It reads:

Dear Ma and Pa,
Guess it is my turn to write but I have been waiting for my coat to turn up, thanks very much it came yesterday. Also, thanks for sending the money on for those shoes, I hope by now the coat has gone.

I am pleased you liked the rabbits, tell Roma to wipe the wet off the skins with a bit of old rag and get 3d of powdered alum from the chemist and just rub plenty of it on the pelt to have the skin stretched as tight as she can and leave the powdered alum on for about a week. She will then find that a thin dry skin on top will pull off but to mind not to tear a pelt when taking it off. Cut out with a razor on the wrong side and mind you get the fur going the right way.

Oh, something inside got torn bad and they stitched me up, but it has not taken right, and I am still losing blood. I feel fine though. Dig says if it does not stop, I will have to go in hospital, and he will see if his sister-in-law will take the baby until I come out. The operation would mean no more children so I guess they would take my womb out, and that makes one grow old quick and life less, seeing that I feel more like my old self I am going to try and stick it out. I do not do any work at all so I may be lucky.

Sorry you have been in bed with flu Ma, I hope you are feeling better now, though the rest would do your feet and legs good. Good old Roma skinning the rabbits, she has got what it takes (plenty of pluck).

Did I tell you Dig bought me a nice navy-blue pram, and I got a pink and green cover with the rabbits on tell Joan very pretty one, and Roma's pink rabbit hung on to.

I think that is all for now as we are all going out. If you write me on Monday Ma or Tuesday, then not again until I write you as I expect to go up to Oxford about Thursday. What a trip it takes from 11am until 6pm. Dig is coming down for us or meeting us halfway. **Dawn is fine though her dark hair has come golden and will be very curly as it grows.**

When you write Owen will you tell him I will write from the new address when I get it.

Love from all to all.

Olga

P.S. If there are any rabbits in Oxford and we go shooting will post some on to you, the others were posted Monday afternoon in Yeovil about 9 miles from here.

The following morning, Sunday, 21 November, Edith Gibbs, fearful that something terrible had happened to the baby, contacted the police. Inspector James Stephen Dunn of the Somerset Constabulary, based at Yeovil, called at the Gibbs, home where he confronted Olga, who was still in bed, and asked her where her baby was. She told him, 'At my mother's in London'. Dunn asked her a series of questions concerning the whereabouts of Dawn. He was not satisfied with any of her answers, told her to get dressed and took her to Milborne Port police station, in the company of Detective Sergeant Thomas Spiller. Once at the station, Dunn began to repeat his questions regarding Dawn and Olga soon broke down, saying, 'I want my baby back, I will tell you all I know'.

The body of Dawn Digby is carried away by detectives from the rabbit hole at Witney Camp where Sergeant Ernest Digby dumped her tiny body.

Digby was the NCO in charge of the guard at Witney that day. He was arrested by Inspector Dunn and driven to Yeovil, where he gave a statement. On Thursday, 25 November, Inspector Dunn, and Chief Inspector Peter Beveridge, accompanied Digby as he led them to a spot just 30yd from his sleeping quarters at Witney, and here they recovered the remains of Dawn Digby from a disused rabbit hole. Her tiny body was carried, in a small wooden box, to the Yeovil public mortuary, where a post-mortem was performed the following day by Professor James Mathewson Webster, director of the West Midland Forensic Science Laboratory. His report describes a healthy, well-nourished and well-cared for little girl, whose death was a result of shock following violence applied to the head. In his opinion, a small round punched out wound at the back of her skull had been caused by a sharp object but was not because of a fall. It is thought that she was killed by blows to the head with the hard corners of the expanding suitcase which Digby had carried out of the cottage, and which Olga claimed she was carrying in the woods as the baby was too heavy.

The Trial

At the beginning of December 1943, Digby was being held at Horfield Prison in Bristol, whilst Olga was kept in Exeter Prison. There now followed a series of court appearances in which they were both accused of murdering the child, both choosing to reserve their defence. Finally, they were brought to trial at Somerset Assizes held in Shire Hall, Taunton, on Tuesday, 25 January 1944, before Mr Justice Singleton. The trial lasted for three days, and the couple was faced with a series of incredulous statements and a mountain of hard evidence. John Francis Claxton, appearing for the Director of Public Prosecutions, stated: 'It is the basis of the prosecution's case that this child was unwanted, that these two people put their heads together with the intention of ridding themselves of it and that they successfully did so by abandoning it in a wood.'

Digby claimed he was carrying Dawn in one hand and a heavy suitcase in the other. He fell behind Olga and when he caught up, Dawn was no longer present. Apparently, Olga did not ask where she was until later that day and Digby assured her that everything was fine. He told the court it was his intention to leave the baby in the wood because he knew the spot was frequented, and he felt somebody might pick her up. They were in considerable financial difficulties, because Hill had given up her employment, and he was making the full army allotment to his wife and three children.

Olga, who collapsed and sobbed bitterly as she took the oath, said it never entered her head that the child should be killed. The damning medical evidence, however, demonstrated that Dawn had suffered several serious injuries to the base of her skull that could only have been inflicted by someone who was determined to end her life. Her head had been wrapped in a nappy to avoid splashing and although she had died rapidly, death had not been instantaneous. The question of what happened to the couple's first child, Doreen, was also raised, although no charges were ever brought regarding her murder. It was purely by chance that their inhuman crime ever came to light. John Claxton said that Hill told the nurse who attended her that she had given birth previously but that baby had been killed in an air raid. 'You will hear in statements references to the birth of an earlier child. The story told in those statements does not agree with the fact that the child was killed in an air raid', he told the court. Olga had lied about what happened to Doreen and her statement of events concerning Dawn was far different from that of Digby. She was with Digby on both the occasions where her daughters 'disappeared', surely she must have known what had happened and, therefore, be complicit?

The final moments of the trial were filled with tension. The jury, made up of ten men and two women, was absent for just 40 minutes before returning with a verdict. The foreman asked the judge for further legal direction as to the position of the woman, if the man alone was guilty of murder. The judge replied, 'you must acquit her', and immediately Digby turned to Olga who was separated from him in the dock by a warder, and appeared to whisper 'you are alright'. As the foreman announced the guilty verdict against Digby, Olga burst into tears and sank down on the chair in which she had been seated throughout the trial. Her surprising acquittal was then announced, and as wardresses led her away, Digby turned and watched her departure. When asked by the clerk if he had anything to say before sentence of death was passed on him, the dark-haired soldier, standing perfectly erect, spoke to the judge with only a trace of a tremor in his voice saying:

> I would like to thank the court for the full way in which the whole proceedings have been conducted and to thank you, my Lord, for your summing up, in which you credited me with a certain amount of sense. Throughout this case I have listened intently to the prosecution and defending counsels and certain points have not been disclosed in this court.

The clerk then adjusted a black cap over the judge's wig. Everybody in the court, apart from the judge, stood up. Digby was emotionless, and stony-faced. The judge, looking at him directly, spoke in quiet tones telling Digby, 'You have been rightly convicted of a cruel murder', followed by the solemn words of the death sentence. The judge spoke in a quivering voice with the final invocation, 'and may the Lord have mercy on your soul', to which the Chaplain to the High Sheriff, Prebendary Harry Freeman, responded 'Amen'. Digby heard the sentence unmoved. He bowed to the judge and said, 'Thank you, my Lord', wheeled around and disappeared from the dock.

The Appeal

On Wednesday, 1 March 1944, the Court of Criminal Appeal heard an application from Digby on the grounds that the judge, in his summing up, had not put sufficient stress on the medical evidence which might have influenced the jury's verdict. Mr Justice Humphreys, giving the Judgment of the Court, said the judge had 'appreciated that the medical evidence was very important. In his summing up he repeated word for word, and he told the jury that they were not bound to accept the evidence of the pathologist called for the Crown.' But the jury did accept the view put forward by Professor Webster, and it was found that there were no grounds for any complaint about the summing up. The documents relating to this dreadful case contain several letters revealing examples of mental illness within Digby's family, and demonstrating a great deal of support for the murderer. This he attempted to use as evidence showing he was not responsible for killing Dawn, and should therefore be reprieved. However, the judges felt there were no grounds for this claim and the appeal was accordingly dismissed. It is interesting to note that the case summary, as always signed by Frank Newsam, the Under Secretary of State at the Home Office, suggests it was unfair Digby should hang whilst Olga was set free. Despite this, he saw no reason to interfere with the course of the law and Ernest Digby was duly hanged on Thursday, 16 March 1944 at Horfield Prison, Bristol, by Thomas Pierrepoint, assisted by Steve Wade. Allegedly, he confessed to the killing of Doreen before his execution.

A Free Woman

Olga, now a free woman, married Ronald Geoffrey Gorham at Brighton in 1946 and moved into her parents' home in Sherriff Road, West Hampstead. She never gave birth again. Unlike her children, she lived a full life, passing away on 13 June 1994 at the age of 80. Doubtless, the tiny, dissected remains of Dawn Digby were disposed of by the authorities with as much dignity as possible. Doreen, however, may still lie in the area between Broadstairs and St Nicholas at Wade. When you gaze upon the name of Sergeant Ernest Charles Digby at Brookwood, spare a thought for them too.

Chapter 5

Gunner Ernest James Harman Kemp – The Cabbage Patch Murder

Panel 3. Column 2
Service Number: 6105471
Unit: 'B' Battery, Royal Artillery Depot – Woolwich
Executed: Tuesday, 6 June 1944, aged 20

The Victim

On Sunday, 21 May 1922, Miriam Deeley (née Cardozo) and her husband, Donald, celebrated her 26th birthday at home in Kirkland Road, nestled in the London borough of West Ham. But there was something more to commemorate that day than usual as, just 24 hours before, she had given birth to their second child, a daughter, whom they named Iris Miriam. Little did they know that day what tragic events lay in store for the little girl, as they looked forward to a brighter future following the war to end all wars. Donald Alan Deeley had served with the 36th Battalion, Northumberland Fusiliers during the First World War and had seen action in France in the closing stages of the conflict. He gained employment as a clerk in a commercial bank and would eventually be promoted to a managerial position. Donald married Miriam Cardozo in 1920 and their first child, Alan, was born a year later, followed closely by Iris, her sister Hazel in 1926 and a fourth child, Raymond,

Iris Miriam Deeley. (*After the Battle* magazine)

would complete the family in 1929. By the outbreak of the Second World War, the family were living in a house in Blake Hall Road, Wanstead, East London.

After leaving school, Iris followed in her father's footsteps, taking up a job as a bank clerk until she joined the Women's Auxiliary Air Force on Friday, 7 August 1942. Described as a friendly and likeable girl, who was prone to trust and converse with members of the fighting services, she was posted to Cornwall, where she met and became engaged to one of the station's radar mechanics, an Irishman, Aircraftsman William Quill. He was seeking promotion and, after his commission had been announced, was posted to a training course at No. 7 Radio School, located in the London Science Museum. Miriam had been posted to No. 1 Balloon Centre at RAF Kidbrooke in South-East London, her last and fateful posting.

The Assailant

The life of Ernest James Harman Kemp was in stark contrast to that of Iris. He was born in Gillingham, Kent, on Thursday, 4 October 1923, the illegitimate son of Alice Louisa Kemp, a war widow whose husband, Private Ernest Richard Kemp, had been killed in the closing stages of the First World War, and a man named James Harman. Adopting his mother's maiden name, he claimed his father had died when he was aged 4, but he is unlikely to have known him. He attended Stanley Street Elementary School in Deptford until the age of 14 after which he lived in New Cross and had several jobs. Initially he worked as a paper boy for W.H. Smith's, then as a porter at the local railway station and finally took up employment as a driver's assistant with Whitbread's Brewery until Saturday, 13 December 1941 when, at the age of 18, he was called up for military service.

Gunner James Harman Kemp.

He joined the 70th Battalion, Queen's Royal Regiment stationed at Maidstone, and served with them at Exeter, Ilfracombe and Taunton, until, on Tuesday, 10 November 1942, he was transferred to the Royal Artillery. Kemp then served at Aberdeen, Cromer, Watford and Woolwich. His service record was not a good one and he was often in trouble with both the military and civil authorities, being reported as having been absent without leave on no less than twenty-five occasions. He was found guilty on Thursday, 28 January 1943 of 'Stealing Home Guard Uniform'. Ominously, just a few months later, on Thursday, 8 April, he was found guilty of 'Indecent Assault on a Female Under the Age of 16 Years', for which he was bound over and ordered to pay a fine of £5. The following day the military authorities placed him in detention for twenty-eight days, for being 'absent without leave'. Lastly, on Tuesday, 30 November 1943, he was placed in detention for eighty-four days, and lost twenty-eight days' pay by order of a Field General Court Martial for 'unlawfully wearing the emblems of an army captain, contrary to good order of military discipline'. It appears he was on embarkation leave awaiting overseas service when he decided to wear the uniform of a captain 'for show'. A civilian, who knew him, reported him to the police and he was arrested.

On Tuesday, 8 February 1944, whilst under military police escort to the dentist, Kemp escaped by climbing through a toilet window at the guardhouse of Woolwich Barracks. Whilst most soldiers in this position would have made every attempt to lay low, Kemp did the opposite. He adorned his uniform with many medal ribbons and emblems, none of which he was entitled to. These included glider pilot's wings, the Military Medal and campaign medals that went back a long time before he was born. He then had the audacity to have his photograph taken in this illegal finery, which he claimed he intended to pass on to his many girlfriends. He may have gotten away with this brazen act, and we may never have heard Kemp's name if it were not for the fact that his path inadvertently crossed that of Iris Deeley on the eve of Valentine's Day.

The Crime

At around 8.30 p.m. on Sunday, 13 November 1944, Iris left her parents' home in the company of her fiancé, the newly promoted Pilot Officer William James Quill. They walked along Wanstead Road until they reached the Green Man public house, where they took shelter due to an air raid. After a while they caught a bus and travelled to the Bow Road Underground station, where they were to part company for the last time. Iris, carrying a copy of Leo Tolstoy's *War and Peace*, boarded an Underground train which would take her to Charing Cross station, where she intended to catch a train to Kidbrooke. Two WAAFs, ACW2 Winifred Allen and ACW2 Betty Blackman, who served with Iris, saw her in the YMCA cafe alone, reading her book. They caught the 11.01 p.m. train to Kidbrooke, but Iris remained in the YMCA for reasons unknown. She then called the camp to explain she had missed her connection and was ordered by Corporal Stanley Weston to get a train to Lewisham, then make her way to Kidbrooke from there.

After getting off the train at Lewisham, she met Margaret Mcgregor and her brother, Andrew O'Sullivan, who were making their way home to Shooters Hill. They overheard Iris asking a railway official where she could get a taxi to Kidbrooke and agreed to share one with her, if they could find one. As they began to make their way through South London's darkened streets, they were joined near Chiesman's Stores by a handsome young soldier, who wore the cap badge of the Army Physical Training Corps, a set of glider pilot's wings and a hefty number of ribbons, including one for the Military Medal. But this was no war hero, it was Gunner Ernest James Kemp, a man on the run. He told the trio that he was also going to Kidbrooke and he chatted to all three as they made their way towards Kidbrooke church, where they parted company. The young soldier offered to walk Iris back to her camp, to which she agreed. As they passed under the railway bridge in Foxholes Lane, the location of a barrage balloon site, the pair were seen by Flight Lieutenant Andrew Howatson, who was making an inspection of the site and was the last person to see Iris alive. As they neared Eltham (Well Hall) station, Kemp tried to kiss her, but she resisted. Very quickly there was a struggle and Kemp held tightly onto the scarf wrapped around her neck. A few moments later, Iris was dead, and Kemp proceeded to molest her limp body. The following morning, Valentine's Day, Special Constable Arthur Belcher, who was on his way to tend his allotment alongside the railway, found the almost naked body of a young woman, laying in a cabbage patch in Sherard Road, Eltham. He felt for her pulse, but there was none, and asked a passing civilian to fetch the police, a woman had been murdered.

The Investigation

Chief Inspector Edward 'Ted' Greeno, the renowned Scotland Yard detective, was called in to head the inquiry. Arriving at the scene, he followed the furrows of trailing feet in the soft earth, and here he found a footprint, which he measured and established was about a size 11. Greeno could see that the young woman, as yet unidentified, had been stripped and robbed. The killer left behind the book she had been reading, *War and Peace*. Carelessly, they had also left behind a khaki glove, of the largest size, snagged on a nearby thorn bush. Later that afternoon, a schoolboy, 13-year-old Ronald Jury, found a set of identity discs that had been thrown into a ditch near where the body was found. Greeno now knew who the victim was, Iris Deeley. Her body had been taken to Lewisham mortuary, where she was later formally identified by her father. He told the police that she had been robbed of a wallet containing £11, a long, heavy, silver cigarette case, which he had given her, and a book of clothing coupons in her fiancé's name. Pawnbrokers across Britain were warned to look out for the case, but the press had become aware of this, and the details were unfortunately released. Greeno now believed the killer would quickly dispose of the case but might hold onto the coupons as nothing had been published about them. A manhunt was now on in what was to become known as the Cabbage Patch Murder. Greeno, who based himself at Eltham police station, obtained what he described as 'an army of policemen' who began questioning people arriving on evening trains at every station from Charing Cross to the ends of Kent. The police were aware that this was a big man, from the size of his footprints and glove, and believed the killer knew the area given the location of the allotments. From the timing, Greeno believed this might be a soldier who was either an absentee, a deserter or on a late pass. The South of England was full of soldiers, and this one could be anywhere by now. He would later recall, 'There comes a time in every murder hunt when everything looks hopeless, and this was it'. But he opted to press on.

As the investigation progressed, there were numerous hoaxes and false accounts from people who had claimed to have seen the killer. Then a one in ten-thousand instance changed the path of the inquiry. Margaret McGregor remembered the young WAAF who was trying to get to Kidbrooke and had a thick book under her arm. She had not only seen the killer, but had spoken to him. He was a rough-tough-looking individual with a light-blonde moustache and his uniform was bedecked with what Margaret described as 'the most amazing paraphernalia of regimental flashes, glider pilot's wings, four medals, sergeant's stripes and a gymnast's badge'. She remembered that the soldier was bragging that he had been in an air raid shelter that night with some Americans who he said were cowering in the corner, so he ordered them out with a pistol. She noted, however, that he was not carrying a pistol. He appeared to hate Americans and said that it was good job he had not brought one home at Christmas as his father was 'a copper and there would have been a murder'. As the four walked along it seems Kemp arranged for him and Iris to fall back a little. When Margaret said, 'Step it out, the Army', he replied, 'I'm trying to keep in step with snow white here.' As they approached the church at Kidbrooke, she heard him say, 'I've been this way before.' That was enough for Greeno, he was sure this was his man.

It was not long before early on the morning of Tuesday, 22 February 1944, a long-serving police sergeant, named Charles Memory, who had served in the First World War, spotted a soldier cuddling a young WAAF at St Pancras station. The soldier was wearing a British army battledress jacket with an impressive collection of medal ribbons, including those for the Northwest Frontier, Afghanistan and Palestine campaigns, which Memory knew had taken place long before this young man was born. He was also wearing American army trousers and carrying an American officer's valise. Once the WAAF had departed, Sergeant Memory questioned the soldier, who claimed he had 'found' the valise at Euston station. At that time, 'stealing by finding' was an offence and Sergeant Memory arrested the soldier and took him to Albany Road police station. Here he was found to have in his possession a wallet, a Waterman pen and a set of clothing coupons with the front cover torn off.

Ted Greeno, after establishing that Kemp was a deserter, asked him to account for his actions over the period of 12–14 February 1944. He found the soldier to be 'very cocky' and, after informing him that he was conducting a murder hunt, Kemp provided a detailed account of the evening he met and walked with the young WAAF until he left her waiting to catch a No. 46 tram. Greeno believed this account to be true, up until the last part. Kemp was unaware that the police had also found a ticket to a locker at Waterloo station which contained a kit bag. When they searched it, they found, in the field dressing pocket of a pair of trousers, the front cover to a clothing coupon book with the name William Quill on it. Kemp was now exposed as the killer. Greeno asked him to remove his boots, which were the same size as the impressions found near Iris's body. Kemp was then informed that he was being detained as a suspect in the murder of Iris Deeley. Aware that he had been uncovered, he admitted the killing, but the callous and boastful murderer claimed it had been an accident and not intentional.

The Trial

On Tuesday, 18 April 1944, Kemp's trial for the murder began at the Old Bailey before Mr Justice Cassels, who had served in the army during the First World War, taking part in actions on the Western Front. He was twice mentioned in dispatches, attained the rank of captain, and is known to have chaired a number of courts martials. The prosecution case was presented by Laurence Austin Byrne and Gerald Howard. Kemp was represented by Mr F.H. Lawson. He pleaded not guilty, and no evidence was presented by the defence.

During his time in prison, Kemp had described how he had had sexual intercourse with two or three girlfriends since he was in the army, but never with prostitutes. He admitted to what was described as 'moderate masturbation' but had not allowed it to 'get hold of him'. He also described how he had been bound over for twelve months after being accused of interfering with a 14-year-old girl. He claimed that she was often out with soldiers and that everyone thought she was aged 19. He also claimed that everything that happened was with her consent and that there had been 'no penetration'. On the night he killed Iris, he had thrown her to the ground where she said, 'don't be silly' and 'if you had any sister, you would not do this'. She struggled with him, so he grabbed her scarf tightly and the next thing he knew, there was no pulse. He undressed her and 'eased himself onto her', but claimed he had 'not penetrated her', which had been confirmed at the post-mortem. On the way to Eltham police station, Kemp told a police officer, 'I deserve all I'm going to get, she didn't have a chance. It was my fault. As soon as I tightened the scarf she seemed to go right out, she wouldn't submit to me at all.' He expressed no remorse at Iris's death, stating there was 'no use crying over spilt milk'. The jury, who took just 16 minutes to come to a decision, found him guilty of murder but added a recommendation to mercy, due to his age. Justice Cassels quickly sentenced him to death by hanging.

The Appeal

Kemp was held in Wandsworth Prison as prisoner No. 9030 and during his stay was monitored by the Medical Officer, who found no evidence of mental instability and no cause as to why the sentence should not be carried out. He now made an attempt to appeal against his sentence, on the basis that the judge had mis-directed the jury. A similar appeal had been made in a recent case whereby the assailant, another British artilleryman, was successful and, even though there was clear evidence that he had raped and murdered a young housewife, he walked free. But that is another story for another time.

In a letter dated Tuesday, 22 February 1944, to his uncle, Walter Henry Hornsey, Kemp fully understands what is in store for him, even though a final verdict on his appeal had not been reached. The letter, somewhat child-like in its content, also has darker undertones as he clearly attempts to make his uncle feel guilty about not visiting him:

Dear Wal,

I guess you have read about the mess I am in being charged with the murder of that WAAF at Eltham and believe me I am in a real mess this time. I was wondering if you could get up to see me sometime, I know you can't get up in the week, but could you manage it one Saturday afternoon as I am allowed visitors every day owing to the seriousness of my charge. I don't expect you will come to see me owing to the fact I am charged with murder, and you don't want to get mixed up in it.

Would you send me £5 out of my money you got for the furniture? I know I can't claim it as it was placed in the bank under your name, but I hope you will send it to me as there are things you can get in here with money. I guess it is big news in the papers now. I have not got a dog's chance and I expect they will condemn me to hang so please send me that money so I can have a few luxuries before I get my lot. I wondered if you could get hold of some of those Wild West magazines and send them to me also some cigarettes. Please try and get up to see me as I need a Pal now more than ever, I needed a Pal in my life.

I am to appear at court again on 13th March and they are supplying me with a lawyer to fight for me, but I don't see how I can get off as all the facts are against me and I have not got the chance in 1 million of getting less than the rope. Everybody here are ever so good to me and the grub is good. But I guess you don't want anything to do with me now and I can't blame you as it is not nice being a relative of an accused murderer. So, I won't hold it against you if you desert me in my greatest hour of need.

If you do visit me, you don't need a permit just ask at the gate for me. I guess there is nothing to live for now that Mum is dead. Well cheerio and goodbye to both you and Nell you were both swell to me.

Love

Ern. xxxx

In a final letter, dated Tuesday, 23 May 1944, to the Home Secretary, Herbert Morrison, Kemp made one more attempt to save his own skin.

Sir,

I do not wish to make myself too much of a trouble to you as I realise in these times of emergency you are a very busy man, but my life is at stake, and I have been advised to petition my case to you as you are now the only person who can decide my fate.

As you know I was found guilty of the murder of a member of the Women's Auxiliary Air Force and sentenced to death. I appealed against my sentence and although my counsel did his best it was of no use and the appeal which was on the grounds of misdirection by the learned judge in his summing up at to [the] jury was squashed.

My trial which was very fair and had only one drawback and that was when the learned judge told the jury to disregard my counsel's defence, which in my opinion and that of my counsel's was entirely bias against me as it is my firm belief that if this direction had not been given I would have only been charged with manslaughter as the word murder means when a foul deed has been premeditated which, in my case was not so.

I know you only have my word for it, and it is only natural that a condemned prisoner would say that he did not intend to [harm] the girl. I admit I was responsible for her death but not knowing my own strength, I attempted to make advances to her, and she struggled and in being possessed with desire to have sexual intercourse with her I grabbed her scarf and pulled it too tight, and I thought she was only unconscious, but later, on feeling her pulse and heart found that she was dead. Whether or not you believe me or not I swear to you sir I had no intention of killing the girl but only to get what I wanted which no man can help at times but she was a real decent girl gave me no encouragement at any time and if I had not been so foolish as to have broken out of my guardhouse I would have never seen the girl and by now would have been over the other side fighting for my country which I regret I will not be able to do now whatever happens. Well sir, I now leave my life in your hands and, if you think my deed which was in the spur of the moment deserves my punishment and I have to die, I hold it against no one, but I think on the evidence I was treated fair. Also, I bring to your notice sir I was given a strong recommendation to mercy from the jury, so my life is now in your hands to do with as you think just. I remain your obedient servant.

Gunner Ernest James Kemp

A final note dated Friday, 2 June 1944 from the Under Secretary of State, Frank Newsam, sealed Kemp's fate, stating that he had 'failed to discover any sufficient ground to justify him in advising His Majesty to interfere with the due course of law'. At 8.00 a.m. on Tuesday, 6 June 1944, as Allied forces fought their way across the beaches of Normandy, the life of Gunner James Ernest Harman Kemp, dressed in plain battledress, was ended by Albert Pierrepoint, assisted by Herbert Morris, at Wandsworth Prison, his muscular body stretching the rope by a full 2in as it dislocated his neck. He was laid to rest within the prison grounds on the same day.

Iris Deeley, however, lies in an isolated grave at the City of London Cemetery and Crematorium, in Manor Park, East London. Unlike those at Brookwood, she does not receive many visitors. Her mother passed away in 1971 at the age of 76 and her father would join her in 1982, aged 86. In a last interview with Winston Ramsey, editor of *After the Battle* magazine, many years after her death, William Quill described how he kept a photograph of Iris in his wallet. This photograph, provided by *After the Battle* and colourised by Doug Banks of Colourising History, is included here (see p. 2 of the colour plates).

Chapter 6

Corporal Hassan Naameh Medlish – A General Court Martial

Panel 5. Column 1
Service Number: PAL/22359
Unit: 1038 Port Operating Company, Royal Engineers
Executed: Monday, 12 July 1943, aged 19

Many of the cases described within these pages have been published to some extent in the past, but perhaps in not quite so much depth. There is, however, one case that does not appear to have been exposed before. Whilst this is a case of murder, the assailant was not tried by a civil court and the manner of execution varies in comparison with all the others. In the period between 3 September 1939 and 31 December 1947, at least forty-four soldiers of the British army were executed for the crime of murder, following sentencing by a General Court Martial or Field General Court Martial. Of these, twenty-seven were colonial or native troops, of which three were Palestinian Arabs. It is estimated that some 12,000 Palestinians volunteered to serve in the British army during the Second World War, the prevailing motivation for a majority being one of financial compensation, rather than any political ideology or overwhelming desire to serve the British monarchy. A large proportion of these volunteers served principally in North Africa and the Mediterranean theatres, and there were a significant number of casualties amongst them. However, as with any military force, a small element of their number was involved in criminal acts, not least of which was murder.

Private Mahmoud Saleh Abbas and Private Hussein Mohamed Ali Trabi were shot by a firing squad for the crime of murder and their names are recorded on the Alamein War Memorial in Egypt. However, the first case of a Palestinian Arab being executed for murder is that of Corporal H. Midlig, Royal Engineers, who was put before a firing squad on Monday, 12 July 1943. Throughout his entire case, for which an interpreter was required, he was referred to by an incorrect name. In fact, he was Corporal Hassan Naameh Medlish, a Palestinian who joined the British army in December 1940 at the age of 16, and was attached to No. 1038 Port Operating Company, a unit of the Royal Engineers. Little is known about his early life, but his career in the British army appears to have been relatively free of any misdemeanours, until spring 1943 when he became actively involved in the hashish (cannabis) trade.

Prior to the Second World War, much of the hashish supplied to consumers in Egypt came through Greece. To compensate for the disruption in the supply caused by the invasion of Greece, smugglers turned to crops from Syria and Lebanon. As a result, Palestine became a central link in the supply chain, and its railway became one of the major routes. In 1942, the line that connected the Egyptian city of Qantara, on the Suez Canal, with Haifa was extended to the Lebanese cities of Beirut and Tripoli. British and French military forces made concerted efforts to disrupt the supply lines, and by 1943 hashish availability in Egypt had decreased, providing a financial opportunity for some in an illegal trade fraught with danger.

The Crime

Based on his statement, on the night of Wednesday, 31 March 1943, Corporal Medlish left the Ritz Hotel in Ismailia, Egypt, where he had been staying for a week, in order to return to the Moascar British army camp, having been absent for almost five months. He was wearing British army issue battledress and was carrying a 9mm Beretta automatic pistol, which he had purchased privately sometime previously. To reach the camp, he had to pass through an area of the town known as the Native Quarter and claimed that, as he did so, he was approached in the darkness by a tall man. It was asserted, he had been approached by a man known as Abdulla El Gharbawi, a fish trader who was also known to deal in hashish. A conversation ensued and the man was surprised to hear the soldier speak Arabic. He apparently congratulated Medlish for serving with the British army and invited him to a cafe for a coffee, to which the soldier agreed. On attempting to leave the cafe, the man insisted on taking Medlish to his home but, aware that some soldiers had been attacked whilst on their own, Medlish declined, at which point he was told, 'I'll make you go willingly or by force'.

Afraid, and in the absence of any other friendly troops, he followed the individual to another cafe, where a second man met them, who he knew as Sourogi. They were then joined by a third man and it was at this point that a hashish deal seems to have been discussed. An argument ensued over the price and Medlish, now fearful that something was about to happen to him, attempted to run away. One of the men grabbed him by the arm, whilst another took hold of him by the throat, the third man placed his hand over Medlish's mouth, and the three men attempted to drag him into a side street. By now, a crowd had started to develop, as the men fought and argued. His attackers began to punch him, and he started to feel faint, at which point he reached into his battledress and produced his pistol. He fired two shots into the air, causing his attackers to run off and the crowd disperse. Still feeling faint, he sat on the ground but became aware of the shape of people starting to gather around him in the darkness and, afraid for his life, he fired another three shots, by which time he was half kneeling, half standing. He then made his way into another street to escape his attackers. Abdel Hameed Abu Egalla, an officer of the Egyptian Police Force, was leaving his house when he heard shooting. He headed towards the sound and discovered Medlish sitting on the ground in the Rue Alexandria, close to the Ritz Hotel, surrounded by about fifty people. His eyes were swollen, and his face battered. Egalla arrested Medlish, who he claimed did not have a pistol with him. It seems that two bullets had struck Abdulla El Gharbawi in the back, seriously wounding him, and he died a short time later. Medlish claimed that no one ever spoke his name and that he knew nothing about hashish. He was taken to the Moascar army camp and placed in custody, where he remained for almost two months.

The Court Martial

On Saturday, 29 May 1943, proceedings for a General Court Martial were ordered by Major General Richard Augustin Marriott 'Ram' Basset MC, CdG, who was at that time commanding No. 18 Area, where the offence took place. A career soldier, Basset had served in the army during the First World War, had been awarded the Military Cross, the French Croix de

Major General Richard Augustin Marriott 'Ram' Basset MC, CdG, who ordered the General Court Martial of Corporal Hassan Naameh Medlish.

Guerre, and was twice Mentioned in Despatches. He served in a series of roles during the interwar period and by 1943 had been appointed as the Commander of No. 18 Lines of Communication Area at Moascar, Egypt, with the rank of major general. He was to hold this appointment until his return to the United Kingdom in March 1945 and retired from the army on 13 February 1946. The General Court Martial was set to take place at Moascar on Monday, 31 May 1943 and was made up from a selection of British officers based in the area, as laid down in the *Manual of Military Law*.

The prosecutor was Lieutenant Lowry Stephen Hart Jackson, Royal Artillery, an experienced barrister at law. Whilst the Defence Counsel was provided by Lieutenant Eric Nevill, Royal Army Ordnance Corps, a solicitor.

President: Lieutenant Colonel Douglas Reginald Edward Shaw, Royal Sussex Regiment
Members: Major F. Lawrence, RASC
            Captain C.J. Bell, RASC
            Major K. Smaje, Royal Engineers
            Captain A.R. Turnor, Kings Royal Rifle Corps

Major Ian Clive Baillieu, Middlesex Yeomanry, was the representative of the DJAG's Staff.
Sergeant E. Caspi, RETD, interpreter
Sergeant R.J. Ford (7887634), Special Investigation Branch
Sergeant George Kiracos, Special Investigation Branch (interpreter)

Kiracos had taken a statement from Medlish on 2 April, two days after the shooting, but did not caution him before doing so. He simply told him that he was acting as an interpreter and had to take a statement from him. This is a point the defence seem not to have picked up.

Witnesses

The prosecution produced twelve witnesses:

- El Sayed Ahmed Faress and Ali El Sayed El Sourogi, both men were known associates of Abdulla El Gharbawi, and claimed to have seen Medlish shoot the Egyptian.
- Mahmoud Mostapha Selim, who lied to the court about being a policeman, and claimed that Medlish had grabbed him by the shirt near the Ritz Hotel.
- Ahmed Fouad Mohamed, a driver, and Mostafa El Sayed El Mohander, a shopkeeper, who both claimed they had heard the sound of shooting but had not seen the incident. These two men were also known associates of Gharbawi.
- Mahmoud Labib Eff, of the Egyptian CID, stated that he had found the dead body of Abdulla El Gharbawi and seen blood stains in the street where he was shot, but there was no evidence supplied as to whom the blood came from.
- Abdel Rahman Hussein Muftah, Commandant of the AIPA (Ambulance Service), who claimed that he had managed to unload the pistol magazine in a struggle with Medlish.
- Mohamed Abdulla Mohamed, who claimed he had found the pistol with a clip in it the next morning. This was an indication that Medlish had apparently replenished his pistol.
- Abdel Hameed Abu Egalla, of the Egyptian Police Force, who had arrested Medlish.
- Abdel Aziz Ali Emara, a detective on the Egyptian Police Force, who claimed to have found two bullets close to where Gharbawi had been shot and that he had handed them to Mahmoud Labib Eff.
- Dr Halim who performed the post-mortem.
- Mr A. Lucas – weapons expert – who examined an automatic pistol and two bullets handed to him by the Egyptian Police.

There were no witnesses for the defence.

Strangely, Dr Halim who performed the post-mortem, and who knew Abdulla El Gharbawi personally, had 'forgotten' his notes regarding the examination and a 30-minute adjournment had to be allowed in order that he could 'refresh his memory'. Having consulted his notes, Halim continued by saying he 'thought' the first wound penetrated the left upper border of the pelvis and that Gharbawi was most likely on the turn when a shot was fired. He stated that this shot had been made whilst the gunman was on the ground. The second shot, however, struck Gharbawi under his left armpit, and came from above. In Halim's opinion, the gunman was now standing. Each shot, he claimed, was fired from a distance of around 10m. This, it seems, was a remarkable feat by Medlish. In the dark, surrounded by a group of people, he fired a shot from the ground and struck a moving target. He then stood up, took aim, and again struck the moving target. No photographs were produced of the post-mortem and the body had been disposed of in line with the customs of the region.

Lieutenant Jackson, prosecuting, believed the case was a straightforward story where a dispute over hashish had resulted in Medlish drawing his pistol and firing. He suggested that there was no doubt the subsequent three shots were fired at the retreating form of Gharbawi. He relied upon the evidence of the post-mortem doctor and the firearms expert who, he felt, had established, beyond all reasonable doubt, that it was Medlish who had fired the pistol. This was despite the fact that the expert had only identified the pistol as a 9mm Beretta and that the bullets were of Italian manufacture. Lucas had undertaken some tests which demonstrated the bullets had the same marks on them as those which had been handed to him by the Egyptian Police. Jackson then claimed that Medlish's story was incredible. The fact he was returning to camp could not be accepted and, if rejected, the only reasonable alternative was that he was there concerning a hashish deal, which disposed of the suggestion he was waylaid by thugs. He would not have been able to have drawn the pistol if he the men were right on top of him. They would not have fled but would have grabbed the weapon out of his hand and, as the defendant had already pointed out, each of these three individuals were considerably bigger than Medlish.

Lieutenant Nevill, the defending officer, outlined the fact that Medlish should be believed. It was inevitable that there should be no other witnesses for the defence and was wholly conceivable that, after a shooting of this nature, there would not be anyone amongst the Egyptian crowd who would not immediately side against the soldier in uniform. The fact that Medlish was in uniform led, inexorably, to the conclusion he was going back to camp. That explained his presence in the location and no significance should be attached to his carrying a pistol, because that was his habit. The court knew the conditions ruling in Palestine at the time and should have no difficulty in accepting this explanation. The prosecution witnesses contradicted each other about the price to be paid for the hashish, which should make the court doubt the whole story. He further argued that if Medlish deliberately intended to kill Gharbawi, he would have done it when he was in front of him and before the others ran away. Nevill asked the court to accept the story as being true. At the very least there must be a doubt about it. The temper of an Egyptian crowd, the fact he had been assaulted and the fact these men were returning once again, possibly to harm him, meant that Medlish believed his life was in danger and, therefore, his actions were those of self-defence which he argued were justifiable.

In his summing up, Major Ian Baillieu, made it quite clear that a total of five rounds had been fired and that Gharbawi was found wounded and later died. No one had witnessed the actual shooting. The evidence of the two witnesses was that Gharbawi was a thug, they were his associates and there was a discrepancy about the price that was being charged for the hashish. An indication that the prosecution witnesses were not being truthful. The evidence given by Dr Halim implied that it was merely an opinion and that it might be unsafe to act on that opinion. Finally, the court had to be satisfied beyond reasonable doubt that it was murder. If they thought it was within reasonable bounds of probability that the killing was excusable or accidental, then Medlish was entitled to be acquitted. Likewise, if they believed it was within the bounds of reasonable doubt that it might have been after provocation and, therefore, without malice they should find the accused guilty of manslaughter.

There is little doubt that Medlish was in some way engaged in trafficking hashish, although no traces of any drugs seem to have been found. He had been absent for five months but had not been charged with desertion. It is reasonable to believe that he fired his pistol to ward off people as they surrounded him in the street, but this only occurred because it seems he and Gharbawi were arguing in a throughfare. The behaviour of the police is questionable, as is the evidence provided by the weapons expert and the doctor who carried out the post-mortem. This was a young Palestinian soldier who, unable to understand what was going on around him, was treated with complete distain. He was at the mercy of people who were, in some way, connected with the Egyptian he is alleged to have killed, and a British military justice system that appears not to have addressed the way it dealt with such cases since those of the First World War, nor the way it treated native troops upon whose service and sacrifice it so greatly depended.

The Sentence

The following morning, Tuesday, 1 June 1943, the court sentenced Medlish to suffer death by being shot but unanimously recommended him to mercy on the following grounds:

- The extreme youth of the accused.
- The fact that he had volunteered for army at the age of 16 years and had a clean record up to the time he admitted going absent.
- The murder appears to have arisen out of the Medlish's participation in the hasish trade, in which his actions were probably influenced by persons older and more responsible than himself.

A submission to the Commander-in-Chief, General Henry Maitland 'Jumbo' Wilson, was made by Revd Brigadier Hugh Scott-Barrett. This clearly indicates that Major General Basset was advised the sentence be commuted to fifteen years' penal servitude. General Wilson, as C-in-C, chose, instead, to follow the final direction given to him by Scott-Barrett.

I think it proper, however, to observe that if the protection of the community be considered it may be thought that there are few menaces to it more serious, or less deserving of leniency, than a deserter, engaged in drug trafficking, who carries a loaded and concealed firearm which he is prepared to use. It is true that the accused was 19 years of age, though that in the case of an Arab is not normally described as extreme youth, and that the deceased was himself a criminal, but the evidence shows that not only did the accused shoot in cold blood a confederate with whom he had quarrelled over a division of the spoils, but that within half an hour he shot and wounded another man whom we apparently thought was going to arrest him.

The sentence was confirmed on Tuesday, 29 June 1943 and on the morning of Monday, 12 July 1943, with all eyes upon the Allied invasion of Sicily, Corporal Hassan Naameh Medlish was executed by firing squad at Moascar. There appears to be no explanation was to why his name was added to the Brookwood Memorial as opposed to one in Egypt.

The Perfect Execution

Strict guidelines were laid down regarding the manner in which a military execution should take place during the Second World War. However, there were some examples of how this could go desperately wrong. In an embarrassing episode for the Royal Navy, a British sailor was shot by a Royal Marine firing squad in Italy and, having not died, had to be given the *coup de grâce* by the commanding captain, who had been specifically trained for this distasteful task. A pistol was placed against the unfortunate man's heart and a shot fired. When the sailor whispered to his executioner, 'bad shot' it was realised that this had not quite worked as defined in the guidelines. He was then shot for a third time, this time in the head. His crime was one of murder, and his final resting place is commemorated with a CWGC headstone.

In a subsequent letter to the Admiralty, a naval legal officer suggested that in future, 'The use of a firing party might perhaps be discontinued in favour of execution by a clamped and fixed Bren gun firing a limited number of shots in automatic mode, or execution by revolver at close range. I think it is desirable to investigate this question with a view to avoiding a reoccurrence of the unfortunate incident.' His suggestion was not taken up.

The guidelines for military execution as laid down by the War Office read:

(a) A provost officer may at any time in war or peace be made responsible for the organization and carrying out of a military execution. There are no firm rules laid down, but notes on a suggested procedure are included here, as this event is more likely to occur in an army of occupation than at any other time. The main object is to carry out the sentence as rapidly and humanely as possible.

(b) Procedure

(i)   Promulgation

The responsibility for promulgation rests with the O.C. unit; usually this is deferred until about an hour or two before the time fixed for the execution.

It must be remembered that the president of the court martial will have already warned the prisoner in writing that the sentence of death has been passed. The promulgating officer should ask the prisoner whether he has any request to make and whether he wants food or drink. He should be allowed, if possible, any drink he asks for and, if desired, a sedative injection by a medical officer. During this stage, the A.P.M. should be in touch with the O.C. unit.

(ii) Place of Execution should be secluded and as near as possible to the place of confinement.

(iii) Time for Execution. The best time is shortly after dawn.

(iv) Action by the Officer of the Provost Service

The A.P.M. of the formation to which the prisoner's unit belongs is responsible for the carrying out of the sentence; he will select the place of execution, fix the time, arrange in conjunction with the C.O. for the attendance of a chaplain, medical officer, firing party (with ten rounds ball and two rounds blank S.A.A.) an ambulance and for the provision and preparation of an execution post or chair, with the necessary straps and ropes, a cap, to be placed over the prisoner's head, an aiming mark for attachment to his uniform, and a stretcher for conveyance of the body to the ambulance. At the place and time of execution the A.P.M. will carry a loaded revolver.

(v)   The C.O. will arrange for the production of the prisoner to the A.P.M., if the latter has not already taken charge of him; he is responsible for the promulgation of the sentence and the delivery to the A.P.M. of the proceedings of the court martial for retention until after the execution. He will arrange for the firing party with ammunition as above, and for rifle-rests, if possible. He will arrange for the burial of the body and for the attendance of a chaplain thereat.

(vi)   The Medical Officer will accompany the A.P.M. He will examine the body immediately after the firing party have fired and before it is unbound and will inform the A.P.M. of the result.

(vii)   The Chaplain will accompany the prisoner from outside the place of confinement to the place of execution.

(viii) Procedure (Note: The prisoner may be shot either standing up strapped to a post fixed in the ground if available or sitting down strapped to a chair.)

A minute or two before the hour fixed for the execution the A.P.M. accompanied by the M.O. and two military policemen will go to the place of confinement and the A.P.M. will satisfy himself as to the identity of the prisoner, whose arms will then be pinioned to his sides with a strap. The M.O. will slip a cap over the prisoner's head and fix an aiming mark over his heart. He will then be led by the two military police to the place of execution, where a strap or rope will be passed around his body to secure him to the post or chair. At the same time, another strap or rope will secure his legs in the same way. The procedure should be carefully rehearsed beforehand so that only the shortest possible time will elapse between the visit of the A.P.M. to the place of confinement and the completion of the sentence.

(ix)   The Firing Party will consist of one officer, the R.S.M. (if possible), one serjeant [sic] and ten rank and file from the prisoner's unit. The rank and file alone will fire.

It is very desirable to arrange rifle rests for aiming some ten or twelve yards from where the prisoner will be placed.

The procedure set out below, including the signals to be used, will be carefully rehearsed beforehand.

The party will arrive at the place of execution in sufficient time to enable the following procedure to be carried out before the time fixed for the execution.

On arrival the firing party will be ordered to load with one live round. They will then ground arms and be marched a short distance away, so that they cannot see their arms, where it will be explained to them that all commands after the appearance of the prisoner will be by signal and in silence, except the command 'fire' and that the greatest service they can render the prisoner is to shoot straight at the mark. Meanwhile, the A.P.M. will change the places of the rifles, unload two and reload them with blank ammunition [marginal handwritten note: live rounds from which bullets have been removed]. The firing party will then be marked back to their rifles and will take up arms and remain perfectly still.

(x)   The Execution

At this point the A.P.M. will proceed to the place of confinement (see paragraph (viii)).

As soon as the prisoner has been secured the A.P.M. will signal to the firing party, who will come to the aiming position, using the rifle-rests, if any.

On a further signal from the A.P.M. to the O.C. firing party, the latter will give the command 'fire' which should be the only word spoken from the moment of the prisoner's arrival until his death.

If the medical officer indicates to the A.P.M. that the prisoner is not dead, it is his duty to administer the 'coup de grace' with his revolver.

Immediately after the firing party has fired the men will be ordered to ground arms and turn about, they will then be marched back a short distance until the A.P.M. has again changed the position of, and unloaded the rifles, when they will return, take up arms and march away to their unit.

(xi)   Burial

After the M.O. has certified that death has taken place, the body will be unstrapped, placed on a stretcher, and carried by the military police to the waiting ambulance, from where it will be removed for burial under arrangements made by the C.O.

Chapter 7

Private Cyril Johnson – A Question of Proof

Panel 10. Column 1
Service Number: 4538424
Unit: 'B' Company, 2nd/5th Battalion, West Yorkshire Regiment (Prince of Wales's Own)
Executed: Wednesday, 15 April 1942, aged 20

A chance meeting, a love of dance music, a lover's rejection and a detective novel were to be the catalysts that brought about the death of a young bank clerk in Ashford, Kent, on Friday, 6 February 1942. Unusually, in this instance, there is far less known about the assailant as opposed to the victim, despite relatively extensive documents having survived which provide details of the circumstances of the case.

The Victim

Maggie Smail was born on Wednesday, 17 May 1911 in Ashford, Kent, the daughter of George Straton and Ellen Elizabeth Smail (née Hughes). Her only sister, Daisy Ellen, was born on Wednesday, 13 August 1913 and, tragically, just a few months later, on the Tuesday, 18 November, their mother died. Their father, an engine driver, now faced life without his beloved wife, and with two young children to raise. Fortunately, he was surrounded by both brothers and sisters, and the girls remained in their care as they grew up. The two sisters had a close relationship, which was to prove invaluable as, on Tuesday, 1 January 1929, their father also passed away, leaving the teenagers orphaned. Maggie, also known by her nickname Mitsy, worked as a clerk in the Ashford branch of Lloyds Bank, and Daisy was the manageress of the Suburban & County newsagents. By 1936, now in their mid-twenties, they had set up home together in a flat above a shop in Beaver Road, a short distance from the home of their aunt and uncle, Albert and Beatrice Smail.

Whilst the sisters often went out together, it was Daisy who had a greater love of dancing. With the outbreak of the Second World War, they found themselves attending local venues where they met soldiers who were billeted in the town. It seems that neither of the girls were particularly serious with anyone, although Daisy had a regular dance partner with whom she had been friends for a short time. In November 1941, she and Maggie went to a dance at the Corn Exchange in Ashford, where Daisy encountered a soldier, Cyril Johnson, who was to bring further tragedy into her life, and that of her sister.

Maggie Smail, brutally attacked and murdered in her own bed by Private Cyril Johnson. (*Robin Matthewman*).

The Assailant

Cyril Johnson was born on Monday, 5 September 1921, the fourth child of Charles and Elsie May Johnson (née Donnellon) of Oxford Road, Horwich, Bolton, Lancashire, who had married on 1 June 1914. He had six siblings; Hilda (b. 1915), Ernest (b. 1917), Evelyn (b. 1919), Arthur (b. 1926), Joyce (b. 1928), Clifford (b. 1929) and Ruth (b. 1932). Records indicate that his father had been a tram conductor for many years, and, at the outbreak of the Second World War, his mother had taken a job in a Royal Ordnance factory near Bolton. During her pregnancy with Cyril, she had been involved in two accidents. In the first she had fallen down the steps of the local town hall and in the second, just three weeks before Cyril was born, a chimney had collapsed at their home and parts of a ceiling had fallen on her. After this, it was claimed, Cyril suffered from hysterical crying fits as a baby and, in his early years, suffered bouts of extreme anxiety.

After leaving school at the age of 14, he worked as an errand boy for a local butcher and as a piercer at a cotton mill. It seems that he did not like the work much and was unhappy at home and, according to his father, had run away on several occasions. With his parents' permission, he joined the army in 1938 at the age of 17 and served with 'B' Company, 2nd/5th Battalion, West Yorkshire Regiment (Prince of Wales's Own), part of the 46th Division. Although his army record was good, he was not popular with his comrades, being described as a 'gigolo' who was vastly more interested in women and dancing than he was soldiering. Johnson only ever served in the United Kingdom and by November 1941 was billeted just outside Ashford, where he met both the sisters. He had particularly befriended Daisy, who apparently felt sorry for him, after he had told her he was heartbroken because his fiancée, Muriel Lilian Golding, had called off their engagement a few months earlier.

The Crime

On the afternoon of Thursday, 5 February 1942, Johnson turned up at the girls' flat unannounced. It seems that he was on leave and had decided that he would not return to his billet until Friday morning. He had brought his dancing shoes and asked Daisy if she would go out with him that night. She agreed, but had to go back to work for a couple of hours first and left Cyril in the flat alone. When she returned from the newsagents, she found him napping with a book by his side. It was a detective novel about the murder of an unpopular pupil who had been strangled in a boarding school, titled *A Question of Proof* (1935) by Nicholas Blake. The pair had a drink and got ready to go out, meanwhile Maggie had returned home from work but declined the invitation to spend the evening with them. Daisy recalled how Johnson seemed to be enjoying himself at the dance, but sensed he was a bit down about returning to his billet that night. He had missed the last train and asked if he could spend the night at the flat, to which Daisy agreed, on the condition that he slept on the sofa in the sitting room. She made it clear that she had to go to work early in the morning, and on the way home from the dance persuaded Johnson to go to the railway station and find out what time his train would be leaving the following morning. A porter told them the first train back to the camp was at 8.00 a.m., and Daisy explained to Johnson that she would have gone to work by then, so he would have to wake himself up, but he could help himself to some breakfast and tea.

When they arrived at the flat Maggie was getting ready for bed and was surprised to see Johnson.

She questioned why he had not gone back to his camp at Wye and was concerned he had deserted his unit. Daisy reassured her that he would get the train in the morning, and Maggie took her hot-water bottle to bed and got into her pyjamas. Daisy made some cocoa for her and her dancing companion and he settled down on the sofa, whilst she went to bed with her sister. The two girls shared a bed and a bedroom. In the morning, Daisy got up at 5.45 a.m. to go to work. Her sister had stirred, but soon went back to sleep. Daisy prepared some breakfast and left it in the kitchen, then crept out of the flat so as not to wake anyone.

When he woke up, Johnson claimed he went to Maggie's bedroom to ask her the time. He said to her, 'Would you like me to get in bed with you?', to which Maggie replied, 'No'. It seems that he quickly became enraged at her rejection and pushed her onto the bed where, as she began to struggle, he grabbed her throat with the intention, he claimed, of frightening her but he had not realised how much force he had used, and she had fallen unconscious. In actuality, Maggie had been struck with a poker, causing two shattering wounds to her skull. Her pyjama jacket had then been forced up under arms and her trousers pulled off. She was sexually assaulted and then Johnson grabbed a red scarf that was hanging on the bedrail and tied it tightly around her neck, in a double granny knot. Her attacker literally choked the life out of her.

Daisy returned home from work just after at 9.00 a.m. and could see by the washing up that only one person had eaten breakfast. She felt that something was wrong and checked to see if her visitor had slept in instead of going back to camp, but found he was not in the sitting room where she had left him. The book he had been reading was left open, half-read, upside down on the fireside kerb. Daisy wondered if perhaps Maggie was still in bed, unwell. As she entered the bedroom, she could see the covers were pulled right up over her sister's face. Daisy approached the bed and gently pulled down the cover and saw blood on her sister's face. The poker from the living room was laying next to the bed. She ran out of the flat, terrified, and went to the chemist next door to fetch the pharmacist, Edward Brotherton, who found that Maggie was dead but her body still warm. He telephoned for assistance and Police Sergeant Arthur John Bones was quickly on the scene. Bones removed the scarf, which he said was 'very tight', and commenced with artificial respiration, most likely for Daisy's benefit, but it was to no avail. The arrival of Dr Reginald Hastings Jones confirmed the worst, Maggie was dead.

Maggie's body was transported to the Kent & Canterbury Hospital, at Canterbury, where later that afternoon the pathologist, Norman Henry Ashton, carried out a post-mortem. He described how he found two small wounds over her right eyebrow, the blood tracks from which indicated she was on her back when the blows were struck. An X-ray revealed a dislocated hyoid bone, which had been caused by a ligature, such as the scarf. He found that there were no signs of any attempt at manual strangulation, thus destroying Johnson's claim that Maggie had fallen unconscious because of his over exertion.

As the police investigated the crime, they established that, after killing Maggie, Johnson had made himself a cup of tea and helped himself to some paper from a writing pad belonging to Daisy, upon which he wrote two letters. The first was to his ex-fiancée, who was living at Fences Farm, Stowbridge, near Kings Lynn, Norfolk, and read:

Dear Muriel,
By the time you get this letter you will see in the papers an account of me doing a murder. All I want to say is this. I'm in love with you, and for the last four months since you jilted me, I've lived in hell, you made me hate females. The girl I've killed was teasing me, just like you did. That's why I did it, and because I hate women.

The second letter was to a female friend, Vera Ward, who was living in Pinfold Lane, Northwold, near Thetford, Norfolk. This was slightly more convivial and reads:

Dear Vera,
By the time you get this you will have seen in the papers what I've done. I did it because I hate women, it seems queer doesn't it after being so friendly with you.
   But all I can say is, thank you for being so good to me, for you are the only one I don't hate.
Goodbye.
Cyril.
PS. Think of me after I've gone.

The killer posted the letters on his way to catch a train back to camp, where he was arrested later that day by Detective Sergeant Harry James Drury. At the time of his arrest, Drury stated that dance music could be heard playing from a radio in a nearby room. On hearing it, Johnson said, 'I don't suppose I'll ever dance to one of those again'. He was right. Once in police custody, Johnson did little to avoid being charged with the murder. He explained that it happened in a 'moment of madness' but was fully prepared to give a statement of what took place, albeit that his version leant more towards it being a passionate accident rather than a brutal assault and murder.

The Trial

Appearing at Ashford Police Court on Monday, 23 February 1942, Johnson was remanded in custody until his case could be heard in the High Court. He was transferred from Maidstone to Brixton Prison on Wednesday, 4 March 1942, in preparation for his trial at the Old Bailey, and it was whilst here he was interviewed by the Prison Medical Officer, Hugh Grierson. He found the soldier was quite rational and well-behaved. He ate and slept quite normally, engaged well in conversation, there appeared to be no sign of any mental impairment and Grierson felt he was able to answer the charge against him.

The trial took place at the Central Criminal Court on Friday, 20 March 1942 before Mr Justice Croom-Johnson. The prosecution, led by Edward George Robey, put forward a case, supported by police evidence, that was particularly strong. The defence, led by Hector Hughes KC, argued that Johnson had been temporarily insane at the time of the murder, but they could provide no real evidence for this. The police had intimated that the killer might be of low intelligence, but doctors found this to be above average for his age. James Davidson of the Metropolitan Police Laboratory at Hendon had examined blood, hairs and seminal stains found at the scene and on the battledress of Johnson, all of which clearly indicated a sexual assault upon Maggie carried out by the soldier. Several extracts from the book he was reading were suggested as being the cause of his actions. However, Justice Croom-Johnson would not allow them to be read out in court. One of them reads: '"Dear me, dear me!" he exclaimed. "Most extraordinary and, er, tragic. No question about it, I'm afraid. Murder or manslaughter. He seems to have been throttled first by his assailant's hands. These bruises, you see. Then a thin cord tied round his neck. You will observe the red line: it has sunk in rather deeply."' This text, it was claimed, may have inspired the young soldier to commit the assault and hinted at manslaughter rather than murder. There seemed to be little explanation for the attack, other than he had gone 'off his head' after reading about a fictional crime. He was friends with Daisy, not with her sister, and he had not shown the slightest interest or attention to Maggie, so why would he attack her?

When she was called as a witness, Muriel Golding stated that Johnson had not seemed that upset when she broke off their engagement, he even said he had been expecting it. In response to being asked why she had broken off her engagement with him, Muriel said:

> I found Cyril Johnson out in various needless lies and he was very spiteful, also he would not tell me anything about his home or parents. He tried to domineer my ways and he was very jealous so that I took a dislike for him and thought it best that we should part, in fact I got so I used to dread him coming to the house. There was no other reason, he behaved himself all the time he was with me.

Citing his young age, the jury found Johnson guilty of murder and recommended he be given mercy, as he was only 20 years old and a serving soldier. The judge disagreed with their recommendation, and he sentenced him to death. In a letter to the Home Secretary dated Friday, 20 March 1942, Croom-Johnson wrote:

> The jury recommend this convict to mercy on account of his youth. The defence was insanity but, in my judgement, there was nothing in this point and it was rightly negatived by the jury in their verdict. The case was a 'sex' one and the offence was committed in circumstances of great brutality, apparently in the course of a rape on a dead girl, and I do not find myself able to endorse the jury's recommendation.

The Appeal

An appeal was filed but abandoned on 31 March 1942. Instead, it seems that Johnson acknowledged his guilt and began petitioning the Home Office for his death sentence to be commuted to life in prison. A number of letters found in the Home Office records, mainly from clergymen in his hometown, show that there were hopeful petitions for Johnson's death sentence to be commuted to life imprisonment giving various reasons

The Smail family grave at Ashford, Kent.
(*Robin Matthewman*)

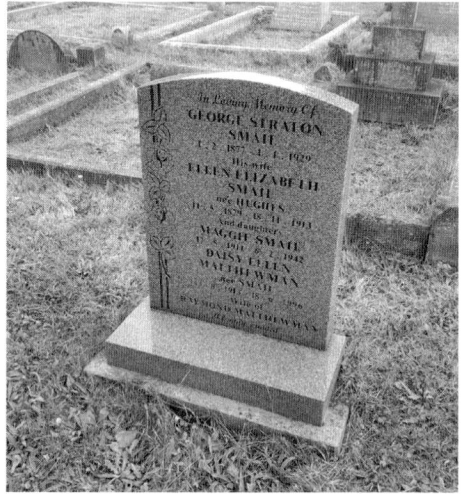

including the respectability of his family, the youth of the prisoner, the 'madness' of the act, the fact that his mother was suffering from cancer and the jury's recommendation for mercy. Each letter is filed with a copy of a personally addressed reply that the Home Secretary had considered the case and found no reason why the law should not run its course. The judge's decision was upheld, and the sentence should be carried out.

Daisy Smail and her husband, Raymond Matthewman, on their wedding day, Saturday, 6 November 1943. She rarely spoke of her sister's murder, blaming herself for Maggie's death. (*Robin Matthewman*)

At 9.00 a.m. on Wednesday, 15 April 1942, Cyril Johnson was hung at Wandsworth Prison by Thomas Pierrepoint, assisted by Henry Critchell. He was buried later that day within the prison grounds. Maggie Smail lays buried with her parents at Ashford Cemetery, Kent.

Daisy carried on with her life as best she could, marrying Raymond Matthewman on Saturday, 6 November 1943. She rarely spoke of her sister's murder, blaming herself for Maggie's death. Upon her own death, on Tuesday, 18 June 1996, she was buried alongside her sister and her parents. Remember them.

Chapter 8

Lance Corporal Walter Clayton – The Morecambe Beach Strangler

Panel 11. Column 1
Service Number: 3606419
Unit: 9th Battalion, Cameronians (Scottish Rifles)
Executed: on Wednesday, 7 August 1946, aged 22

By spring 1946, the process of demobilisation was well underway across the United Kingdom. The country had undergone six years of hardship and there was a shortage of many of the basic essentials including food, clothing and housing. Returning servicemen and women also faced all kinds of personal challenges as they reverted to civilian life. Aside from the institutional problems of release, husbands and wives had to adjust to living together again after many years apart. For those who had seen service in the Far East, the readjustment was particularly tough, taking a heavy toll upon relationships and lives. Despite the grim austerity of post-war life across the country, Joyce Jacques, a pretty 22-year-old brunette, was determined to enjoy herself. She had done her bit, and now

Joyce Jacques, the former WAAF who was strangled by Lance Corporal Walter Clayton on Morecambe Beach.

she wanted some fun, but little did she know, as she entered the doors of the Ship Hotel in Morecambe on Friday, 5 April 1946, that the bronzed man who caught her eye would soon be the last face she would ever see.

The Victim

Joyce was born, illegitimately, on Friday, 3 August 1923. She was raised from a baby by her grandparents, Ernest and Ada Jacques, at their home in Mawfield Road, Barnsley, Yorkshire. Her grandfather was a carpenter by trade and whilst the family endured tough working conditions in an era of austerity, Joyce seemed to have led a relatively conventional life, attending the Gawber National School and becoming a member of the Girl Guides. Her mother, Nellie, married Adam Alexander Thompson on Wednesday, 11 April 1934 and, when she was 17 years old, Joyce moved into their home, a seaside boarding house in Westminster Road, Morecambe, Lancashire. In 1940, Joyce joined the Women's Auxiliary Air Force (WAAF) being stationed in South Wales and the West Midlands and was eventually to rise to the rank of Flight Sergeant. On Wednesday, 27 October 1943, she was discharged from the service with a foot condition and her character was described, rather surprisingly, as 'unsatisfactory'. It would appear that Joyce enjoyed life, seemingly keen on drinking when she was on leave and being referred to on occasions as 'wayward'. She was, to all intents, a party girl.

After leaving the WAAF, Joyce became restless. She would spend time living at Westminster Road helping to run the boarding house, but then would spend weeks away from home. She had been unemployed for six months after leaving the forces but then began a job as a trainee nurse at the County Mental Hospital in Lancaster. Working in an environment many patients described as 'disagreeable', it was not unsurprising that she only remained there for three months, before seeking her release from the job. In summer 1944, Joyce returned to Morecambe and again worked in the boarding house, but in the latter part of the year she started a job at the Fairfield Laundry in Heysham. This lasted until January 1945, when she moved away again, not telling anyone where she was going. On Friday, 13 April 1945, her mother passed away and Joyce moved back to help her stepfather with the boarding house. This did not last long, and on 12 July she told him that she was leaving 'to have a good time' and moved into lodgings in Christie Avenue, Morecambe. This is where she was living when she met Walter Clayton, and where the couple would stay during their brief association.

The Assailant

Walter Clayton was born on Saturday, 22 September 1923, the son of James and Ada Clayton (née Bilsborough) of Woone Lane, Clitheroe, Lancashire. His father was a mill worker and also deacon of the local congregational church. Walter attended the St James School and the Ribblesdale Senior School in the town, and was described by his headmaster, Harry Gregson, as being somewhat below average intelligence, but his attitude towards other children was quite normal. Upon leaving school, at the age of 14, he gained employment as an apprentice painter with Lofthouse & Son of Chatburn Road, Clitheroe. He had quickly shown some promise at the job, but it only lasted for a short period of time due to what was described as a 'technical issue' between the employers and the local trade union. On 22 September 1939, his 16th birthday, Clayton took up employment with the C.W.S. Poultry Farm at Mitton, near Clitheroe. He was remembered by his employers as being a rather stubborn and headstrong boy who could not be driven, but he held down the job until Wednesday, 4 June 1941 when, now almost 18, he enlisted in the army, joining the Border Regiment at Blackburn, Lancashire. Just a month into his basic training, a report was initiated from a Royal Army Medical Corps psychiatrist describing the young soldier as 'a pale youth in rather flabby condition. He shows evidence of psychoneurotic traits of an obsessional nature and is emotionally underdeveloped'. The report indicates that he could not keep up with other recruits, was afraid of the dark and felt faint when he changed posture. It was suggested that he would improve but might benefit from a transfer to a Young Soldiers Battalion, but this never happened.

Despite the initial difficulties, Clayton completed his training and returned to Clitheroe where, on Tuesday, 3 February 1942, with his parents' permission, the teenager married his sweetheart, Barbara Stones. She was the 23-year-old daughter of Joseph and Annie Stones of Pimlico Road, Clitheroe, and was serving in the WAAF at the time of their marriage, prior to which she had worked as a shop assistant with the Maypole Dairy Company. Following their honeymoon, the couple returned to their respective units and only saw each other on the rare occasions when they were on leave. It was perhaps no surprise, as Clayton did not want to be parted from his wife, that a charge of desertion was made against him on Tuesday, 10 November 1942, for which he received a sentence of twenty-eight days' detention. A further charge, for another case of desertion, was made on Tuesday, 13 April 1943, which this time brought a heftier sentence of eighteen months' imprisonment. However, just five weeks later, on Thursday, 27 May 1943, he was transferred to the 9th Battalion, Cameronians (Scottish Rifles) and posted to the Far East theatre. As the 9th Battalion only ever served in Europe, it is believed that he actually joined the 1st Battalion, which had been serving in Burma and India since 1942.

On Tuesday, 1 June 1943, as he made his way to South-East Asia, he received the news that his mother had passed away as a result of myocardial degeneration and chronic bronchitis. Clayton was apparently devastated at her loss and never really got over it. He spent the next three years serving with the battalion, particularly in India, and, despite suffering malaria, blackwater fever and typhoid fever, appears to have fallen in love with the country. By 1944, the battalion were serving in Burma, as part of the famous Chindit campaign, unique in the way troops would carry out a series of small attacks to form a prolonged raid on the Japanese army. During the time they existed, the Chindits helped to keep vital supply routes open, all the time fighting against an experienced enemy. There is some indication in the case records that Clayton liked to describe the way he killed enemy troops and seemed to enjoy killing. He was admitted to a military mental facility in India and there is little information as to how long he actually served in a combat role.

In 1945, as the war drew to a close, Joseph and Annie Stones moved to Balmoral Road, Morcambe, on the Lancashire coast, where they opened a boarding house, not far from the home of Joyce Jacques. Barbara moved in with them, having been demobilised from the WAAF, and waited for Walter to return home from South-East Asia. He arrived home on 11 March 1946, and the scene was about to be set for a murderous event.

The Crime

Following his return to the United Kingdom, Clayton claimed he wanted to remain in the army, but it seems that his recent spell in a military mental facility may have prevented this from happening. Although he returned to Barbara, he, like Joyce, was restless and sought excitement. He drank heavily and behaved badly towards his wife. Eventually, on Friday, 5 April 1946, they had a quarrel and he walked out. Tanned from his service in the Far East and looking physically fit, he entered the Ship Hotel in Morecambe, where he met Joyce Jacques. The couple began drinking together and a short, intense and passionate affair soon commenced, during which Clayton spent every night at her lodgings. On the evening of 10 April, he quarrelled with Joyce, and she talked about leaving him. The following morning, he returned home to his wife and showed her a love-letter from Joyce. She threatened him with a divorce unless he 'pulled himself together'. This prompted

Lance Corporal Walter Clayton.

him to return to Joyce and the two began a drinking bout which lasted until 10.00 p.m. that evening. They returned to her lodgings in a taxi, by which time Joyce was so intoxicated that she had to be carried into the house.

On the evening of Friday, 12 April, the pair continued their drinking spree, calling at five different hotels and pubs, starting with The Battery in Marine Road West and finishing in The Elms in Bare. Joyce was feeling the worse for wear and so the couple decided to go for stroll along Marine Road East. At some point, they ventured onto the beach and a quarrel began. It seems that Joyce intimated that she no longer wished to see Clayton. Whether it was premeditated or just an instantaneous response, we will never know, but Clayton took the scarf Joyce had given him a few days earlier and twisted it tightly around her neck, jamming it up behind her right ear. He held it there until all life was extinct, then simply walked away leaving her laying on the pebbles.

After another drink he went to the Central Pier, looking for his wife, who was out for the evening dancing. When he found her, they went for a walk, and Clayton told her all about Joyce and how he had just killed her. He said that his wife then 'asked me to go home with her for the last time'.

At 9.35 p.m., a passer-by spotted the body of Joyce Jacques lying on the foreshore near a bus stop, just under the sea wall on Marine Road East opposite the Channings Hotel. The Police were called, as well as

The Battery Hotel in Morecambe where Joyce Jacques and Walter Clayton began their drinking spree on the night he murdered her.

a police surgeon. In the early hours of the following morning, Clayton was arrested at his home. He made a voluntary statement in which he confessed to strangling Joyce and was charged with her murder.

Clayton wrote to his father on 7 July 1946, unrepentant for his crime and explaining that he had confessed to murdering Joyce to avoid, in some way, a family disgrace:

Dear Father,

Hoping this letter finds you in the very best of health, I hope also that you're not taking things too bad, I'm okay and happy go lucky as ever. So, there's nothing to worry about at this end, I will probably make an appeal for the sake of you people, though I don't think it will be much use, still I will try just the same. But don't worry Dad I'm quite prepared to go through with it when the end comes taking it with a smile just like I always have done.

I'm not sorry for what I have done, so that's something to put your mind at rest. By the way Dad I'm going to ask for permission for Jack to come and visit me. The prison will notify you on what day he may come, but don't come along yourself it's the best that way. Don't send any cigarettes because I get cigarettes and beer every day,

I've got two prison officers with me all the time, we spend our time playing cards and other games. Though we are laughing and joking most of the time. Well Dad my trial was over in quick time without the truth being told it was the best way out. It will save you a lot of disgrace so please realise by doing this I was thinking of you as well as myself but also Dad I was thinking of Joyce. So, you see I'm true to my colours which is something for you to be proud of.

Well Dad I'm going to close there and will write again soon. So, God bless and keep you safe. And remember I'm okay and smiling as always so don't worry too much.

With love and respect from your son

Walter.

Cheerio Dad

xxxxxxxxxxxxxxx

The Trial

Walter Clayton, fully aware of his actions and wanting to get on with matters, wrote to his solicitors on Wednesday, 22 May 1946, whilst detained in Liverpool Prison, curtly instructing them on how he wanted to proceed and stating that he did not wish to appear at Manchester Assizes. Despite his request, he appeared at Manchester Assizes on Tuesday, 16 July 1946 before Mr Justice Stable, where he pleaded guilty, in what must have been a near-record time for a murder trial – just 3 minutes – and he was just as rapidly sentenced to death.

A psychological report, dated 29 July 1946, paints a revealing picture of Clayton as a purposeful liar whose untruths served nothing but his own ends, and whose statements were often contradictory. He appeared to hesitatingly consider his replies to any questions about the murder but was not deemed to be a pathological liar. However, he gave the Prison Medical Officer, Dr James Hunter Murdoch, a variation of explanations as to why he had murdered Joyce. On various occasions he claimed to have killed her because:

- They had a quarrel.
- He thought she might have given him gonorrhoea.
- She threatened to disclose their relationship to his wife.
- She had dared him to do it.

It seems that Clayton was, in fact, diagnosed with gonorrhoea some six days after he murdered Joyce, but whether this infection came from her is unclear. He declared a love for her in some correspondence, but in other letters, such as one he wrote to his mother-in-law, he stated that he had 'done the public a great service' by killing her. He also declared immense respect and affection towards his wife, yet he told a prison warder, following a visit to see him, that she was a 'fucking old cow'. The general impression was of a violent-tempered, conceited, boastful, unreliable and untruthful individual with no concern for anyone except himself. There was also a strong indication that he had been 'shamming' his mental illness whilst serving in the Far East and that he had fooled the army psychiatrists.

The Appeal

Despite his admission to killing Joyce, the death sentence handed to Clayton provoked a great public outcry and many letters and petitions were sent to the Home Secretary demanding that his sentence be reduced to one of imprisonment. Revd Charles James Stranks, who resided at St Barnabas Vicarage in Morecambe, and who had presided over Joyce's funeral, pleaded for clemency in a letter written on the same day that the psychological report had been produced. In this, he founded his plea on the basis that Clayton's mind had been affected by his overseas service, that he was 'not a criminal type', that he had been brutalised by his service to his country and that Joyce was a woman of 'low character', who gained her living by associations with men. Had he read the report before writing the letter, or seen the photographs of Joyce in the mortuary, he may have wished to amend this judgemental view. All the letters and petitions were, however, of little use.

Walter Clayton was hung at Walton Prison, Liverpool, on Wednesday, 7 August 1946 by Albert Pierrepoint, assisted by Harry Allen. His body was buried the same day within the prison grounds. Joyce Jacques had been buried, in secret, on Wednesday, 17 April 1946 at the Torrisholme Cemetery, Morecambe, her body placed in an unmarked grave close to her mother's. There were just five mourners at the graveside, her stepfather, grandparents and two aunts. One wonders, when reading his letter of 29 July and his opinion of Joyce, what words of comfort the Revd Stranks gave to the family as she was lowered into her lonely grave.

Chapter 9

Private David Miller Jennings –
A Murder in the NAFFI

Panel 12. Column 1
Service Number: 3654402
Unit: 1st Battalion, South Lancashire Regiment
Executed: Thursday, 24 July 1941, aged 21

Three victims of the Brookwood Killers were in their senior years. Mark Turner was the oldest at 82 years of age, murdered by a Canadian deserter, Jane Coulton was the 69-year-old victim of a brutal robbery and Albert Edward Farley, who was 65 years old, lost his life in a tragic shooting. He is the only victim who had seen active service in the First World War and was performing civil defence work when he was killed. Because his death was not as a result of 'enemy action' his name is not listed in the Civilian War Dead Roll of Honour, something that applies to many members of the voluntary services and perhaps should be reviewed. The case was to see controversy both before and after the event, some of which is still unresolved.

The Victim

Albert Edward Farley was born in Devizes, Wiltshire, on Tuesday, 8 June 1875, the son of William Henry and Eliza Farley. His father was a tailor by trade and after leaving school Albert also entered the tailoring trade. However, it seems that he later took up a job as a domestic groom, caring for horses on a local farm. When he was 21 years old he married Kate Maria Harding at the Dorchester registry office on Thursday, 19 November 1896, and their first child, Albert Hedley Charles, was born a few months later. Five more children were to follow: Kathleen Maud, George Edward, Vera May, Hettie Kate and Joan Marjorie.

With the outbreak of the First World War, Albert was amongst the initial wave of enthusiastic volunteers, enlisting in the army on Friday, 16 October 1914, as a member of the Army Service Corps, with the Regimental Number T2/016056. His skills as a groom were much needed and he was posted to France on Monday, 12 July 1915, serving with 17th Divisional Train. Initially, the division, having concentrated at St Omer, saw a period of front-line service in the southern area of the Ypres salient. It remained on the Western Front throughout the war, taking part in many significant actions across Belgium and France in locations such as the Somme, Passchendaele, Cambrai and Ypres. Albert attained the rank of lance corporal and was eventually discharged from the army on Monday, 26 May 1919, returning home to Dorchester. He was awarded three campaign medals, the 1914/15 Star, British War Medal and Victory Medal. It is uncertain if his experiences with horses during the war had any sort of effect upon him, but after leaving the army he again took up the trade of tailoring in Dorchester and kept a watchful eye upon his family as they grew up.

By September 1939, Albert and Kate were living at a house in The Grove with their daughter Joan and son-in-law Arthur Edwin Bellinger. Albert was in good health and had been employed as a coffee-bar assistant at the Holy Trinity Institute, in Princes Street, which was being used by the Navy, Army and Air Force Institutes (NAFFI) as a canteen for service personnel. In January 1941, the recruitment of civilian men and women into part-time fire-watching and fire-party duties became compulsory for those under 60 years of age who were not in military service, but volunteers were also accepted from men up to age of 70. Albert quickly volunteered for the role of fire watcher, the main responsibility of which was to deal with incendiaries as far as possible and call upon the assistance of the fire and rescue parties as need be. It was a generally unpopular duty as watching buildings in case of an enemy air raid was tedious, involving long nights. Albert was due to sleep at the NAFFI on alternate nights as both the caretaker and fire watcher but, sadly, his first night as a fully trained member of the Civil Defence Service was to be his last.

The Assailant

David Miller Jennings was born on Tuesday, 2 March 1920 in Severn Street, Chopwell, a village close to Gateshead, Tyne & Wear, the eldest son of Fred and Sarah Annie Jennings (née Miller). His father worked as a miner in the local colliery, and he had two siblings, Robina (b. 1924) and Rowland (b. 1932). Jennings joined the army in 1938 serving with the 1st Battalion, South Lancashire Regiment and, with the outbreak of the Second World War, served in France as part of the 12th Infantry Brigade, 4th Division, commanded by Major General Dudley Johnson VC. The battalion was sent to the border between France and Belgium as part of Lieutenant General Alan Brooke's II Corps of the British Expeditionary Force and had to escape the invading German forces before being evacuated from the chaos of the Dunkirk beaches on Wednesday, 31 May 1940. By November 1940, the battalion was stationed at the Marabout Barracks in Dorchester, and here Jennings shared a room with five other men, Privates Anelay, Bowker, Hall, Hood and Kay.

On Sunday, 26 January 1941, Jennings spent the day training on the barracks rifle range. He had, apparently, received a letter from his girlfriend ending their relationship and, after reading it, decided to go on a pub crawl with his pal, Private James Torkington. The soldiers first visited the George Hotel, and then moved on to a couple of popular pubs, the Antelope and the Old Ship, where they met up with two other men from their unit, Corporal Frank Leith and Private Joseph Gerard Riley. During this drinking session Jennings, who regularly borrowed money from his comrades, paid for all the drinks, and is known to have consumed at least five half-pints of beer with whisky and several half-pints of mild beer. Afterwards, the group went to a local milk bar where they enjoyed a cup of tea and a pie, then moved on to a fish and chip shop. The group returned to the barracks at about 10.30 p.m., with Jennings being described as 'not drunk, just merry', where they then consumed their chips and prepared for bed. All except for Jennings.

The Crime

As his comrades settled down for the night, Jennings changed out of his army boots and put on a pair of gym shoes, telling his roommate, Private Wilfred Bowker, that he was 'going out on a break'. Bowker and another roommate, Private Hall, tried to stop him, but he pushed them out of the way, picked up his rifle and ten rounds of live ammunition, and then left the billet. Allegedly, his comrades reported this to an officer, but it appears that little was done about it.

Walking out of the barracks, carrying his service rifle and ten rounds of ammunition in his pocket, he made his way across town to the Army Recruiting Centre in Princes Street, unchallenged. Here, it seems, he was aware a safe was located. He broke into the office by pushing the muzzle of his rifle through a pane of glass in the door, then lit a match, and could see the safe in the corner of the room. Placing the muzzle of the rifle to the safe door, he fired six rounds with the intention of shooting out the lock. The .303 bullets, incapable of penetrating the steel door, caused a shower of sparks and metal shards to explode across the room, one of which struck him on the cheek. Quickly realising that his efforts were useless, he left the premises and walked across the road to the NAFFI at the Holy Trinity Institute, a place he used regularly and knew well. His intentions were to steal the cash box, but he was not aware that a nightwatchman was on duty in the form of Albert Farley. Having first entered a garage gate, he went to a side door where he fired several shots at the entrance to the canteen to shoot out the lock. It is uncertain if Farley was behind the door and was struck by one of the rounds, or if Jennings fired at him as he tried to chase off the soldier. Jennings later claimed that he heard a voice shout inside the building and tried to get away, but on reaching the road saw someone opening the front doors from the inside. The explanation in his statement reads: 'I turned and fired my last round at the front door, not intending to harm but just to scare anyone who might be there. I then went away. Through my mind, being hazy through drink, I did not realise I might have hurt anyone. I did not hear anyone fall or call out after I fired.'

Either way, Jennings had entered the premises illegally, stole most of the contents of the cash box, discharged his rifle in two separate locations and run back to the barracks, still unchallenged. Upon arriving back at his billet, out of breath and with blood flowing from one side of his face, he ran to his room. Corporal Frank Leith attempted to speak to him, but Jennings slammed the door in his face. Leith managed to gain access to the room where he asked Jennings what had happened, he said, 'I tried to do a bust. I've killed a man.' In his statement, Leith claimed that Jennings later changed this to, 'I don't know whether I killed him or not.'

Sergeant Walter Murch was called for and asked Jennings to account for the cuts on his face, and he said, 'I have been trying to blow a safe'. When asked why he did it he said, 'Tell you the truth Sergeant, I am broke. I am short of money.' Jennings was placed under arrest and taken to the guardroom and both Sergeant Murch and Corporal Leith made their way to the NAFFI, where they found Albert Farley laying in the entrance doorway, he was dead, a bullet wound in his left breast. The air was filled with the smell of gas and Leith stemmed the flow from a pipe which had been struck by a bullet. The two soldiers moved the body into the canteen and called for the police.

Following notification of the shooting, Police Sergeant Harry Lill made his way to the NAFFI where he found the body of Albert Farley. The presence of some food on the table suggested that he had been disturbed when having a meal. Farley was removed to the nearby Dorset County Hospital and later that day, Sergeant Lill escorted Kathleen Maude Thorne, the daughter of Albert Farley, to the hospital mortuary where she identified the body of her father. After this, Lill went to the Marabout Barracks and arrested Jennings, who was still being held in the guard room. When he charged him, the soldier put his hands over his face and exclaimed 'Oh my God.' Lill felt that he was not under the influence of drink, though his breath smelt of liquor.

The Trial

On Monday, 3 February 1941, Jennings made his first appearance in court, before the magistrates in Dorchester, chaired by the mayor, Mr A.R. Jeffery. The event was a strange one, as the electricity supply had temporarily failed, and the courtroom was blacked out. In a scene reminiscent of Dickensian times, an oil lamp was burning on the solicitors' table, the mayor's bench was illuminated by two candles and the press bench by a further six. Standing in the dock wearing his battledress, the 20-year-old stated that he was not guilty and reserved his defence. He indicated, through his solicitor, Philip Howard Morton, that he did not desire to give evidence or call any witnesses at this stage. A remand was ordered, and Jennings was sent for trial.

A month later, on Monday, 3 March 1941, Jennings was transferred from Dorchester to Brixton Prison. Here he was observed by the Senior

Medical Officer, Hugh Grierson, who felt that the young soldier had been affected by his experiences at Dunkirk. He explained how the boy's parents had described his demeanour whilst he was on Christmas leave, in that he had been unable to sleep, was moody and not himself at all. Despite this, Grierson felt that the young soldier was not mentally impaired in any way and was fit to stand trial. The following morning, Jennings complained about a small irritating abscess on his left cheekbone. The prison doctor examined him and saw something protruding from the area, which he then removed. This was found to be a small metal splinter, debris from when he had fired his rifle at the safe in the recruiting office. The splinter was retained by the police as evidence, should Jennings ever try and deny he was at the scene.

Eventually, Jennings came to trial at Dorchester on Monday, 2 June 1941, before Mr Justice Charles.

The jury, consisting of ten men and two women, was presented with the two scenarios. Had this soldier deliberately and callously murdered an elderly man, or had he accidentally shot him in a desperate effort to frighten off his challenger and escape. Jennings again claimed he had fired at the door of the premises to frighten the person inside, that he had fired from the hip and had not taken aim from the shoulder. Evidence was produced to demonstrate that the shot, his last round, had been aimed, from shoulder height, at less than a metre away. Witnesses stated that they heard sounds like thuds and shots, the last one louder than the rest, possibly because Jennings was in the street by then, trying to make a getaway. If this was the case, he most likely encountered Farley after he had stolen the money from the cash box.

Medical evidence was provided by Dr Gerald Osbrey Taylor, who described the cause of Albert Farley's death:

> The direction of the wound was downwards and backwards, caused by a .303 bullet. It entered the abdominal cavity, lacerating the small bowel in two places, one laceration was 3 inches long. It then struck the spine and left the body immediately to the right of the spine in two different exits. In my opinion death was due to shock and haemorrhage, the haemorrhage being due to ruptured blood vessels.

It would seem that, irrespective of how he received his injuries, his death was not instantaneous and is likely to have been a painful one.

On Tuesday, 3 June 1941, the jury gave its verdict, guilty of murder. They did not make a recommendation for mercy and the judge wholly agreed with their verdict. In his summing up he was extremely critical of the army saying, 'I am shocked that a man in running shoes and carrying a rifle could get out of his billet and return without any interference by the military authorities. If there had been the control, there ought to have been this would never have happened.' The death sentence was then read out and Jennings, standing to attention, said, 'I did not intend to kill this man.' He was then led away between two warders.

The Appeal

Jennings submitted an appeal in which he claimed he had been drinking heavily and, after leaving the confines of the pub, his head had become 'hazy'. He had lived a decent, clean and straight life up until that point and would never have considered breaking into the premises. This was something that was contended after his execution. His appeal was dismissed on Monday, 7 July 1941. The following day, the failure of the both the army authorities and the War Office to provide clear guidelines as to how a convicted member of the army should be treated when sentenced to death was highlighted in a note from the prison governor, John Rutherford, regarding a request for the return of Jennings' uniform and gas mask. The note reads:

> That if the Army authorities supply a suit of plain clothes for this man, he shall be executed in such clothes and the uniform returned to the military authorities. Should a suit of private clothing not be supplied, Jennings would be executed in military uniform, all service badges and buttons being first removed and retained as unclaimed property. The clothing in which the man is executed will be burned as laid down in SO185. The GS respirator to be returned to the Army authorities.

Unlike the Royal Navy and the Royal Air Force, who ensured that murderers and rapists convicted in a civil court were executed as civilians, and thus did not disgrace the King's uniform, both the army and the War Office were somewhat erratic in their approach. Consequently, some of those executed were not recognised as serving members of the armed forces, whilst others presented the CWGC with an insurmountable issue, in that they were entitled to have their names recorded in perpetuity.

The Time is Nigh

Time was now rapidly diminishing, and pressure was beginning to mount upon the Home Secretary, Herbert Morrison, and King George VI to commute the sentence to a period of imprisonment. On Friday, 11 July 1941, Jennings' mother wrote to the King and made an impassioned plea for the life of her young son. The letter read:

> Dear Sir,
> I beg to appeal to you to exercise your influence to commute the sentence of death past [sic] upon my son, Private David Miller Jennings 3654402 1st Batt. South Lancashire Regt. I am his mother and from that fact and with all a mother's feelings I implore you to have mercy and exercise that clemency according to the feeling of mercy in you. It has been explained to me that acting on a momentary impulse a person may win a Victoria Cross and in other circumstances commit a crime as my son has done. I could be proud of his death if he could die on the field of battle, put him in the front line and in points of greatest danger as a soldier and I will be forever thankful to you.
> I am your humble servant.
Annie Jennings

The following day, Major William Bamford of the Salvation Army submitted a petition for mercy to the Home Secretary, containing some 4,372 signatures collected from the residents of Warrington and Chopwell. Even in the last hours before his execution, telegrams continued to be sent to the only two men who could save him from the gallows. One referred to Flying Officer Jack Lynch-White who, whilst under the influence of alcohol, had shot and killed his wife and been sentenced to fifteen years' imprisonment for manslaughter on the day before Jennings was due to be executed. Despite the intensity, all the pleas for clemency were to no avail.

Private David Miller Jennings, standing at 5ft 6 ½in and weighing 144lb, was hung in Dorchester Prison at 9.00 a.m. on Thursday, 24 July 1941 by Thomas Pierrepoint, assisted by Alex Riley, and in the presence of

Mr John Rutherford, the prison governor, Sir Claude Schuster, the High Sheriff, and Cannon Markby, the prison chaplain. His executioners, in a last-minute change, extended the length of the drop. The rope stretched a further 2in as it broke his neck. He was the last man to be executed in the prison and his body was buried the same day within the prison grounds. The body of Albert Farley, however, rests in an unknown location, with little recognition of the manner in which his life was taken whilst serving his country for a second time.

Controversy

Aside from the comments made by Mr Justice Charles regarding the army's lax security at the time of the incident, documents contained within the case papers reveal there was some controversy both before and after his execution. The first of these, dated 11 February 1941, describes how Revd Corin, the regimental chaplain, attempted to see Jennings just three days after his arrest. Despite all efforts, he was prevented from seeing the soldier by the prison governor on the basis that the prison chaplain, Cannon Markby, dealt with all spiritual matters. Later, on 10 February, Revd Corin again attempted to see Jennings, this time accompanied by the senior chaplain, Revd Young. The pair were again rebuffed and during a conversation about access, Corin asked the governor, 'Was it about the diary? – the Police have it.' The governor appeared to have no idea what Corin was referring to and felt that his intentions related to more than just spiritual ministration. No reference was ever made throughout the court case to a diary, but it appears that documentation exists which could have benefitted the imprisoned soldier. In the Home Office case review notes it states that the day after the murder, the police had taken a statement from Private Robert Anelay, Jennings' roommate and best friend, claiming that on the night of Saturday, 25 January, the two soldiers had taken a poker, broken into the NAFFI and each of them had taken a handful of money from the cash box. On the following day, Jennings paid for his mates' drinks using this money, but claiming that it was the cash he had saved for his wedding, that was now not going to take place. Not only was this alleged crime not reported, but the statement was not brought before the court, and could have demonstrated the insecurity that existed in the NAFFI, and the fact that the cash box was always left unlocked, something confirmed in court by the NAFFI manageress, Dorothy Warren. The notes indicate that Anelay's statement would have been against his own interests and, therefore, could be taken as true. The final entry in the review notes, ignoring this fact, simply states, 'In my opinion, the law should take its course.'

Further controversy arose after Jennings' execution when Cannon Markby, in direct contravention of Home Office rules, revealed to a reporter from the *Dorset County Chronicle* the final message he was given by the condemned man. The dictated message was subsequently published in both that newspaper and the *Dorset Daily Echo*. It reads:

> To my comrades;
> I have been talking to the Chaplain of the prison and wish to give you the following message.
> During my time in prison God has forgiven me my sin, and I pray and beseech you to turn at once to the Lord and leave the drink strictly alone as it has been part of my ruin.

Markby was forced to apologise to the county and police authorities for this grave error, which he did on 9 August 1941.

This, however, is not the end of the Jennings' controversy. Following the closure of Dorchester Prison in January 2014, proposals were submitted to build 185 homes on the site. Fears that new homeowners may end up living on top of a graveyard brought an outcry from the public, led by award-winning screenwriter Julian Fellowes. In February 2019, the Bishop of Salisbury gave the developer consent to remove the bodies buried in the prison grounds and rebury them in consecrated land. This means, under the current guidelines, David Miller Jennings will be entitled to have a CWGC headstone erected over his grave, which will provide a place to honour a convicted murderer. Could the same consideration not be applied to Albert Farley?

Chapter 10

Private Arthur Peach –
The Killing of Kitty Lyon

Panel 12. Column 1
Service Number: 4918596
Unit: 11th Battalion, South Staffordshire Regiment
Executed: Friday, 30 January 1942, aged 23

For the majority of modern society murder is perceived to be a heinous crime, however, it is perhaps motiveless killing that is considered most abhorrent. A violent and unprovoked assault on an unknown victim, aimed at taking their life, is often referred to in contemporary terms as a 'thrill kill'. One such case concerning the Brookwood Memorial is that of 18-year-old Kitty Lyon.

The Victim

Kitty was born in Walsall, Staffordshire, on Thursday, 23 August 1923 the daughter of James and Mary Maud Lyon (née Perrins). Her parents married on Sunday, 31 March 1907, and it seems that tragedy would strike them early in their marriage. Their first child, Charles, was born in 1908 and a daughter, Winifred Maud, was added to the family in 1910. Sadly, Charles died in 1912 at the tender age of 4. The couple then had two more children, Doris who was born in 1915 and finally Kitty, a late addition to the family. Her father was employed in Walsall as a brass caster in a local foundry and, eventually, her mother was to enter the same trade.

After leaving school Kitty was employed at the Grove Laundry in Walsall, where she worked as a steam-press operator. As the country emerged from the austerity of the Depression, tragedy was to strike the family for the second time when, on Saturday 1 April 1939, her father died at Walsall General Hospital as a result of a cardiac arrest, peritonitis and a gastric perforation. Devastated, Mary was left alone to face life, with only Kitty for company, as both Winifred and Doris were now married.

The Assailant

Arthur Peach was born on Tuesday, 7 May 1918, the son of David and Louise Peach. His father had served in the army during the First World War and been discharged in June 1917, having been injured. Home life appears to have been somewhat chaotic and his father, an abusive drunk, spent periods in prison. Arthur enlisted in the army on Sunday, 10 December 1939, at which time his father was serving a sentence in Stafford Prison. After completing his basic training at Lichfield, he was posted to Norfolk, where his battalion was set to defend the East Anglian coast. The regiment, part of the 144th Brigade, 48th (South Midland) Division, was then transferred to Tavistock, Devon, and whilst stationed there a .45 Webley pistol was stolen from the weapons store. Peach was apt to absent himself on numerous occasions and deserted his regiment totally in August 1941, returning to the Walsall area.

The Crime

Violet Richards was best friends with Kitty. She had been born in Walsall on Wednesday, 19 September 1917, the daughter of James Frederick and Elizabeth Richards. The family home was in Tantarra Street where Violet lived quietly with her parents and three siblings and, like Kitty, was employed by the Grove Laundry as a sorter.

On Sunday, 21 September 1941, just two days after Violet had celebrated her 24th birthday, Kitty said goodbye to her mother and left the house to call for her friend.

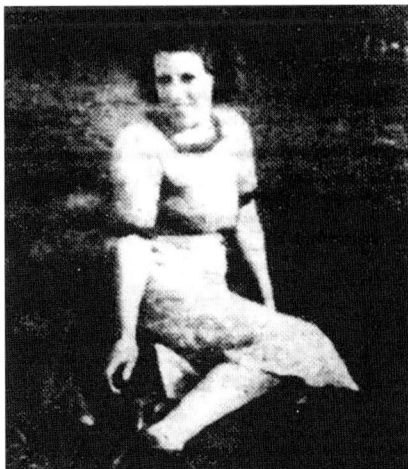

Violet Richards, who was shot and beaten by Private Arthur Peach during a Sunday morning walk with her friend, Kitty Lyon.

The two girls had planned to go for a walk, with the intention of doing nothing else other than gathering blackberries. They walked along Tantarra Street, into Union Street and then along the top of Mellish Road. From here, they turned down Leigh Road, past Rushall church and across the footpath that ran towards Daw End. The footpath passed through a cattle arch under the railway.

At this point, they saw a soldier walking towards them. He turned around and went back through the arch and, just after the girls passed through it, they saw him standing by some bushes. Violet said to her friend, 'What's the matter with him? He has got wild look about him.' Just after they passed him, a shot rang out and Violet felt a searing pain in her chest. Kitty, just 5ft 3in tall, began to run up the pathway, but the soldier chased after her, held a pistol to her head and pulled the trigger. Kitty, who had held her hands up to her face, slumped to the ground, shot through the skull. The soldier then returned to Violet, who he could see was still alive, and began brutally hitting her around the head with his pistol until she fell into unconsciousness. When she came around, the soldier had gone, her handbag had been stolen and her dear friend lay dying on the ground a short distance away.

John Short, a 16-year-old confectioner's assistant from Borneo Street, and his 6-year-old brother were making their way to Park Lime Pits. As they passed Rushall church, he had a clear view of the cattle arch and the path. Suddenly, he heard two shots but was distracted for a moment by a low-flying aircraft. When he looked back, he could see a man struggling with a girl on the footpath. She fell to the ground, and he was hitting her around the head, but he suddenly looked around and saw Short watching him. The man ran off towards the co-operative field and John made his way to the arch, where he found Violet Richards laying on the ground, covered with blood. He ran to the pits to fetch his brother-in-law, Eric Leonard Smith, who was fishing. When they returned, David Bickley, an aircraft engineer from Litchfield Road, was also there. They found Violet still unconscious and soaked in blood. Around the corner of the track lay Kitty, Bickley determining she was dead. He sent for assistance and at 12.10 p.m. Police Constable (No. 74) Albert Lee arrived at the scene. Detective Sergeant Samuel Dallow followed 5 minutes later. Constable Lee took Kitty to Walsall General Hospital, in the vain hope that she might not quite be dead.

By this time Kitty and Violet arrived at Walsall General Hospital where Dr Werner Paul Hirsch, a 25-year-old German from Charlottenberg, was the casualty house surgeon that day. He could see that Kitty was dead with a bullet wound behind her right ear, blood pouring from her left ear. Her friend was very badly wounded, a bullet having passed through her left shoulder and exited via her breastbone. She also had a total of twenty-two wounds to her head, including a compound fracture of her skull, both of her forearms were broken and two teeth were missing. These, he said, were all caused by the butt end of a revolver. At the Lyon's home in Union Street, there was a knock at the door. When Mary Lyon opened it, she found Elizabeth Richards standing there. The two women quickly made their way to Walsall Hospital, where Mary's husband had recently died, to be told the terrible news. Kitty was dead and Violet was clinging on to life. Mary was asked by Detective Sergeant Dallow to identify the body as that of Kitty. She confirmed that this was her youngest daughter.

A witness, Horace Arthur Wilson of Bloxwich Road, now came forward regarding the suspicious behaviour of a soldier he had seen when he was walking along Cartbridge Road towards Lichfield Road. As he did so, the man came trotting towards him but suddenly, opposite No. 14, a bungalow, he dropped something. Daisy Robinson, of Cartbridge Road, was looking out of her window at the same time. She saw the soldier going by and noticed he was carrying a lady's black handbag. He dropped this on the grass verge, stooped down and picked it up, then continued until he was out of sight.

On Monday, 22 September, the police established that there was now another witness, Thomas Thomas, a retired tailor of Dartmouth Place. He had been walking in Cartbridge Lane when he saw a soldier, walking very fast, crouched down. He watched as the man crossed the meadow and climbed a railway gate. As he did so, he threw something to his left. He then carried on, past some old farm buildings and disappeared into Cartbridge Crescent. The following day Thomas accompanied Police Constable Charles Jones to the location. Here, he recovered a slime- and mud-covered revolver, with part of the vulcanite palm plate missing. The weapon was quickly identified as a Webley Mark VI .45 dated 1917 and numbered 263097, and was easily traced, having been stolen between 20 and 23 July 1943 from the guardroom of the 11th Battalion, South

Staffordshire Regiment stationed in Tiverton, Devon. This information led to a check being made on all the men absent without leave from the unit. It was on the same day that Dr James Mathewson Webster, Director of the West Midland Forensic Science Laboratory, carried out a post-mortem on Kitty at Walsall General Hospital. He determined that she was a rather plump but healthy young woman who had a supernumerary sixth toe. She had suffered a devastating injury to her brain, and he recovered a .45 bullet from her skull, where it had come to rest in the ceiling of her mouth.

Kitty was laid to rest in the Ryecroft Cemetery, Walsall, on Friday, 26 September 1941, following a service in St George's Church, amid a mass of floral tributes. The Revd T. Nigel Hulme officiated. The sizeable congregation included many of Kitty's fellow employees, and at the grave a large crowd attended, composed almost exclusively of women.

Now, as quickly as they could, the police set about the task of trying to trace the missing man. Every available member of the force was soon engaged in a search within the borough, and a description of the assailant, which Violet Richards had been able to give, was circulated to other forces. He was aged about 23 years old, height 5ft 7in or 5ft 8in, medium build, light-brown hair, inclined to be fair, blue eyes, fresh complexion, clean shaven, dressed in army uniform with a narrow blue band on one arm, believed to be the left arm. He wore army pattern boots, no headdress and may be in possession of a service rifle. Very soon, inquiries were being made over a wide area, which was further extended later in the day with road, rail, and canal transport closely scrutinised. In the town and surrounding district members of the Home Guard and military units assisted, and throughout Sunday, during the night and again on Monday large numbers of motor vehicles were stopped, and their drivers questioned.

However, unbeknown to the police, the killer was already in custody. At 2.30 a.m. on Monday, 22 September, Police Sergeant Charles Smith knocked at the door of a house in Green Rock Lane, Bloxwich. He found a soldier sitting on the couch in a downstairs room. Smith, after issuing a caution, told him that here was a warrant for his arrest, for being an army deserter. This was 23-year-old Private Arthur Peach. Smith told the soldier to get dressed and that he was taking him to Walsall police station to be returned to his unit. As Peach got dressed, Smith noticed that the right-hand pocket of his battledress trousers was torn. The tear was deliberate, and one that could only have one purpose. To conceal a weapon.

Scotland Yard was asked for its assistance in the inquiry and Chief Inspector Arthur Davis arrived at Walsall police station on Tuesday, 23 September, having been informed that a deserter had been arrested, who happened to fit the description of the man wanted for the attack on Violet Richards and Kitty Lyon. On arrival, he interviewed Peach, who initially denied the attack or possessing the revolver. Over the next two days, Davis interviewed Peach on several different occasions and, each time, he changed his story. Eventually, he admitted stealing the revolver but continued to deny the attack. Later, he claimed he was in the vicinity but had not attacked the girls. Davis did not believe him and, eventually, Arthur Peach was charged with murder, attempted murder and robbery.

The Trial

Peach was brought to trial on Monday, 24 November 1941, at Stafford Assizes, before Mr Justice MacNaughton, who was also to try another murderous soldier commemorated on the Brookwood Memorial, Private August Sangret.

Colour Sergeant Edward Foran Courtenay, a professional soldier who has served with the East Surrey Rifles in the First World War, Lance Corporal Robert Haveron and Private Peter Sells explained that they had served with Peach's regiment, stationed at Tiverton, Devon. A Webley Mk.VI revolver with the serial number 263097 had been issued to the stores on Saturday, 15 March 1941 and was reported missing on Friday, 25 July. Peach, it was claimed, would visit the stores regularly, usually with the laundry for the Regimental Police, where the revolver was kept in a press with other revolvers, but this was not locked.

Winnie Grice of Newport Street was 'seeing' Peach and she described him as always wearing khaki, mostly with a badge on that said, 'Special Police', and how he would often carry a revolver with a lanyard attached to it. On the day of the shooting, she had been out and when she came home, Peach was waiting for her in her house. He seemed perfectly normal and was not phased when she told her there had been a shooting. Winnie, her girlfriend and Peach then went to the cinema, after which they went to the Vine public house and had some drinks. Peach said he was on 'special leave' at the time, but he had by then actually deserted his regiment.

Frank Cowlishaw, the licensee of the Alma Inn on Bentley Road, had known Peach since he was a baby. He recalled that a few days before the shooting, on Wednesday, 17 September, Peach had come into his pub for a drink. He was wearing a yellow armband with the letters 'M.P.' in black on it and had the initials 'S.P.' embroidered on his battledress. When he was asked about them, Peach explained that they denoted Military Police and Service Police.

Peach, who had pleaded not guilty, initially claimed that the revolver had been stolen from his coat. He later changed his story and said that he had sold the revolver to another soldier for 7s., and he only knew him as 'Jock'. He had arranged to meet this soldier at the cattle arch, and it was whilst this man was testing the weapon that the girls were shot. Frederick Alexander Griffiths of Lichfield Road had passed through the arch just a short while before the girls and had seen a hatless soldier go under the arch but did not see him on the other side. Griffiths stated that the soldier had distinctive hair and was alone when he saw him, there was no other soldier present. James Doughty, a bridle cutter, of Daw End Lane, Rushall, also saw the same soldier, who he identified as Peach. They had spoken to each other as they passed, and he confirmed that the soldier was alone. Harold Cooper, of The Butts, described the badge he had observed on the battledress of a hatless soldier he had observed walking towards the cattle arch a short time before the attack.

There was, however, one thing in Peach's favour. Detective Sergeant Dallow carried out an identity parade on Saturday, 4 October 1941. Eleven men were lined up, including Peach, and twelve people were brought in, one at a time, to confirm the man they had seen. Only seven were actual witnesses, the other five were not. Of the seven witnesses, only one picked out Peach. The others picked a different man. In his summing up, Judge MacNaughton stated that anyone who heard the evidence must have been convinced that Peach's story was untrue and that he alone shot Kitty Lyon. He was quickly found guilty and sentenced to death.

The Appeal

On Wednesday, 14 January 1942, Peach appealed against his sentence in the Court of Criminal Appeal. He was in uniform. His counsel, Mr J.P. Bourke, said that one of the grounds for the appeal was that the judge had misdirected the jury regarding the evidence of Violet Richards. He also criticised the judge's answer to questions the jury put regarding a print that was taken of Peach's palm. Mr Justice Humphreys said it was remarkable, given her injuries, that Violet Richards lived to give evidence. She was the only person, apart from the murderer, who could give account of this apparently inexplicable attack on the girls. It was proved that Peach stole the revolver from regimental stores and that it was in his possession on the day of the crime. There was evidence on which the jury was entitled to come to the conclusion it did, and there was no misdirection the judge.

With his appeal lost, Arthur Peach was hung at Winson Green Prison on Friday, 30 January 1942 by Thomas Pierrepoint, assisted by Henry Critchell. He is buried in the prison grounds but due to the fact he was in uniform when he was executed, and not discharged from the service, he was eligible for recognition by the CWGC. Peach is remembered in perpetuity, in a beautifully maintained cemetery. Kitty, however, lies in an unmarked grave that has no visitors. Violet Richards survived her ordeal and eventually married Albert Walker in 1947. She passed away in 1974 at the age of 56.

A Lesson Learned

One of the most vehement appeals for Peach's life came from the chaplain of Winson Green Prison, William Jenner, described as 'a young man with ideas and sincere religious views', who had only been in post for eighteen months at the time Peach was executed. He wrote an impassioned letter to the Home Secretary, outlining numerous reasons why the soldier could not have committed the crime and how his father had been seriously injured in the First World War. On the day Peach was executed, Jenner again wrote to the Home Secretary stating that he was resigning his post.

Chapter 11

Lance Corporal Frederick James Austin – I Didn't Know it was Loaded!

Panel 16. Column 1
Service Number: 6008711
Unit: Royal Army Service Corps
Executed: Thursday, 30 April 1942, aged 29

For many people across the country the effects of the Second World War would be very profound. Massive social upheaval, population displacement, food and supply shortages, combined with the ever-present threat of death, took their toll on society. But family separation, even amongst those who did not experience combat, was perhaps amongst the most damaging. Long days, and lonely nights, combined with the hardships of daily military and civilian life could have a devastating effect upon relationships and, in some of the worst cases, lead to an individual taking their own lives, or those of others. In contrast, there were those who used their newfound freedom to seek out fresh relationships, both short and long

Lance Corporal Frederick James Austin. (*Anneliese Rimmer*)

term, at home and abroad. Only a handful of passers-by paused to read the notice posted outside Horfield Prison, Bristol, on Thursday, 30 April 1942, which indicated that Driver Frederick James Austin had paid the extreme penalty for the murder of his wife. Their story is one that was repeated on numerous occasions throughout the war, some with a similar outcome, whilst others escaped the ultimate consequence.

The Victim

Lilian Dorothy Pax Hardman was born on Tuesday, 1 July 1919 in Prusom Street, Wapping, East London, the daughter of John Barksdale and Dorothy Bertha Hardman (née Page). Her father had his own business as a boot repairer, whilst Dorothy ran the family home and took care of their children, John (b. 1916), Tom (b. 1920) and Ernest (b. 1923) and Lilian. There was another child, Mary, who was born in 1929, but sadly she passed away in 1931. Lilian grew up at a time when the state of the economy was poor, wages low and there were high levels of unemployment. It was a struggle to make ends meet but the family appear to have grown up in relative security. On 16 October 1937, 18-year-old Lilian married Frederick James Austin, at Arbour Square Registry Office in Stepney, East London. At this time he was a serving soldier with the Essex Regiment, stationed at the Tower of London, awaiting his discharge after seven years of service both at home and abroad. She looked forward to a happy life with him.

Lillian Dorothy Pax Austin (née Hardman), shot dead in front of her 4-year-old son. (*Anneliese Rimmer*)

The Assailant

Frederick James Austin was born in Colchester, Essex, on Tuesday, 28 January 1913, the son of James William and Constance Jessie Austin (née Cranfield). He was one of seven children, the others being: Beatrice (b. 1912), Lillian (b. 1916), Arthur (b. 1919), Iris (b. 1922), Ronald (b. 1925) and Kenneth (b. 1926). His father had served with the Royal Navy from 1896–1900, and had also served in the 2nd Battalion, Essex Regiment during the First World War, eventually being discharged on Wednesday, 22 January 1919, at the age of 38.

On Saturday, 31 January 1931, just three days after his 18th birthday, Fred followed in his father's footsteps and enlisted in the Essex Regiment as a musician. He served in the United Kingdom for two-and-half years, during which time he was hospitalised on several occasions with fairly minor ailments, and once with appendicitis. However, by Thursday, 14 September 1933, he was sufficiently fit enough to begin a lengthy period of overseas service, commencing in India, where he remained until 26 October 1935. He was then posted to Egypt for a period of six months after which, on 18 March 1936, he arrived in Sudan where he would spend almost a year, before returning to the United Kingdom in February 1937. His time overseas was not without discomfort, being admitted to hospital on no less than ten occasions. A troublesome anal fissure had plagued him during his service in India, boils were also to be a source of irritation for him throughout his service and those age-old soldier's ailments syphilis and gonorrhoea were visitors both in India and Sudan. Once he had returned to the United Kingdom and fully recovered, he married Lilian and was posted to the Army Reserve on Saturday, 15 January 1938, finally becoming a civilian. But the clouds of war were forming over Europe, and over their relationship.

The Unhappy Couple

Initially, the newly married couple rented a bedsit in Commercial Road, Stepney, but later moved into another one in Flower and Dean Street, off Brick Lane, famous for its connection to the Jack the Ripper tales. Then, having left the army, the couple moved to Colchester, Fred's hometown. Now separated from her family, Lilian found herself frequently being left alone. She wrote to her mother telling her how unhappy she was, and that Fred was out drinking all the time, and getting involved with other women. Her mother suggested she returned to London, but Lilian wrote back telling her they had made things up and she would be staying where she was.

The couple later moved to Brentford, Essex, but things began to get worse. She would often turn up at her mother's home sporting a black eye or cut lips from where Fred had hit her. On top of this, frequent arguments between the couple caused landlords to terminate their tenancy, so they seemed to be constantly on the move. Her mother made continued efforts to get her to move back with her, but each time Fred would turn up at the house and charm Lilian into going home with him, an apparent regular event. Eventually, following another beating from her husband, Lilian, who was now heavily pregnant with their first child, applied for a separation order at Thames Police Court. However, after just a few weeks she returned to Fred for the sake of her unborn child. Their son, Ronald Bevan Austin, was born on 22 August 1938, and life seemed to get a little sunnier for the couple, for a while.

With military conflict now looking increasingly likely, Fred was called back to the army on Friday, 16 June 1939, and posted to Royal Army Service Corps. Just a few weeks later, with the outbreak of the Second World War, he was sent to France as part of the British Expeditionary Force (BEF). Lilian and Ronald, who were then living in Worthfield Road, Dagenham, Essex, were again left alone, awaiting news. Fred came home on a seven day leave pass at Christmas 1939, but was soon back on the Continent. Tragedy then struck the family, when Lilian's father died on Saturday, 23 March 1940. Fred came home on leave for the funeral and, by a stroke of good fortune, was admitted to hospital. Upon his release he was sent to a holding company at Woking to take up the role of drill instructor, and did not have to return to France, or run the gauntlet of the Dunkirk evacuation.

Lilian, who was now pregnant for a second time, and Ronald moved home again to be close to Fred and by the first week of September 1940, the couple were living in Victoria Road, Knaphill, near the Inkerman Barracks and, ironically, not far from Brookwood. Here William Thomas Austin, their second son, was born. Tragically, just seven weeks later, on

Thursday, 31 October, the baby would die from the effects of bronchitis and his tiny body was buried in St John's Cemetery two days later.

In January 1941, Fred was attached to a Regimental Training School at Clifton College, Bristol. Lilian had managed to secure a job as a porter at Temple Meads Great Western Railway station and the couple were looking for lodgings, but most landlords refused to rent to them because of the child. Eventually, they found a landlady, 51-year-old Marie Adele Leat (née Picquet), a French widow who lived in a house in Montrose Avenue, who agreed to let them her attic room for 10s. a week. The cramped, rather squalid, little room, containing little furniture, was to be their home for the next twelve months, and was to be the place where more arguments would take place, and Lilian's life would end violently.

A Summer Affair

Marion Alice Hendy lived with her family in Witley, a small village on the outskirts of Godalming, Surrey. The 20-year-old was employed by the RFD Company at their factory in Catteshall Lane, manufacturing barrage balloons. She often attended local dances, and, in summer 1941, she met a handsome soldier, Lance Corporal Frederick James Austin. It was a chance meeting that would lead to a court appearance for her, one where he would be charged with murder. The couple regularly went to the cinema and to dances and, within two weeks of meeting her, Fred asked Marion for her hand in marriage, despite the fact he had a wife and child. Marion readily agreed and soon after an intimate relationship developed. At the same time, Austin began to get into trouble with his commanding officer. He was frequently late for duty, most likely due to late nights with Marion, and eventually lost his lance corporal stripe, reverting to the rank of driver.

During this period, an incident occurred whilst the couple were standing in a queue outside a cinema in Farncombe, just north of Godalming, when Marion noticed a woman staring at them intently. Fred, looking rather surprised, went to speak to the woman, who promptly burst into tears. He then left the woman standing where she was and went into the cinema with Marion. A short time later, a request was flashed onto the cinema screen asking Austin to report to the box office. Here he was promptly escorted back to his billet by two military policemen. On the way, he informed Marion that the woman was his wife, Lilian. In total shock at this terrible news, Marion returned home, devastated. Although they continued to exchange letters for a period of time, she never saw him again.

As a result of this incident, and his overall drop in efficiency, Austin was posted to a holding company in Leeds for a short time, to help improve matters in his personal life. His commanding officer at the time, Major Michael St John Packe, a well-known English cricketer and historian, who went on to serve with 1st Airborne Division as a lieutenant colonel, regarded Austin as a 'broken man' due to his circumstances. His health was poor because of his ongoing issues with boils and his relationship was in a bad way. Packe stated that on one occasion Austin was sporting a black eye, which he claimed was given to him by Lilian. He was then referred to the Chaplain of the Forces, Norman Alexander Cairns, who arranged to see Lilian. She brought Ronald with her, and Cairns recalled how well cared for the child was. It seems that she was genuinely concerned for her husband's well-being and the chaplain, who felt that Lilian was of 'sub normal intelligence', formed the opinion that there was a form of reconciliation going on between them due to Ronald having been extremely ill at the time. It could not have been further from the truth.

Fred, completely infatuated with Marion, wrote to Lilian on Monday, 6 October 1941, to explain how he felt and seeking a divorce. The letter, a key piece of evidence in the case, reads:

Dear Lil,
No doubt you will wonder why I haven't written to you lately. Well, this is the reason. I have been courting a girl for some time now. She knows I am married, but it doesn't make any difference we have fallen in love with each other, and we want to get married. As you know already, I could never be happy with you.

God knows how I have tried to make the marriage a success. I wish now that I have kept away from you when I had the separation, but it was my love for the kiddie that made me go back to you. You know that I have tried several times before to get away from you. This is my last time of asking. I want my freedom so that I can marry her. I know I should be happy with her, so I want you to start proceedings against me as soon as possible.

I have been intimate with her on several occasions, and she would state the same if interviewed, so this letter should be ample proof of my misconduct which is all the evidence you require. Well, I am sorry it had to happen this way to you, but it is the best thing to do. We could never be happy together. Hoping I will hear about what you are going to do soon.

Goodbye

From your husband

Fred

P.S. I sincerely hope that Roland [*sic*] is quite well. Let me know.

Sometime later, he wrote to Lilian again, but on this occasion he described how his previous letter was only a joke and professed total love for her, it reads:

Dear Lily,

Just a line or two hoping they will find you and Roland [*sic*] okay. I have been expecting a letter from you, but I suppose you do not want to write to me. I want you to write to me and let me know exactly what you are doing. Even if you don't want to divorce me you could write to me not write to the OC.

The only reason I wrote that letter was because I heard you was going out with somebody else, which I do not believe, so I wrote that letter to make you write back to me telling me it was not true. If you love me as you say you do, you would tell me not somebody else. I know I was a fool writing what I did but I did not mean it so if you love me, please tear it up and write to me.

I hear the company is starting leave next week, so I will be having mine in about a month's time. I hope you will let me come down with you and Roland. Please write and let me know.

Cheerio for the time being,

Love,

Fred

P.S. please remember Darling that I only made that letter up and everything I said in it was not true.

(I love you) Fred.

The Crime

On 25 January 1942, with his company stationed at Ramsbury, Wiltshire, and preparing to be posted overseas, Austin began a seven-day period of embarkation leave. The time with his family appears to have been relatively uneventful until 28 January, when Lilian found a love letter from Marion Hendy in Austin's haversack. An argument ensued and, at one point, it seems he placed a live round in his rifle and pointed it in her direction, with the intention of frightening her. She told him not to be silly and to forget all about it, but it seems that neither of them could do that.

The next two days passed without incident and then on the afternoon of 31 January, the last day of his leave, Marie Leat was in her kitchen on the ground floor of the house when she heard a loud bang. She went into the hallway, where she saw Austin coming down the stairs. In a very agitated state, he said, 'Please get a doctor quickly. I was cleaning my gun and I shot my wife. The gun went off.' When Mrs Leat asked him why he had not put the safety catch on he replied, 'I didn't know it was loaded.' Shocked at what had at happened, Mrs Leat asked Austin to repeat what he had said to Horace Bidmead, an accountant who was also lodging at the address. On this occasion, Austin added, 'Honestly, I was cleaning it.'

Bidmead climbed the stairs behind Austin and upon entering the room he saw Lilian laying on the floor, soaked in blood. He grabbed the rifle, took it downstairs, and locked it in another room. He then telephoned for assistance and within 15 minutes both Dr Harold Bishop Logan and Inspector George Pickering of the Bristol Constabulary arrived at the address. Dr Logan examined Lilian, who was laying on her right side with her back to the fireplace. He could see that she was dead, and blood was sprayed on the wall behind where she had been sitting. He asked Austin, 'Did she fall into that position?', to which he replied, 'No, I pulled her there.' Logan would later tell to the police that there were no blood smears on the floor, so Austin could not have moved her after she was shot.

Inspector Pickering began to question Austin about what had happened, and his suspicions were soon raised. He escorted Austin to the Bristol Central police station, where he made this statement:

At about 6:10 by my clock – I believe it is 15 minutes fast – I was in my furnished room on the third floor with my wife. I was standing near the chest of drawers and had my rifle against my right-hand side. I was cleaning the outside of it with some cloth, a piece I use for cleaning. I had not taken the bolt out or examined the safety catch, nor the magazine. I don't know whether my hand touched the trigger, but it suddenly went off and my wife was sitting down darning some stockings and the bullet hit her. I rushed to her put my hand around her to lift her up and felt a lot of blood, so I rushed downstairs and called Mrs Leat and told her what had happened. I got some hot water and took it up and tried to dress her wounds.

Pickering then cautioned Austin and told him that he would be charged with murder of his wife, at which point he said:

I realise now that I am in a jam. That statement I made is true but there is more to it than that. About three days ago my wife found a letter in my kit. She asked me about it. It was a letter written by a girl to me. The letter was in my trousers when I was searched. I said to my wife, 'I should forget about it', but she kept nagging. I said, 'There is nothing between me and the girl.' It was then that I put the round in the rifle. I was going to frighten her. She said, let's forget it, so I put the rifle down. Today I started to clean the rifle and she said, 'What have you done with that letter?' I said, 'It's in my pocket. Haven't you forgotten about that letter? You keep bringing it up.' She was sitting down at the time and swore at me and said, 'It's a good job when you do go back.' While we were still talking to each other I still carried on rubbing my rifle. She said something, I can't think what it was, and the rifle went off. As soon as I realised what I had done I rushed downstairs to get help.

When Pickering formally charged Austin he replied, 'I'm not guilty of murder. I plead not guilty. That's all.'

The Trial

On Monday, 2 February 1942, Austin made his first appearance in court and was remanded until 16 February. He then appeared at the Bristol Police Court before Mr G.F. Jones and Alderman T.H.J. Underdown. He is described as having laboriously ascended the stairs leading to the dock, where he slumped down, his head bowed. He rose slowly to his feet when charged and made a plea of not guilty, reserving his defence. He appeared to be overwhelmed by the proceedings and stumbled back to the cells having been committed for trial at Winchester Assises.

Austin finally appeared at Hampshire Assizes, held in Winchester, before the Lord Chief Justice, Lord Caldecote, on Monday, 2 March 1942. The case for the Crown was opened by Mr Geoffrey Roberts KC, and the defence by John Trapnell KC. Austin maintained that his wife had become angry when she found a letter from another girl in his kit. To frighten her he put a live round into his rifle and, three days later, whilst cleaning it the rifle went off and she was hit. Herbert Frank Stevens, the managing director of gunmakers George Gibbs Ltd, described how the P.14 service rifle he had been asked to examine was standard army issue and required a 'double pull' to trigger it, and an experienced soldier like Austin, he stated, would have ensured the safety catch was

Policewoman Beatrice Mitchell helps a member of the ATS at Temple Meads Great Western Railway station, Bristol. She was one of last people to see Lilian Austin alive. (*Pen & Sword*)

on, the magazine removed and the breach empty before he started to clean it. Major Norman John Culver, commanding 98th General Transport Company, RASC, who had served with the Artists Rifles and the King's Royal Rifle Corps in the First World War, explained how Austin had been transferred to him on 24 January 1942, but he had not seen him as he had left on embarkation leave the following day and was not due back until 1 February, but he made it clear that Austin had no right to have live ammunition in his possession.

Beatrice Mitchell, who lived in Birchdale Road, Knowle, Bristol, was a policewoman in the employ of the Great Western Railway Company. She described how she had known Lilian for almost eight months and that she had confided in her about her private life. Fred never gave her any money, expected her to keep him in cigarettes and would hit her if she asked

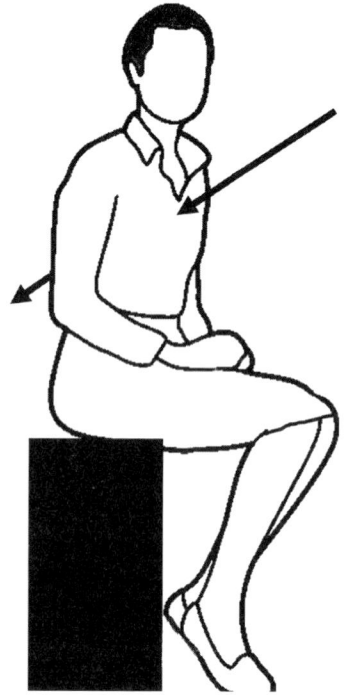

The angle at which the bullet entered Lilian Austin's body was proven to have been fired from a rifle held at shoulder height.

for money. On one occasion Fred turned up at the railway station and told Lilian that he had received a letter, informing him that her mother was not well. He told her she could not see the letter until she handed over her week's wages, which she did. On the afternoon of the murder, Beatrice asked Lilian if she had any money for food and offered to give her some. Lilian refused, saying that if her husband found it, he would take it away. He had come home just after midnight that day and demanded that she get out of bed and make him some supper. When she refused, he hit her. Beatrice said that Lilian was a very decent, hardworking woman, who showed a very big regard for her child.

Dr Edward Burdon Parkes, director of the Bristol Forensic Science Department, and Dr James Mathewson Webster, the director of the West Midland Forensic Science Laboratory, based at Newton Street, Birmingham, gave damming evidence concerning the bullet hole in Lilian's chest, the marks in the room and the line of the trajectory. They had performed the autopsy and found Lilian to be a young, healthy woman, whose death was caused by shock and haemorrhaging due to a bullet having passed through her heart, right lung and liver, and that death was almost instantaneous. There was a small entry wound in her chest, and a much larger one in her back.

Tests showed that the rifle, a .303 P.14 type, had not caused any scorching to Lilian's clothes or body and, therefore, must have been at least 12in away from her when it was fired. In their opinion, it was said:

> Bearing in mind the height of the accused, the butt of the rifle must have been at shoulder height. If the rifle had been discharged in the cleaning position it could not have caused the line of trajectory. A table would have been in the way, and the bullet would not have passed over the table but through or below it.

Clearly, Austin was not cleaning his rifle and was pointing it directly at his wife when it was fired.

The landlady, Marie Leat, whose husband, Rueben, had served as a Second Lieutenant with the 8th Battalion, Wiltshire Regiment during the First World War and had died on 25 April 1930, gave evidence indicating that during their tenure at the address there had been many arguments, some violent, usually over money and she had threatened to evict them if they did not behave. Lilian had confided in Mrs Leat over the letter her husband had written to her and was terribly upset about the matter. On the day before the murder, Austin had asked to borrow money from Mrs Leat and when Lilian came home from work, she explained that he had been to her place of work, but she had managed to avoid him. It was pay day, so she knew he would try and take her wages.

It did not take the jury long to determine an outcome and they returned having found Austin guilty of murder. Perhaps somewhat questionably, they also gave a recommendation to mercy 'owing to provocation received'. In an extract from his case notes, Frank Newsam, the Home Office Assistant Secretary, states that Austin 'was excessively provoked by the nagging of his wife over a love affair that had terminated. The prisoner is <u>not a man of bad character</u>'. This was an astonishing statement given he was aware of the evidence concerning how Lilian had been treated.

The Appeal

An appeal was launched at the Court of Criminal Appeal on Thursday, 16 April 1942 before Justice Humphreys, Justice Oliver and Justice Cassels on the basis of misdirection. Austin, standing in the dock in his battledress, made a plea that, at the most, the verdict should have been one of manslaughter. The court felt that there were no grounds to uphold the appeal and, as such, it was lost. Personal appeals and petitions were submitted to the Home Secretary, Herbert Morrison, in the days running up to the execution date but these were to no avail and Frederick James Austin was executed at Horfield Prison, Bristol, on Thursday, 30 April 1942 by Thomas Pierrepoint, assisted by Harry Kirk. His body was buried the same day within the prison grounds. He was unaware, at the time of the murder, that Marion Hendy had married Kenneth Soutar, an Irishman serving with the Royal Artillery, just a week before he killed his wife.

Throughout the entire case papers, it fails to mention that at the time of the murder their son Ronald was in the room. One can only imagine the impact on the little boy's life. He was taken into public care and remained in a children's home until the age of 11, at which point he was adopted and his surname changed to Furness. He built a life in the Lancashire town of Southport. Ronald passed away on 25 September 1994, at the age of 56. The location of his mother's burial is at present unknown. Remember them.

Chapter 12

Private Theodore John William Schurch – I Have Played My Game and Lost Fairly

Panel 17. Column 3
Service Number: T/61711
Unit: Royal Army Service Corps
Executed: Friday, 4 January 1946, aged 27

Amongst the names recorded on the Brookwood Memorial is the only serving member of the British army to be executed for treachery in the Second World War. The life of Theodore John William 'Teddy' Schurch was a mixture of fact and fiction, the features of which occasionally rivalled those of any imaginary international secret agent. He was born in Queen Charlotte's Hospital, Hammersmith, London, on Sunday, 5 May 1918, the son of Theodore and Henrietta Schurch (née Chapman). His mother was British and his father, a Swiss citizen, worked as a luggage porter at the world-renowned Savoy Hotel. In order that his son could obtain Swiss citizenship, the birth was registered in the village of Rohrbach, his father's place of birth. First living in Stoke Newington, the young family later moved to Stamford Hill and finally settled in West Court, North Wembley, Middlesex, Schurch's last known address in the United Kingdom.

Educated at an elementary school in Tottenham, Schurch was subsequently employed as a

Theodore Schurch as a young boy.
(*Schurch family*).

costing accountant for several firms in the Wembley area, including the Glazier Metal Company, the Philco Radio and Television Company and the Lancegaye Safety Glass Company. It was whilst he was working here that the 17-year-old met the firm's telephone operator, a lady he claimed was named Irene Page. She, he alleged, came to work every Saturday wearing a black shirt and began to get him interested in the British Union of Fascists, eventually taking him to political party meetings in a house in Willesden. He always claimed that he never wore a black shirt, due to the fact his parents, who objected strenuously to the teenager's late-night absences, were unaware of his political activities. Eventually, he was approached about becoming a member of the fascist secret service, which Schurch initially thought was a joke given his age and his limited educational achievements. However, he was soon persuaded that intelligence gathering was simply a question of being in a position to gain information and that his scholastic abilities were of little importance. It seems that, after this, he readily agreed to undertake 'missions' on behalf of the party, firmly believing that his activities were accomplishing nothing more than supporting the movement in achieving its political aims, as opposed to any subversive activity. He also claimed that, apart from senior members of the movement in his area, he had met Sir Oswald Mosley, the leader of the English fascist movement, but this has never been verified.

Schurch claimed that a man named Bianchi, a member of the fascist intelligence service, suggested he would be in a good position to obtain information regarding military movements if he joined the British army. So, on Wednesday, 8 July 1936, he walked into the recruiting office in Whitehall, London, and enlisted in the Royal Army Service Corps (RASC), signing up for six years with the colours and six years with the reserves. Initially, he was posted to Buller Barracks, Aldershot, where he spent three months learning basic soldiering, followed by an eight-week RASC driver training course at Feltham, Middlesex. During the time he was undergoing basic training he was contacted by Bianchi who arranged to meet him at Frascati's Restaurant, Oxford Street, London, a venue celebrated for its cosmopolitanism, luxury and excellent cuisine. This was a sumptuous and elegant setting for the instigation of international espionage, where Schurch was to be offered money for the first time. He was apparently given £5 to pay for his dress uniform, and so began his career as a paid member of the fascist intelligence service. The fascists maintained contact with him during his time at Aldershot through a man he claimed was named Edward King who worked for Spinks, the well-known antiquities dealer. Schurch stated that, in December 1936, he was invited by King to afternoon tea at the Savoy, but he could not accept the offer, as his father worked there, so the two men met at Lyon's Corner House on the junction of Coventry Street and Rupert Street in Piccadilly. At this meeting he was given £15 and told to let King know what company he was being posted to.

On the completion of his training, he joined No. 9 Company, RASC, at Bordon, Hampshire, with the rank of driver, and in June 1937, he saw a company notice asking for volunteers for overseas service. He wrote to King telling him about this, and it was suggested he volunteered for service in the Middle East. And so, on Thursday, 11 November 1937, he boarded the *HT California* heading for Palestine. Upon arrival at Haifa, he joined No. 14 Company, RASC, in Jerusalem, and became a staff car driver at GHQ under General Wavell. Whenever Wavell travelled from Jerusalem to Haifa, he would be accompanied by at least two armoured cars, usually from the 11th Hussars. The drivers would draw their fuel from the same location where Schurch drew his, and whilst talking with them he managed to obtain small amounts of information. Two drivers, Corporals Hurrell and Heath, were assigned to the general, as well as a relief driver, named Swatridge. They all shared the same barracks with Schurch, and he was able to extract a great deal of information from them concerning the general's movements.

In January 1938, Schurch was approached by an Arab contact and told to gather as much information as he could on the officers of the General Staff and pass it on to a man named Homsi, a wealthy Christian Arab, who was believed to have had a European education and was highly respected by the British Palestine Police. He would see Homsi at least once a week between February 1938 until the end of 1940, and after handing over any information he had collected, would receive whatever payment he requested. It seems, however, that much of the information Schurch collected was turned over to the Arabs rather than the Italians.

Early in 1941 Schurch was compulsorily posted to Genefa, Egypt, where he found it impossible to contact Homsi, as all mail was censored by the commanding officer, Major Whittaker. Schurch asked the

CO for a ten-day leave pass to go to Palestine, on the pretence that he had not had any leave for a long time. His request was refused, so the next day he obtained a pass form on which he forged the name of Captain John Richards, a name he was to use on numerous occasions to trick captured British servicemen into revealing any information they possessed. That evening, he travelled by train to Ismailia and then crossed the Suez Canal to Palestine, evading military police by carrying the luggage of an officer who was travelling on the train. After reaching Tel Aviv he contacted Homsi, explained that he had absented himself from his unit and could not be away from it for more than twenty-one days. He was given money by Homsi and told that he needed to provide information regarding motor transport supplies for the entire Middle East. Ten days later, Schurch made his way back to his unit, where he reported to RSM Hoffman, who then placed him in custody. After being brought before the CO, he was awarded fourteen days' field punishment for his unauthorised absence. Major Whittaker then interviewed him to ask why he had gone AWOL. Schurch stated that he had been refused leave, did not like the men in his unit as they were new recruits, some of whom had been promoted whilst he was still a private. Whittaker assigned him to 'more interesting work', this being in the Central Receipts Office, which dealt with ship movements and bills of landing for machinery and equipment coming into Egypt. The perfect role for an aspiring intelligence gatherer.

Shortly after taking up this new role, he was contacted by his old friend Bianchi, who was allegedly residing at the Continental Savoy Hotel in Cairo. Schurch made a request to go to Cairo on the pretence of visiting the Swiss Embassy to obtain a Swiss passport, but this was refused. As before, he went AWOL and after making a short visit to the Swiss Embassy to make his absence appear genuine, he contacted Bianchi at Groppi's Rotunda Cafe. Here, he was told that it was yet to be decided what information would be required from him in the future, and that he should visit the Continental Savoy Hotel if he needed to contact Bianchi. When he attempted this, Schurch was told that Bianchi had never been heard of and may have, in fact, left the country. In an effort to contact the Italian intelligence service he began pestering his commanding officer for a posting to a front-line unit. He volunteered constantly in the hope that his persistence would eventually bring success.

A 30cwt Morris commercial van similar to that used by Schurch to cross between the British and Italian front lines.

Finally, after about eight months, he managed to get a posting to No. 432 Company, 201st Guards Brigade of the 7th Armoured Division in the Tobruk area. He had only been with the unit for a week when the Germans captured Tobruk, and on Thursday, 18 June 1942 he became a prisoner of war. After a couple of weeks in captivity, he was hospitalised in Benghazi with Koch's disease, and upon recovery approached an Italian officer and asked to be put in touch with the Italian intelligence service, who were under the control of Lieutenant Colonel Mario Revetria. Following the completion of security checks with Rome, he was driven to a location at Ainga-Zala where he met with Revetria. Here, he was given the task of obtaining information from Allied prisoners of war, particularly officers, as well as crossing the front lines to acquire specified information on the movement of British forces, in particular, elite units such as the Long-Range Desert Group and the Special Air Service. Schurch used a 30cwt Morris commercial van from a unit of the Royal Corps of Signals for his journeys. He carried out this dangerous manoeuvre on more than one occasion, crossing into the German/Italian sector and then returning, but was never caught.

On Sunday, 13 September 1942, having been provided with a British officer's uniform, he was given the task of questioning prisoners from HMS *Zulu* and HMS *Sikh* who had been captured during a Commando raid on Tobruk. Posing as Captain John Richards of the Long-Range Desert Group, he mingled with the prisoners at Derna Prisoner of War Camp, obtaining as much information as he could, which was quickly passed on to Revetria, who was apparently incredibly pleased with the outcome. However, with his strong cockney accent, and inability to explain himself, suspicions about the unknown British officer were quickly raised amongst the prisoners and he was suspected of being a 'stool pigeon'. One British soldier who encountered Schurch was Private John Elliott Bowman, who was serving with 'B' Squadron, Special Air Service, when he was taken prisoner at Gussabat near Tripoli on Monday, 21 December 1942. Unwashed and bearded, he found himself locked alone in a cell at the Italian interrogation camp located at Tarhuna, Libya. The following day, a British officer entered his cell and began to ask him some military related questions. When Bowman asked the man who he was, he identified himself as an officer of the Long-Range Desert Group. Unfortunately for Schurch, Bowman knew exactly who he was. He had served with Schurch in Palestine in 1937, and knew him by his nickname, 'Issy'. When Bowman challenged Schurch, he denied being the soldier who had served with him and quickly made arrangements for an Italian guard to extract him from the situation.

The Italian Campaign

By February 1943, Schurch found himself in Rome where, acting as a civilian, he was given the task of locating a purported British wireless station operating out of the Vatican City, but his efforts came to no avail. At this point, he was placed in a special prisoner of war camp where he was given a new assignment, that of obtaining information from Colonel David Stirling, the commanding officer of the Special Air Service. As so often, he posed as Captain John Richards of the RASC, and his mission was to establish who Stirling's successor would be following his capture. This, he discovered, was Captain 'Paddy' Mayne. Stirling always maintained that he knew Schurch was a stool pigeon and never gave him any information the Italians did not already possess. But there are those who choose not to agree with this, believing that Stirling was fooled by Schurch and, in combination with documents captured from SAS troops at the time, the entire Special Forces operation was revealed. At the same time, the British intelligence services became aware of Schurch's alleged treason, and his name appeared in a list of British subjects who were believed to be aiding the enemy. MI9 contacted his mother to establish if she had a photograph of her son. She was very distressed at the time as she had not heard from her son since receiving official notification that he had been taken prisoner, nor had she been given an address where she could write to him. It was explained that a soldier with the same surname had been taken prisoner and a photograph was required to help identify him, which she willingly supplied. Now they could put a face to a dangerous traitor.

In September 1943, Schurch went to Perugia, again dressed in civilian clothes and taking his British army pay book with him, with the intention of contacting Italians who were supposed to be working for British intelligence. However, owing to the Italian Armistice being signed, he was arrested by German troops who believed he was an escaped prisoner of war and was taken to a prisoner of war camp at Spoleto. Here, he made strenuous efforts to convince the Germans that he was working for the Italians, but they seemed disinterested, and he was placed on a train destined for Germany. There were thirty-two men in his carriage and, just 20 minutes into their journey, a corporal of the Scots Guards and a private of the New Zealand Army managed to get the cattle-wagon door open. The train was moving at around 30mph and the men began to jump out, with Schurch injuring his ankle. He set off on foot with four other prisoners of war but needed to get away from them to get back to Rome. He began to make a nuisance of himself, and several arguments broke out. Eventually he told the others he was making his own way to the British lines, but instead walked to the Terni–Rome road, where he stopped an Italian supply truck with a German guard. He convinced the guard that he was an RAF officer

Colonel Otto Helfferich, head of the Abwehr in Italy.

who had been shot down whilst bombing Milan, and was taken to Rome, where he was quickly handed over to German police stationed at Caserma Castro Pretorio. The following morning, he was driven to the Albergo Flora, the headquarters the German Secret Service, where he met Colonel Otto Helfferich, head of the Abwehr in Italy. On confirming his identity, Schurch was given a bath, had his injured ankle treated and was taken to lunch at the Excelsior Hotel. Now he was working for the Germans.

Working for the Germans

The activities undertaken by Schurch on behalf of the German intelligence service in the period between September 1943 and March 1945 involved mainly attempting to ascertain which Italian civilians were acting as Allied sympathisers in and around the city of Verona. He spent a large proportion of his time mixing with members of both German and Italian high society, the well-educated elite who were often busy detaching their fascist links. In summer 1944, he left Verona to go to San Remo, close to the French border, helping to contact German agents coming in from France. By the beginning of October 1944, the Abwehr had been absorbed by the Sicherheitsdienst (SD), and Schurch claimed he had a salary in excess of 20,000 lire a month, plus expenses and bonuses. He was living the high life and was in very little danger.

In December 1944, he was sent to Rome to obtain military information regarding the morale of the British troops, particularly the 8th Army. The Germans had received reports to the effect that many members of the 8th Army were deserting at the front and going AWOL to Rome, a fact that was true. On the night of Friday, 5 January 1945, he left German SD headquarters in Verona and was taken to a minor airfield, from where was flown in a small aircraft to the outskirts of Rome and dropped by parachute, which he then buried in the field. Making his way on foot and carrying 5000 lire in old Italian banknotes, Schurch claimed that when he arrived in the town of Aquapendente he was recognised by an Italian girl whom he had met when the town had been under German occupation. He decided to abandon his mission and claimed that he travelled north, living on vitamins which he had brought with him, not daring to stop at any houses along the way for food for fear of arousing suspicion since he looked either German or English and did not speak fluent Italian.

He arrived in Florence on 8 January, made his way to the coast, where he then crossed the lines into German territory on the morning of 10 January.

The Beginning of the End

From this point on Schurch did very little but pass the time away. He stayed in Verona until 29 March 1945, after which he was sent on his last mission. This time he was again told to go to Rome where he was to learn of Archbishop Spellman's activities, and to establish if any pacts were being made between the Vatican and Russia, especially in Catholic countries which had been occupied by the Russians. The Germans wanted to know what the relationship was between the Vatican and the Allied military commanders in Rome, what England was doing about the enmity between de Gaulle and Franco, and how the Vatican may have intervened in the matter. As a sideline, he was to note anything of military interest, establish the cost of living in Rome, obtain details regarding the morale of the Italians both in the city and in the Vatican and determine whether there was a political party in existence in the Vatican which was working against Russia. He was to bring back copies of Roman newspapers, American weekly magazines and find out what political parties existed in Rome, who their heads were and what their strengths were.

Schurch arrived in the town of La Spezia on 1 April 1945 in preparation for his mission. Here he was to travel by Italian motor torpedo boat (MTB) to a point along the coast where he was to then use a small, motorised rubber boat to take him to the shore. However, engine trouble with the MTB caused the operation to be abandoned and he returned to La Spezia where, on the evening of Sunday, 22 April 1945, a British intelligence officer, Major Gordon Lett, arrived by jeep in an effort to contact local dignitaries and establish who was running the town. Schurch, now pretending to be an escaped British prisoner of war, saw this as an opportunity to ingratiate himself with the Allies and offered to assist with finding accommodation and contacting the local political parties. However, amongst the Allied officers who arrived in the town was a member of the American intelligence service, who became suspicious of Schurch and his intentions, and believed he recognised him from a time when he himself had been a prisoner of war. Schurch was eventually arrested by the US intelligence service. He was then interviewed and interrogated by members of the Special Investigation Branch, and eventually admitted to his acts of treachery. Somewhat naïvely, he seemed to think that he was supporting fascism without really realising the impact this may be having upon Allied troops.

Court Martial

Schurch was brought back to the United Kingdom to be tried by court martial at the Duke of York's Headquarters in Chelsea, London, on Monday, 17 September 1945, Major Melford Stevenson presiding. He was charged with nine counts of treachery, five of which related to his activities in North Africa during 1942, and four relating to his later time in Rome during 1943. He was also charged with desertion. The prosecutor was Major Richard Arthur Loraine Hillard of the Judge Advocate General's Office, whose brother, Second Lieutenant Eustace Arthur Peter Hillard, had been serving with the Royal Marines when he was killed in a German air raid on Monday, 26 August 1940 at Fort Cumberland, Eastney. Hillard

Lieutenant John Henry Bromage, Commanding Officer of the British submarine HMS *Sahib*. Theodore Schurch revealed his true identity to Bromage possibly in the hope of saving himself.

called several ex-prisoners of war to identify Schurch as the person who had been asking them questions about what they had been doing and where they were serving prior to capture.

Amongst these were Lieutenant John Henry Bromage, the Commanding Officer of the British submarine HMS *Sahib*, who had been taken prisoner by the Italians on Saturday, 24 April 1943 after being depth-charged in the Mediterranean. Bromage identified Schurch as the man he knew as Captain John Richards of the RASC, but also stated that on Monday, 3 May 1943, the treacherous soldier had asked for a private meeting with him in which he confessed who he was. He claimed that the Italians had become aware of his German ancestry and had threatened to 'frame' his parents if he did not co-operate with them. Upon asking advice from Bromage about what he should do, he was told to apply for a court martial in which he could then state his case. Schurch did no such thing. Lieutenant G.G. Hardy, RNVR, was another witness who had unwittingly helped Schurch a great deal whilst he was masquerading as Captain John Richards. They were together all day, every day, and Hardy would start arguments as to whose submarine was the best, his or Bromage's. These arguments brought forth information that Schurch required, such as the details of supply ships for the Mediterranean area. They also discussed officers of other submarines in which the German and Italian naval commands were very much interested. Schurch was able to give the Italians a complete list of 'S' squadron submarines operating in the Mediterranean area because of his work.

The defence was headed by Lieutenant Alexander Brands KC, who stressed that Schurch had suffered a persecution complex from an early age, and it was this that caused him to be so treacherous. He was, they claimed, 'a poor, uneducated fool who was caught young when he knew no better and jockeyed into a position from which he could not recover'. It was clearly demonstrated that his main objective was his own personal comfort, rather than any political cause. Schurch did not call any witnesses in his defence.

After being found guilty of all charges he received the only sentence available under the Treachery Act, death. He appealed twice, and petitioned the King for a reprieve, but all to no end. Major Edward James Patrick Cussen of MI5 made this comment regarding Schurch's last grasp for a reprieve, 'This man's history shows that he has no loyalties to anyone, and I do not feel that I am justified in suggesting that the information which he gave was of such value as to affect any recommendation which may be made to the King regarding confirmation'. It was claimed that he was gifted with an innate shrewdness and natural intelligence which compensated for his obvious lack of education. Undoubtedly, the renumeration and the easy living were mainly responsible for his activities with the various intelligence services for whom he worked.

Theodore Schurch was hung on Friday, 4 January 1946 at Pentonville Prison by Albert Pierrepoint, assisted by Alex Riley. He was the last person to be executed in the United Kingdom for a crime other than murder, and his body was buried on the same day within the prison grounds. He was the only British soldier to be executed for treachery during the Second World War. However, Duncan Scott-Ford, a 21-year-old merchant seaman and former member of the Royal Navy, had been hung for treachery at Wandsworth Prison on 3 November 1942, also by Albert Pierrepoint, under the 1940 Treachery Act. His death was not as a consequence of enemy action and, therefore, as a civilian seaman, his name is not recorded on any memorial maintained by the CWGC. Conversely, Captain Patrick Stanley Vaughan Heenan of the 16th Punjab Regiment, was convicted of espionage after spying for Japan during the Malayan campaign of 1942. In his case, it is claimed, he taunted his British Military Police warders in Singapore by telling them that he would soon be freed by the Japanese. He was allegedly shot by his guards on Friday, 13 February 1942, and his body dumped into the sea. As a serving British officer, his name is recorded on Column 263 of the Singapore Memorial.

Despite detailed investigations, the British security services could not find any trace of the men Schurch claimed had been his contacts, and their opinion of his activities were that they had achieved very little. They did, however, interview Irene Page who vehemently denied ever knowing or working with Schurch. Records show that she did work at the same company, and even had a small number of shares in the business, but there is no evidence regarding her political views or activities. It will never be known if the information Schurch passed to both the Italians or Germans had any significant impact, but if it caused the death of just one member of the British or Commonwealth forces, it could be argued that his execution was justified. Tania Szabo, whose mother, Violette, was a decorated member of the Special Operations Executive, murdered at the Ravensbruck concentration camp and whose name is also listed on the panels of the Brookwood Memorial, is recorded as asking, 'If it is absolutely conclusive that a person betrayed the Allies of their own free will during the Second World War then they should be erased from public monuments.' A sentiment many will no doubt share.

Chapter 13

Private Terence Casey –
A Case of Mistaken Identity?

Panel 17. Column 3
Service Number: 7399163
Unit: 'A' Company, 160 Field Ambulance, Royal Army Medical Corps
Executed: Friday, 19 November 1943, aged 22

The developments made in the field of science and technology throughout the Second World War were, in many cases, to bring advancements that would forever change life in Britain and help make present-day technology possible. Wartime medical advances, initially developed by the military, would eventually become available to the civilian population, leading to a healthier and longer lived society. But some developments were seen, at the time, as nothing more than science fiction. The electroencephalogram (EEG) was one such device, an apparatus for making graphic records of the human cerebrum where two or more electrodes were placed on different parts of the skull or scalp. The difference in electrical action within the brain was traced by styluses writing on a continuous paper strip. In 1943, the EEG was regarded by many in the medical profession as simply a 'gadget', and little reliance could be placed upon it, except by those who operated it. Initially, it was used on soldiers who were suffering from serious mental disorders, shell shock, suspected epilepsy or who had committed acts of violence without any apparent reason. It was very much in its infancy and one of the first times it was used was in a British murder trial, the case of a soldier whose name today appears on the Brookwood Memorial.

The Victim

Bridget Nora Milton was described by the Police as 'mysterious'. She was born illegitimately in Clonmel, County Tipperary, Ireland, on 27 May 1898, her birth name believed to have been Agnes Cook. She was raised, it was claimed, by a family whose name was Carey, which is the name she used until she came to England as a domestic servant in 1918. She never married but had three children as a result of what was described as an 'association' with a married man, Philip Milton, with whom she had lived for two years. In July 1925, Bridget gave birth to twin daughters, who she struggled to care for. They were raised at Nazareth House, Isleworth, a home for poor, orphan and destitute children – primarily Roman Catholic girls – until the age of 16, when they returned to the care of their mother. A third child was born on Sunday, 21 January 1934, but such were her mother's circumstances that she was taken into care by the local authorities.

At the beginning of July 1943, Bridget rented two basement rooms in Cambalt Road, Putney, for her and her daughters. The owner, Ethel Day, agreed that she could have the rooms for a fee of £1 a week and after two weeks she could live there rent free on the basis that she carried out cleaning and odd-job work at the premises. Described as a respectable, hard-working woman, who had daughters she could be proud of, she had high morals and a final entry in her case papers explains that her fear of soldiers – and strange men generally – was such that on the night of Tuesday, 13 July 1943 she would never have voluntarily entered the garden where her body was to be found.

The Assailant

Terence Casey was born at the Queen Charlotte Hospital, Marylebone, London, on 18 January 1921, the son of William Rubert and Ellen Casey (née Toole). He was one of seven children, the others being: Cyril, Desmond, Albert, Kathleen, Iris and Denis. His father had served a total of seventeen years in the Royal Marines, after which he worked as an attendant in the Bath Club, Piccadilly, one of the few gentleman's clubs that admitted women. Sadly, he died from the effects of tuberculosis on Boxing Day 1927, leaving Ellen and the children to face a bleak future. Casey attended the Lillie Road School until he was 11 years old, after which he went to the Fulham Central School, until the age of 15, when he began full-time employment. On Monday, 10 February 1936, he started working for Twinings Tea Merchants at their head office in central London. Described as shy and retiring, he had little to do with the other members of staff but was found to be a good employee. He was a Spiritualist by religion and, with the outbreak of the Second World War, informed his employer that he was a conscientious objector. He chose to leave the company on Saturday, 10 May 1941 to take up civil defence work, in an effort to avoid military service, and obtained a job with the Universal Construction Company based in Lambeth, which was involved in the clearance of bomb sites. He remained in their employ until Monday, 1 September 1941 when, having registered as a conscientious objector, he was brought before a tribunal where his grounds for exemption were not allowed and he was required to undertake military service.

On Thursday, 11 September 1941 Casey joined the British army, becoming a nursing orderly with the Royal Army Medical Corps (RAMC). Initially, he trained with 'H' Company, No. 1 Depot at Boyce Barracks, Church Crookham, Hampshire, after which he was posted to No. 18 Company, RAMC. A few weeks later, on 1 January 1942, he was posted to the Military Isolation Hospital in Harrow, where he served for almost eighteen months, performing some very unsavoury tasks. On Saturday, 15 May 1943, he received his final posting, to the 160th Field Ambulance, based at Panteg House, Griffithstown, Pontypool, Wales. Although his medical category was given as A1, he was listed as a TB suspect, due to the fact his father had died from the disease. His conduct record was clear and his commanding officer, Major Littler, described him as a good worker who had proved himself to be a trustworthy and reliable nursing orderly.

The Crime

On the evening of Monday, 12 July 1943, Casey left his unit and travelled to his mother's home in Hannell Road, Fulham, London, where he planned to take ten days' leave. The following evening, he joined his older brother, Albert, and another soldier, Rifleman Joseph Palmer, with the intention of having a few drinks. The three men first visited the Duke's Head public house in Putney, followed by the White Lion, where they were joined by a sailor. The four men then returned to the Duke's Head, where they met with a man and two women. Finally, the four servicemen and one of the women walked to the Quill pub in Charlwood Road, Putney, where they spent the rest of the evening.

At the same time, Bridget Milton, who had spent the early evening with a friend, Ernest Charles Littleboy, known to her daughters as 'Uncle Ernie', a widower living in Landford Road, was making her way home, and called in at another friend's house, that of Phillip Watson Tyrrell, a 61-year-old Irishman living in Quill Lane. They had not known each other for very long, but got on well, as they both drank at the Quill pub and were Irish. Their relationship was purely platonic and she called at his home that night to see if he wanted to go out for a drink. As he really did not want to, she went out and returned with a bottle of stout. He estimated that she was only at his address for about an hour and during this time he had given her two glass decanters and a red glass biscuit barrel, which he wrapped up in a copy of the *Evening News* from that day.

The former Quill public house. It was from here that Private Terence Casey began to follow his victim.

The licensee of the Quill, 32-year-old Elizabeth Violet Davis, and one of the barmaids, 40-year-old Freda Gibbons, recalled a woman they knew as the 'little Irish lady' coming into the pub. She drank a glass of Guinness, purchased a bottle of Toby Stout and then left. They also remembered seeing three men in the Saloon Bar, two soldiers and a sailor, despite the bar being busy. Freda recollected how one of the soldiers made 'a suggestion' to her and told her he would be waiting for her outside, Freda told him, 'Don't be so silly, I'm old enough to be your mother', and thought no more of it. At 10.30 p.m., as the pub closed, Casey's brother suggested they make their way home, but Terence said he wanted to 'hang around for a bit'. A witness, schoolmaster William Taylor, said he had seen a soldier, looking agitated, opening the pub door slightly several times, as though he was looking for someone, but when he realised he was being watched, he walked off quickly. As Freda Gibbons left the pub that night, she used a different exit to normal, and noticed a soldier standing in the doorway to the Public Bar, where she would usually leave from. Disturbed by this, she asked another barmaid, 52-year-old Gladys Jane Miller, if she could walk with her, and the pair began to stroll along Quill Lane. As they passed No. 2, they noticed Bridget Milton talking to a man they knew as 'Paddy' who lived at the address. Bridget, upon seeing the two women, said to Phillip Tyrell, 'Those girls are afraid of the soldiers.' He then saw a soldier who was walking at an easy pace when he first spotted him, but then quickened his step as he went down Quill Lane towards Quill Bridge. Tyrell watched as Bridget Milton, and then the soldier, disappeared from view, the time was 11.10 p.m.

At 11.25 p.m. that night, John Walton, a newsagent of Coalcroft Road and a volunteer air raid warden, was on patrol with another volunteer, Lionel Hunter Weaver, in Gwendolen Avenue, when he heard a sound that, at first, he thought was an air raid siren beginning. He quickly realised that this was not the case and, as he approached the front garden of No. 8, the home of 74-year-old Ernest Quick and his family, Walton saw the shrubbery moving and, believing that this was an animal of some sorts, he flicked on his torch. In the dim light, he saw a woman, face down on the lawn, her dress pushed up around her shoulders and her underclothing disarranged, her naked legs and buttocks visible. Laying across her, with his head in the shrubbery, he could see a soldier. At that moment a police patrol car, containing PC Charles Nelson and PC

The lawn in Gwendolen Avenue, Putney, where Bridget Milton was attacked and murdered. (*The National Archives – Crim1/1538*)

William Kimberley Kewell of 'V' Division, drove down Gwendolen Avenue, and Walton flagged them down. At first, Nelson thought the couple were dead, but as he approached, he could see the soldier moving and, pulling him to his feet, said, 'What's going on here chummy?' The soldier said, 'She cut rough, so I bashed her.'

At this point, PC James Hyde arrived and asked the soldier who the woman was. He replied, 'I don't know, I met her in The Quill, and we had a few drinks.' Hyde placed the soldier in his radio car and drove him to Putney police station. He noticed that the soldiers trouser fly was open, and he had a bloodstain on the front of his uniform. In the meantime, PC Nelson had turned the woman onto her back, her chest was exposed, and there was blood on her lips and ear. Her breathing was shallow and her pulse weak, but it seemed she was alive, although not much could be done for her. Dr James Wilson Clyne then arrived on the scene, but he was too late, she had died a few moments before. A handbag nearby contained an identity card in the name of Phyllis Milton, but this was her daughter's card. It was not long before they established that the dead woman was, in fact, Bridget Nora Milton.

At first, the police believed that the crime had 'the appearance of a man, encouraged by a woman who, when the time came, refused to satisfy his sexual craving, killed the woman in his unsatisfied frenzy by attempting to gain his ends by force'. They quickly realised that it was, in fact, a brutal murder committed in an attempt to rape. Upon his arrival at Putney police station, Casey was in a dishevelled state, his trouser fly was open, there was mud on his knees, blood stains on his battledress blouse and he had dried blood on his hands. PC Albert Edward Morris asked him why he had an iris leaf sticking out of his battledress blouse. He replied, 'I tried to get a bit of under, she refused, so I bashed her.' This was deemed to be the most truthful and damming statement that Casey made throughout the whole case.

Detective Inspector Dorey and Detective Sergeant Palmer visited the crime scene, and found Bridget was still laying in the front garden where she had been killed. Her arms were doubled up under her body, the ground around her was disturbed and it was clear she had put up a tremendous struggle. They found her clothing in complete disarray, a sanitary napkin ripped off, her top dentures some distance away and all around were shattered pieces of the red glass biscuit barrel that Phillip Tyrell had given her. The ground was soaked in blood and faeces but her assailant, who's red and navy forage cap was found at the scene, had not achieved his aim. The detectives accompanied Dr Clyne back to Putney police station, where the soldier had been identified as Private Terence Casey. The doctor examined him and found that his breath smelt of alcohol, although he was not drunk, his pupils were dilated and his pulse rapid. However, it was felt that he was fit enough to be detained.

Casey then gave a statement in which he described how he had met a girl in the Quill public house, and they were drinking together. Although his brother had tried to get him to go home at closing time, he had chosen to stay with the girl and had offered to walk her home. On arriving at her house, they entered the garden and had begun to kiss and cuddle and although there was some initial resistance, it was only temporary. She led him to believe he could have sexual intercourse with her but then she began to struggle, and they fell to the ground, where she started to scream. He placed his hand around her throat and squeezed but not sufficiently enough to render her unconscious. He was sorry if anything had happened, but he had been drinking since 7.30 p.m. and must have lost control of himself. He had never met the girl and did not know her name.

In the meantime, Bridget's body had been transported to Battersea mortuary where she was identified by her 18-year-old daughter, Josephine. At 6.15 a.m. on the morning of Wednesday, 14 July, the day when the war film *For Whom the Bell Tolls* was released across the United Kingdom, Dr Keith Simpson, a Home Office pathologist, carried out a post-mortem at Guy's Hospital. In a very graphic and detailed report, he describes how Bridget had suffered cuts and bruises in the violent struggle with her assailant, which had taken place in an area between the front door of the house through to the low front wall where she was found. There had been an attempt to have both sexual and anal intercourse with her and there had been multiple attempts at manual strangulation. Bridget had suffered a total of five fractures to her voice box from what Simpson described as 'a repeated grip of most unusual force'. Later that day, after being charged with her murder, Terence Casey appeared before the magistrate, Claude Mullins, at the Southwestern Police Court. He was remanded in custody until Thursday, 22 July 1943.

Brain Test

On Thursday, 9 September, Casey was taken to Sutton Hospital where Dr John Denis Nelson Hill, a psychological medicine expert from St Thomas' Hospital, put him through a series of tests over a two-day period using an electroencephalograph. Essentially, after eating a normal breakfast, Casey was given water to drink at the rate of four pints an hour, to replicate the twelve pints of beer he had consumed on the night of the attack. Hill examined Casey at the end of each hour, and he was also taken for a 5- to 10-minute stroll, to reproduce the exercise he had when he walked from one public house to another. At the end of each test Casey was subjected to 3 minutes' deep breathing to recreate the exertion his body would have been going through at the time of the attack. Hill's examination found no trace of bad temper or abnormal traits, but the electroencephalograph did show an irregular rhythm which appeared with considerable frequency. This type of record, it was suggested, indicated that the person was susceptible to a variety of medical disorders, the chief of which was epilepsy and an epileptic-like state in which aggressive

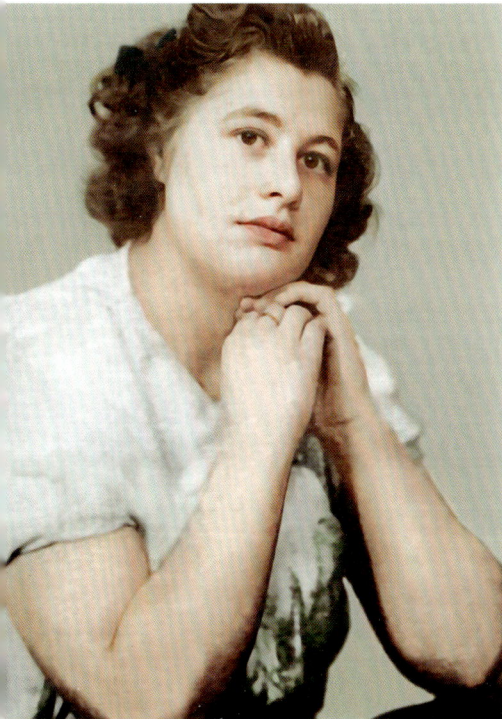

Kitty Lyon, the 18-year-old shot dead by Private Arthur Peach. She lays in an unmarked grave whilst his name is recorded in perpetuity on the Brookwood Memorial. (*Colourised by Doug Banks – Colourising History*)

The insignia of the 48th (South Midland) Division with two red bars denoting the 144th Infantry Brigade. This distinctive sleeve badge helped to identify Private Arthur Peach.

Iris Deeley, murdered by Gunner James Ernest Kemp near Well Hall railway station whilst she was making her way back to RAF Kidbrooke. (*Colourised by Doug Banks – Colourising History*)

Driver Theodore Schurch following his capture. He was the only member of the British armed forces to be executed during the Second World War for treachery.

Aircraftswoman 1st Class Marguerite Burge, murdered by Private Charles Arthur Raymond and buried at the Havant and Waterloo Cemetery, Hampshire.

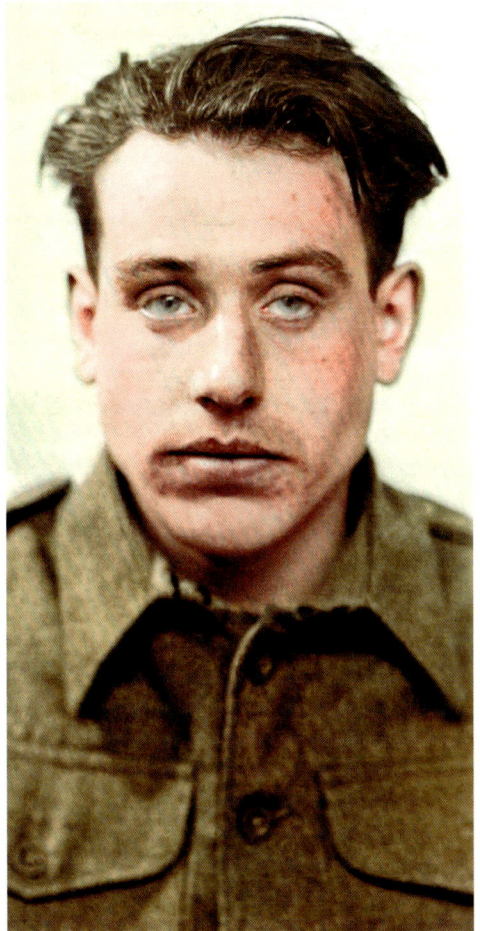

Private Charles Arthur Raymond. (*Colourised by Doug Banks – Colourising History*)

Lance Corporal Frederick James Austin, who shot dead his wife, Lilian Dorothy Pax Austin, in front of their son, Ronald, who was just 4 years old. (*Anneliese Rimmer. Colourised by Doug Banks – Colourising History*)

Maggie Smailw, brutally murdered by Private Cyril Johnson in a sexually motivated attack. (*Robin Matthewman. Colourised by Doug Banks – Colourising History*)

Field Marshal Henry Maitland Wilson, 1st Baron Wilson, GCB, GBE, DSO.

Corporal Salameh, who is alleged to have been present at the murder of Private Abdel Ghaffa Mohamad Mansour. (*The National Archives – WO71/1087*)

Dr Keith Simpson, Home Office pathologist, with the skull of Joan Pearl Wolf and the British army jackknife alleged to have been used to murder her by Private August Sangret.

The site on the Halnaker Road where the body of ACW1 Marguerite Burge was found by two members of the Home Guard. (*Martin Mace*)

The lane in Porthcawl where Lily Griffiths was shot by her bigamous common-law husband, Bombardier Joseph Howard Grossley.

crimes were common. However, in his final report, Hill stated that 'the effects of such instability of the cerebral rhythms would be to impair his capacity for controlling judgement upon his actions, yet these tests do not provide evidence that he did not know what he was doing, or that it was wrong', a point that would be seized upon by Casey's prosecutors. The EEG, having been developed from its early uses, is still used in the United Kingdom today to help detect and investigate the causes and treatment of epilepsy.

The Trial

On Tuesday, 14 September 1943, following the outcome of the tests, Casey appeared at Central Criminal Court before Mr Justice Singleton. The prosecution was led by Laurence Austin Byrne KC, a former Labour Corps officer during the First World War, and Stephen Gerald Howard KC, who had served with the RAF for a short time in 1918. Casey was defended, under a legal aid certificate, by Benjamin Yahuda and the suggestion was made that, with regard to his abnormal brain, he was not responsible for his actions and had acted 'like an automaton'. Casey himself attempted to claim that he could not remember what had happened on the night and that, additionally, his father's sister, Mabel Casey, had resided in West Ham Mental Hospital for eighteen years. As such, there was a history of insanity within the family. The prosecution, however, deemed the attack on Bridget Milton had been nothing but a brutal murder and attempted rape of a hard-working mother. It had been proven that Casey was caught, literally red-handed, at the scene of the crime, and his comments made at Putney police station indicated he was fully aware of what he was doing. The 'brain tests', despite indicating an abnormality, showed he was well aware of the difference between right and wrong.

Despite the mountain of evidence against him, there was to be one further blow. His brother, Albert Edward Casey, with whom he had spent the evening drinking, gave a statement in which he said that at the closing part of the evening, Terence had moved away from the group and was not seen drinking or talking with anyone else, and certainly not a woman. The police believed that Casey intended to follow Freda Gibbons as she left the pub but had either followed Bridget Milton in error or just happened upon her in his search for the barmaid. He blatantly lied about the circumstances of the crime and the assault upon Bridget was motivated by nothing other than wanton lust. After an absence of just 45 minutes the jury announced a verdict of guilty to murder but gave a recommendation to mercy. Justice Singleton said he did not see how the jury could have come to any other conclusion and sentenced Casey to death.

The Appeal

Initially, the execution date was set for 14 October, but Casey submitted an appeal that was heard on Monday, 1 November 1943 before the Lord Chief Justice, Mr Justice Charles, and Mr Justice Hallett. Again, represented by Benjamin Yahuda, there were eleven grounds for appeal, one of which called for the introduction of further evidence. In his speech, which lasted over 3 hours, Yahuda invited the court to reverse the jury's decision and replace it with one of either guilty but insane, or one of manslaughter. This was on the basis that the judge had misdirected the jury regarding medical evidence concerning the electroencephalograph and that the intent to commit felony was absent. Mr Justice Charles gave the verdict of the court, stating that the offence committed was one of 'plain stark murder'. The judge had given an accurate and comprehensive summing up and they saw no reason for interfering with the verdict of the jury and the appeal was accordingly dismissed.

Terence Casey was hung at Wandsworth Prison on Friday, 19 November 1943 by Albert Pierrepoint, assisted by Henry 'Harry' William Critchell. His body was buried within the prison grounds. Bridget Milton's body had been conveyed to the Church of St Simon's in Putney where a service was conducted by Canon Pritchard, after which she was interred in the cemetery. Her daughters were cared for by Ernest Littleboy for many years at his home in Landford Road until his death on Friday, 20 August 1971.

Chapter 14

Private John Gordon Davidson – A Skilful Interrogation

Panel 19. Column 1
Service Number: 14425572
Unit: Royal Army Ordnance Corps
Executed: 12 July 1944, aged 19

In spring 1944 there was an air of great anticipation, as the United Kingdom and her Allies prepared for the impending invasion of Europe. The Battle of Monte Cassino was underway in Italy, an increasing number of U-boats were being sunk in the Atlantic and the British government announced plans to build 300,000 houses after the war. For the civilian population, virtually every household item was either in short supply or unobtainable and a seriously depleted workforce across the country saw women become ever more crucial to the war effort. Soldiers, newly recruited into the British army, were finding themselves now being held in dreary wartime camps across the country and sought out every opportunity for some relief from the drab surroundings. A few, however, such as Private John Gordon Davidson, would find their efforts to fulfil their desires spill over into a murderous situation.

The Victim

Gladys May Appleton, like many other young women in wartime Britain, was to lead a very average life, despite the privations of rationing and the continued limitations placed upon British citizens. She was born in St Helens, Lancashire, on Saturday, 18 November 1916, the daughter of Frederick and Sarah Maud Appleton (née Moore). A single woman, she lived quietly with her parents and her elder sister, Doris, in the family home in Bishop Road. Described as a slightly built girl, she had, since

Gladys May Appleton, found on the lawn of The Elms, Cowley Hill Lane, with 20in of scarf stuffed into her mouth.

1941, been employed as a cleaner at the offices of the St Helens Co-Operative Industrial Society in Baldwin Street, prior to which she had worked as an usherette at a local cinema. Her health was not particularly good for a woman of her age, and she had undergone both an operation on her stomach and suffered appendicitis in 1943. She was also, like so many other young people at that time, burdened with a full set of dentures. Despite this, Gladys was in an intimate relationship with a local man, George Leslie Barker, who lived in Knowsley Road. Although not officially engaged, the couple, who had been together for almost four years, were planning to get married. Due to what was described as 'an upset with her parents', he rarely visited Gladys at her home, but she would make the journey to his house most evenings. George, an electrician's labourer by trade, suffered with bronchial difficulties, which prevented him from performing military service. On Monday, 13 March 1944 he had to have some teeth removed and, suffering considerable face pain, told Gladys that he would be staying at home over the weekend to recover.

On the evening of Sunday, 19 March 1944, with local newspapers reporting continued successes by Allied forces around the globe, Gladys left her home and walked to Knowsley Road, where she spent the evening with her boyfriend. The couple, who were described as very fond of each other, played bagatelle, ate cold-meat sandwiches, cake and drank tea. At around 10.30 p.m., Gladys prepared herself for the short walk home, donning a light brown coat over her blue frock and topping it off with a plum-coloured hat, rabbitfur gloves and a red and white woollen scarf, which she always wrapped around her neck twice and crossed over her chest. After spending 10 minutes in the doorway saying good night, Gladys left the house to begin her journey. She was a nervous girl and would usually wait for someone who was walking in the same direction and then follow behind them, and only ever walked along with someone she knew. As she disappeared into the night, it was to be the last time anyone ever saw her alive.

The Assailant

The life of John Gordon Davidson was filled with tragedy and deceit and may have been completely different had it not been for one of the most significant events of the twentieth century, the First World War. He was born in a maternity home in West Princes Street, Glasgow, on Saturday, 11 April 1925 and regarded as an orphan, brought up with a foster parent, Annie Wardrope. Records show that his mother was, in fact, Madge Gordon Gilmour, a schoolteacher at the Auchanachie School House in Keith Parish, Banffshire. Her maiden name was Sim and on Tuesday, 25 May 1915, at the age of 22, she had married Williejohn Oberlin Gilmour, a 30-year-old master at the Leith Academy. He enlisted as a trooper in the Scottish Horse on Friday, 7 August 1914, and was soon serving overseas, attaining the rank of quartermaster sergeant. It was at this point he was offered a commission as an officer, being posted to Gallipoli, and serving with the 13th Battalion, Black Watch (Royal Highlanders). Upon the evacuation of the Turkish peninsula, he proceeded with his regiment to Egypt, where he was attached to the Lanarkshire Yeomanry for a period of time. After re-joining the Black Watch, he was posted to Salonika in October 1916, where he acted as the battalion adjutant. He was then attached to the South Nottinghamshire Hussars for cavalry work and it was whilst serving with this regiment that he was killed on a patrol, near Kakaraska, on the Struma Front, on Tuesday, 15 May 1917. Williejohn Gilmour has no known grave and is commemorated on the Doiran Memorial, Greece.

Madge and Williejohn had a son, James Gordon Gilmour, who was born on Wednesday, 22 March 1916, and would become a half-brother to John Gordon Davidson. Following the death of her husband, Madge subsequently married Robert Davidson, a railway signalman, on Saturday, 12 February 1921. It seems that Robert decided to go to the US to gain employment, but Madge refused to join him and, consequently, he divorced her. She then reverted her name back to Gilmour. The war widow, now a divorcee, then found herself in a brief relationship with William Downie, a local farm grieve, who was responsible for running a nearby farm. This liaison resulted in her becoming pregnant. She took up a job at Rise School House, Hull, Yorkshire, for a while, then moved to Glasgow where she gave birth in the maternity home run by a nurse whose sister was named Annie Wardrope. When he was just 2 days old, Madge took him to Annie's home in Kerse Road, Grangemouth, where it was agreed she would bring him up as her own, despite her advancing years. Madge told Annie that the father was a farmer from Yorkshire and that her husband, Robert Davidson, had died, both of which were untrue. She registered the birth of the child on Friday, 17 April 1925, and did not name the father, giving the baby the surname of Davidson or Sim. Madge returned to Auchanachie and never saw the child again.

At the age of 5, John Davidson joined the Dundas School in Grangemouth, where his attendance and educational abilities were regarded as being very good. However, he became involved with petty crime early in his life and his first appearance in court was at the tender age of 10, when he was charged at Grangemouth Juvenile Court on Monday, 16 December 1935, along with five others, with stealing pens, pencils and face cream from a local shop, for which he was placed on probation for twelve months. A further misdemeanour occurred when, on Monday, 21 March 1938, now aged 13, he appeared in the same court charged with two cases of theft after stealing money from local houses and was, again, placed on probation for a year.

Davidson left school at the age of 14 and took a job at Grangemouth airport as a stores assistant for Scottish Airways, but was discharged from the job in 1940 when the RAF took over the aerodrome. He then went to work for the Petroleum Board at Grangemouth but eventually left this job after a year to obtain a better wage. Instead, however, he took up a series of bar jobs in pubs in and around Grangemouth and Falkirk. On Saturday, 1 August 1942, he ran away from home to go to London but quickly became destitute and, a few weeks later Annie Wardrope received a phone call from the Metropolitan Police informing her he was stranded in the capitol and asking her to pay his train fare home, which she agreed to do. He obtained work at the Regal Cinema in Falkirk during December 1942 but was dismissed after three weeks for dishonesty. His last civilian job was at a timber merchants named Christie & Vesey in Falkirk between January and April 1943. Despite being in employment, he was involved in more petty crime and on Tuesday, 4 May 1943, now aged 18, faced a more serious charge following the theft of a camera and a case of cutlery from the house of his foster mother. Appearing at Grangemouth Court, he stated in his defence that it was his intention to join the army the following day and he was therefore only admonished. He was drafted into the Royal Army Ordinance Corps and at the latter end of 1943 was given a period of compassionate leave to care for his foster mother, who was by now a virtual invalid. During this absence, he obtained a job as a taxi driver working for the Queen's Hotel Garage in Grangemouth but was dismissed when he was found to be driving whilst under the influence of alcohol. He appears to have spent most of his spare time going to the cinema, never attended dances, was rarely seen in the company of women or girls and was never convicted of any offences of a sexual or indecent nature.

The Crime

On the evening of Sunday, 19 March 1944, Davidson, now based at Rainford camp on Merseyside, and his pal Private John Hunter Sanderson slipped out of camp without permission, planning to visit a couple of pubs, and eventually ended up in the Rifle Corps Hotel in St Helens. Here they met up with a soldier from their company, Lance Corporal James Thomas Green, and stayed drinking until about 10.00 p.m. The three soldiers then left the pub in the company of three women, one of whom appeared to be middle-aged. As they walked along Sanderson and Davidson were interested in the same girl and, after a few words, Davidson became annoyed and said, 'You can have her.' He then walked off, alone, back towards the pub, his route taking him past the Capitol Cinema.

At around the same time Jeannie Galvin, whose husband was serving overseas, was walking back to her home in Gamble Avenue, after visiting her mother-in-law. She was suddenly approached by a soldier with a strong Scottish accent, who began to walk along with her. He told her that he was a welder in the REME and was stationed nearby. On reaching her home, Jeannie closed the front gate keeping the soldier on the other side. He said, 'You are going home to a nice soft bed', she turned and began to walk away when he said, 'I'll walk down the path with you.' When she asked him why, he said, 'I want to kiss you goodnight.' Jeannie now became frightened, as he claimed he was going to stay there until she kissed him. She ran across the lawn and flower beds, with the soldier chasing her, but managed to make it indoors and slam the door shut. He

The Elms in Cowley Hill Lane, where the body of Gladys Appleton was found by postwoman Betsy Baines.

departed but left a large boot print in the flower bed, one that was to be his undoing.

A short a time after, a couple were walking home and, as they reached Bishop Road, were approached by a young soldier with a Scottish accent who asked for directions to the town centre. He said, 'If I get to the Capitol, I shall know my way.' He walked off in the direction of Cowley Hill Lane. As he reached the crest of the hill, he met a young woman coming the other way, Gladys Appleton. At that moment, Martha Leigh, a spinster, was also walking home and, as she turned into Windle Street, she heard a funny scream. She described it as an awful sound, at first a full scream, which seemed to be smothered and ended in a moan. She had no idea where it came from but, in the pitch black of the night, it frightened her.

At 7.30 a.m. the following morning, Monday, 20 March, Margaret Allsopp arrived at The Elms in Cowley Hill Lane, where she worked as a cleaner. The house, just a short distance from Jeannie Galvin's home, was being used as the district headquarters for the National Fire Service. As she entered the gateway, she found a black suede handbag on the rockery. She took it into the house with the intention of establishing who it belonged to. However, 15 minutes later, Betsy Baines, the local postwoman, was delivering mail to the house. She entered the building by the front door and, as usual, left the mail on a desk in one of the offices. As she began to walk back down the drive, she noticed what she thought was a wax model laying on the grass in front of the house. She looked at it for a moment and then went back to the house and called out, 'Is anyone about?' Margaret Allsopp responded to the call and was asked, 'Have you been using models for practice?' The two women then went outside where, to their horror, they realised this was the body of a woman.

Leading Fireman Arthur Leslie Trevor called the police and within a short time Superintendent James Ball and Detective Inspector John Maddocks of the St Helens Borough Police were on the scene. They found Gladys laying on the lawn with her head towards the road, her eyes bulging and her face bloodstained. She had been dragged across the soft ground, her corset and underclothes had been torn off, exposing her body, her scarf was tightly wound around her neck and had been stuffed into her mouth. Her body was then removed to the local mortuary, where a post-mortem established she had been strangled and raped, and a total of 20in of her scarf were found to have been rammed into her mouth. Standing at just 5ft 3in in height and weighing 8 stone, Gladys was no match for the burly soldier who had forced her tongue down her throat. Red ridges found on her neck demonstrated just how tightly her scarf had been twisted at the same time.

Superintendent Ball quickly realised that he was going to need some expert assistance to solve this horrendous murder, and Scotland Yard were contacted, resulting in the arrival of veteran detectives Chief Inspector Arthur Philpott and Sergeant Frank McGinn. They got to work straight away, but there were virtually no clues at the murder scene that could be of assistance. Very quickly things looked bleak, but then there was a break. The local police had been made aware of the attempted assault on Jeannie Galvin and had taken a plaster cast of the footprint left in the flowerbed. At first, they did not connect the two incidents, but when Philpott and McGinn heard about it, they knew they were onto something. The cast was of a square-toed shoe, with protector studs, which were not army issue. Enquires then began which would result in visits to apartment and lodging houses, dyers and cleaners, and transport companies. Long-distance drivers, mental patients on parole and persons convicted or suspected of indecent offences were interrogated and their stories verified. House-to-house enquiries covering the route taken by Gladys, or that which could have been taken by her killer, were made. A total of 9,000 soldiers were interviewed, including some 350 absentees.

The investigation then focused on the nearest army camp, Rainford. Police were given the names of two young soldiers who had been absent without leave on the Sunday night and attempted to interview them, but Davidson had gone on leave on Wednesday, 22 March for seven days. He returned a day early but, by now, was aware that the police were looking for a soldier, most likely from his camp. He slipped away again and hid at 2 Station Cottages, Rainford, the home of Ruby Herd and Martha Scarisbrick, two married women whose husbands were serving overseas and who were described by the police as being of 'questionable morals'. He stayed there until 31 March when he returned to Rainford Camp in the company of Corporal Thomas Patrick Clarke. Initially, he did not want to go but Clarke persuaded him it was for the best. Once there, he was ordered to report to the acting sergeant major, which he failed to do. He was subsequently placed in the guardroom for being absent without leave and not complying with an order.

That evening, Detective Inspector Maddocks went to Rainford Camp to inspect the kit of soldiers who had been on leave. When he opened Davidson's kit bag he found a pair of brown leather shoes, with square toes and protector studs, that exactly matched the prints found in the garden of Jeannie Galvin. She was later able to positively identify him. This was their man, all they had to do was prove it. Davidson was taken to St Helens police station where he was questioned about his movements on the night of the murder. When he was asked about the incident involving Jeanie Galvin, he initially denied any involvement. Davidson was then left with Detective Sergeant McGinn and Detective Sergeant Spedding and, now faced with a significant amount of evidence, he placed his head in his hands and began to sob. When Sergeant McGinn asked him what the matter was, he replied, 'I did it. I did it. That poor girl. What made me do it. My god, how shall I die.' The death of Gladys Appleton was then coldly described by Davidson.

I came out and started to walk and then I met that girl. I asked her to show me the way to the Capitol and I took her in that gate. I kissed her. She didn't like it. I choked her with my hands. She struggled. I put her on the ground. I took her over the grass. I killed her there. I just choked her. I tore her clothes and tried to ride her. I just put it in and tried a little bit. Then I ran away. I went to the theatre and stopped there till morning, when I went back to camp. It would be about half past six. I have been worrying all the time.

When asked why he had lied about the matter, he told the police he did not want to get mixed up in any murders.

In the meantime, his clothes had been taken to the Home Office North-Western Forensic Science Laboratory in Preston where Dr James Brierley Firth examined them in detail. He found bloodstains on Davidson's greatcoat that were the same group as Gladys. Rabbit hairs matching those from the gloves she was wearing and blue fibres from her dress were found on his trousers along with seminal stains, that matched those found on her body.

The Trail

Davidson appeared at Manchester Assizes on Monday, 8 May 1944 before Mr Justice Hilbery. His defence was one of insanity and he claimed he killed Gladys in a state of post-epileptic automatism due to the amount of alcohol he had consumed. Dr Firth gave evidence that Gladys had been the victim of a violent sexual assault described as 'animal' in its ferocity. There were no witnesses called on behalf of the defence and Davidson spent most of the time with his head in his hands, crying. The jury did not accept his defence, as no firm evidence could be produced to prove it. However, they did recommend mercy, on account of Davidson's age. Upon being found guilty of murder he was sentenced to death.

The Appeal

On Monday, 26 June 1944, Davidson appeared before the Court of Criminal Appeal, headed by the Lord Chief Justice, Mr Justice Humphrey, and Mr Justice Oliver, and was asked to provide grounds as to why he should not be executed. His appeal makes desperate reading:

My Lords,

I, John Gordon Davidson, respectfully wish to present my appeal against the sentence passed upon me at Manchester assizes. The following grounds are here with written and presented to you.

A. I would like to put before you my condition prior to this crime occurring. I had been drinking heavily and not capable of knowing what I was doing, and I think that the amount of drink consumed had affected my normal balance, because I know in my own mind and heart that had I been normal and in my right mind that I could never have committed a crime of this kind. I would with respect like to point out that the fact was not given enough consideration by the judge at the trial and sufficient stress was not made to the jury. I think the verdict was unfair on account of the fact that I was drunk, was not given enough consideration and that the judge did not consider this enough in his direction to the jury.

B. I am an orphan and illegitimate child, a youth just turned 19 years of age. Through not having any parents I never had a good start in life, and I think that this too should have been given consideration at the trial. I am young with all my life before me and I would never have done what happened had I been in my normal senses, and I cannot make myself believe that I did this. I was never accustomed to drinking beer or spirits, it was in the Army I got a bad habit under the influence of older men, listening to the tales they tell, all this must have gone to my head. My normal allowance was a couple of pints and the most I ever had was between four and six. On the night of the crime, I had more than my normal amount of beer and so far as I can remember I had about a dozen pints of beer and could not have been capable of realising what I was doing.

In conclusion I earnestly request that my appeal will be given your most kindly and considerate attention.

I am, my lords, yours respectfully,

John Gordon Davidson

There were a great many appeals for mercy from the public, given the age of the young soldier, but there were also those who demanded his life be taken. Gladys had been identified by her father following the discovery of her body and had been quietly buried on Saturday, 25 March. On the eve of D-Day 1944, as thousands of troops prepared to land on the Normandy coast, her mother wrote an impassioned letter to the Home Secretary, Herbert Morrison, pleading for the execution to go ahead, it reads:

Dear Sir,

I am just writing a few lines to you to ask you to help us in our great trouble, as regards to the petition sent into you for Davidson who so cruelly and so violently took my daughter Gladys's life. It says in the Bible a life for a life and my husband has been ill ever since it happened and I myself.

I don't know how to go on, as my nerves are a wreck, I also have a son in Italy, and he has been away 5 years next month in HMF and he wants to know is this what we are fighting for. We all desire his death sentence to be carried out and hung. It would not be right for him to live, and my daughter gone, even if he gets imprisonment, he will still have his life and my husband and myself will never be the same again if he is not hung, and also my daughter at home wishes the same as we do as he took her sister's life.

We hope that you will help us and that we are not being too personal to you, but that is our great wish, also my son's wish, so please help us as we are her parents, her mother and father and we have always tried to do the right and just thing in our lives and then for this to come, this awful tragedy we hope we are not too late trusting you will help us kindly.

Gratefully yours
Mr & Mrs Appleton

Just eighteen months after Gladys was murdered, on Thursday, 13 December 1945, her mother became a widow after her father died as a result of a perforated gastric ulcer and peritonitis.

Although 18-year-olds were normally reprieved at this time, the Home Secretary, Herbert Morrison, decided against it in Davidson's case as he was only three weeks away from his 19th birthday at the time of the murder. The appeal was dismissed and on Wednesday, 12 July 1944, as the American 116th Infantry Regiment seized Hill 147 and British troops continued their advance towards Hill 112 during the Battle of Normandy, John Gordon Davidson was hung at Walton Prison in Liverpool by Thomas Pierrepoint, assisted by Alex Riley. His body was buried on the same day within the prison grounds.

Postscript

The outcome was regarded as a very satisfactory ending to what, at first, might easily have resulted in an unsolved crime, as not a single clue could be found at the scene. The police had no idea who Gladys had met after she left her boyfriend's house that evening. On a practically pitch-black night it was, perhaps, only the footprints left by the soldier who chased Jeannie Galvin that were of the upmost importance, in fact the only conclusive clue obtained to the murder. It was simply the skilful interrogation by the Scotland Yard CID that brought the matter to a successful conclusion, something that was reflected in a letter of gratitude from the Chief Constable of Lancashire, Arthur Cust. The murder of Gladys Appleton was a great tragedy, but the story of Madge Gilmour, having lost her husband in the First World War, who would produce two sons who never knew each other, and who would both lose their lives in the Second World War, is perhaps the greatest untold part of the whole terrible event. John Davidson was executed for murder, but his half-brother, James Gordon Gilmour, who had enlisted in the Royal Artillery and attained the rank of Second Lieutenant, was to be reported missing on Sunday, 22 February 1942 at the age of 25, whilst serving with the 5th Battery, 25th Mountain Regiment. His name is recorded on Face 2 of the Rangoon Memorial, Burma. When you look upon John Davidson's name at Brookwood, remember them all.

Chapter 15

Corporal Dudley George Rayner – Guilty, Sir!

Panel 20. Column 3
Service Number: 13900160
Unit: Pioneer Corps
Executed: Wednesday, 31 March 1943, aged 26

M urder is an unthinkable act for most of us, but its roots lie in human emotions, and jealously rates amongst one of the greatest motives. Those who fall victim to bitter aggression are often the female partners of jealous males and, where women kill, it can be argued, they typically act in self defence against the male partner's envious rage. The case of Corporal Dudley George Rayner is one such example amongst the Brookwood Killers, a cold-blooded and premeditated murder resulting from nothing less than jealously.

Private Josephine Rayner of the ATS, murdered by her husband, Private Dudley Rayner, in a fit of jealousy.

The Victim

Josephine Colaluca was born in South London on Friday, 23 February 1923, the daughter of Raffaile 'Harry' and Ruth Colaluca (née Dock). Her father, a Sicilian ice-cream vendor, and mother had married in 1909, and the couple were to have seven children. Tragedy struck the family in 1924 when their eldest daughter, Domenica, suddenly died at the age of 16, a devastating blow for the family. A further shock was to come just three years later when Ruth, aged 36, died shortly after giving birth to their daughter Celeste, leaving Harry to face raising six children alone. There is no real indication as to how a working man during the Depression era would manage in this situation, but it is likely that there was some form of family participation. In addition, the older children would have been expected to help in many ways, particularly with the younger children, and it seems that Josephine formed a strong bond with her older sister, Juliette. Eventually, Harry met another woman, Alice Victoria Adams, and the couple married in 1933. They went on to have a further six children and Harry was faced with the costs of caring for his ever-growing family. The large family appear to have lived in relative poverty and some disharmony so, perhaps not unsurprisingly, petty crime was an occasional event in their lives.

Josephine's older brother, Angelo, had been sent to an approved school at a comparatively young age and, after leaving the facility, became involved in minor crime, appearing at Penge Juvenile Court in March 1940 charged with stealing bicycles. The 19-years-old's criminal behaviour began to escalate, and, on Monday, 16 December 1940, he was involved, together with his nephew, 19-year-old Charles D'Archambaud, in the theft of groceries from a lock-up shop in Coventry Road, South Norwood. It seems the two youths took their haul back to a flat in nearby Albert Road, which was then raided by the police. There was a struggle at the front door, which later continued in the back garden. The police alleged that fists, feet, a milk bottle and a broom were used on them in the affray. Angelo worked as a labourer with an ARP demolition party and was described by the police as a bad workman, who was not wanted for the army because of his Italian ancestry. He was sent to borstal for three years, however, despite his criminal record, he was drafted into the army, entering service with the 3rd Battalion, Parachute Regiment, taking part in the airborne assault on Arnhem, Holland, on 17 September 1944. He was taken prisoner on 24 September, being held in captivity at Stalag XIb, Fallingbostel, from where he was eventually released.

Tragedy would also strike the heart of the extended family. Having lost his eldest daughter and his wife, Harry was to suffer further heartache. Alice had given birth to twins on Friday, 21 June 1940, Judy and Shirley, but just seven weeks later, whilst sleeping in a pram in their back garden, Shirley died. In the meantime, Josephine's life seems to have been slightly haphazard and she had left the family home on several occasions, but always seemed to return. In May 1941, the teenager met a Burmese man, Esoof Khan, who had joined the British army at South Norwood and was serving with the Pioneer Corps, and a courtship soon began. Perhaps spurred on by Josephine, he changed his name on Monday, 9 February 1942 to Dudley George Rayner, and the couple planned to get married.

On Sunday, 23 August 1942, Josephine, her older married sister Juliette D'Archambaud and a friend, Janet Thomas, were involved in stealing a quantity of bed linen and other household articles, the property of Frank William Young, from a house in Minden Road, Penge. Thomas described how she was in financial difficulties and was expecting a baby. After breaking into the house through a basement window, Juliette and Janet stole several cups, saucers, plates, saucepans and other articles from the house over a period of a week, which they took home and then sold. Josephine had kept watch whilst the burglary took place and sold some of the stolen goods. Just two days after the break-in, on Tuesday, 25 August, Josephine married Dudley Rayner at Bromley Register Office. She was later arrested and charged with receiving stolen goods and bound over for a period of two years. She had not told Dudley about the crime, and he only found out when he read about it in a local newspaper. He was furious and blamed Juliette for leading her sister astray.

In November 1942, the couple began to share a bedroom on the ground floor in her father's house in Weighton Road, Anerley, as she and her husband had no home of their own. Things were not going well with their marriage and, with encouragement from her sister and father, she applied to join the Auxiliary Territorial Service (ATS). Despite her criminal activity, Josephine was accepted into the ATS on Friday, 15 January 1943 and began her service with 'A' Company, at No. 7 ATS Training Centre, Queen's Camp, Guildford. She had asked that Dudley not be told about her entry into the army and, as he could not find her on his return home, he went to Penge police station where he reported her as missing. Eventually, having discovered she had joined the ATS, he traced her to Guildford and travelled there to see her. It was clear that he was unhappy, and her actions to evade him would be the catalyst which would lead her life to a devastating and murderous conclusion.

The Assailant

Dudley George Rayner was born Thursday, 16 March 1916 in Rangoon, Burma with the birth name Esoof Khan. His life prior to enlistment in the army can only be described as vague but he claimed that, before the war, he worked for his brother-in-law, who was a racehorse trainer. He had joined the Merchant Navy at the outbreak of the war and had made two journeys to Britain, working as a steward. On the second journey, he claimed, his ship was torpedoed. He left the SS *Staffordshire*, part of the Bibby Line, at Newcastle to join the army. He travelled to London for a medical assessment and to finalise his enlistment, joining the army at Upper Norwood on Friday, 9 May 1941. He met Josephine at the same time and, in February 1942, changed his name to Dudley George Rayner. The couple married on 25 August 1942, but his wife had been involved in a criminal act, for which he blamed her sister. Married life was not quite what Dudley expected it to be and there were often arguments over money, and Josephine would often come off worse, usually at the end of his fist or boot. On Thursday, 14 January 1943, Josephine wrote to her husband's commanding officer, Major Stanley, asking for advice and complaining of his cruelty towards her. She informed him that she was going to run away as she could not stand any more of his kicking and punching, and how she was afraid of her husband. There was little that Major Stanley could do in these circumstances, but Josephine's fears were soon to be well founded.

The Crime

On Saturday, 6 February 1943, Josephine came home on a 48-hour pass. Her husband, whose unit was stationed at Arthur Road, Wimbledon, joined her later that day and, it seemed, they were quite happy. In the evening they went to the cinema together and on the Sunday, they went dancing. There were no apparent quarrels, but Alice Colaluca knew that Dudley was a violent man and jealous of his wife serving in the ATS, so she was expecting trouble but nothing like what was about to occur.

Just after breakfast on Monday, 8 February, Alice was at home with her five young children, Harry having left for work at 7.30 a.m. Dudley was polishing Josephine's shoes whilst she was preparing to return to camp.

She went into the bedroom at the back of the house, her husband followed her, and closed the door. Alice then heard several terrible screams and when she rushed to the bedroom door, she found it locked. She sent one of her daughters for help and shortly after a policeman arrived at the house, War Reserve William Allen Austin. As he approached the bedroom, Dudley Rayner stepped out and said, 'I have killed my wife. I wish to give myself up.' Then he went back into the bedroom. Austin entered the room and saw Josephine lying on the floor, dressed in her uniform, apparently dead, with her right leg curled up and her head in a pool of blood. Alice was standing at the front gate and Rayner called out 'Mum, I can't live without her. She was going one way and I am going another. It's the best way out of it, now we'll both go together.'

Detective Sergeant Edward Marsh then arrived on the scene and immediately recognised both Josephine and Dudley Rayner who said, 'Good Morning, Sergeant Marsh.' As Marsh bent down to examine the body, he thought Rayner was going to say something, so he cautioned him and took him into the adjoining front room where he said, 'I couldn't stand it any longer, being apart. I hit her with the hammer. The head came off. I hit her with my fist. I kicked her.' Marsh saw that Rayner was wearing army boots and on the right-hand side of the right boot was some congealed blood adhering to the sole. He removed Rayner's boots and passed them to Detective Inspector Sidney Jones, who had also arrived at the scene. Jones described how he found Rayner sitting in a chair near a window, with his hands covered with blood. There were also two skin abrasions on the knuckles of his right forefinger. Jones informed Rayner that he had seen the body of his wife in the next room, and he asked, 'Is she dead?' He was told that she was and that he would be taken to Penge police station and charged with wilful murder. He said 'Yes, yes, all right.' Rayner then made the following statement, revealing his cold and violent nature:

> I made up my mind that if we were going to be parted, we would go together. I hit her with a hammer, but it came off the handle. I hit her with my fist, and she fell down. I kicked her in the head with my boot. The only thing I am sorry about is if I caused her any pain before the end. I should have brought my rifle home and I could have finished it off properly, I could have made a clean job of it.

Dr Guy de Houghton Dawson, who had served with the British Red Cross and the Royal Army Medical Corps during the First World War, arrived at the house a short time after the murder. He found Josephine lying curled up on the floor of the bedroom, near the bed. The room was very dark, as the black-out curtain was still up. It was obvious that she was dead and had been so for about a quarter of an hour. Her body was still quite warm and rigor mortis had not set in. There were injuries at the back of her head, the hair being matted with blood. Bleeding had ceased, but there was about half a pint of blood on the floor. Her body was then removed to the Penge mortuary.

The Inquest

The day after her murder, a post-mortem examination was conducted by pathologist Dr Edward Burnett. Detailing the injuries, he spoke of extensive bruises about the face, a bruise on the left shoulder and a smaller one on the right arm. There were thirteen scalp wounds, three of them being lacerated incised cuts right through the scalp to the bone, 2in long, slightly curved and obviously inflicted by the same implement. The most serious wound was immediately above the left ear and was depressed sufficiently to accommodate the bulb of his finger. He opened the skull and found a fracture of the lower part of the left temporal bone. A portion of the inner surface of the skull was detached and pressing upon the brain. The striking feature of this wound was the extremely small amount of blood, which showed that death had been instantaneous. The cause of death was shock, due to the fractured skull and multiple injuries. The injuries were consistent with being caused by a heavy boot. One bruise on the head was undoubtedly caused by a hammer which he had seen. Burnett stated, 'The distribution and extent of the injuries shows that she has been the victim of considerable savagery.'

Later that day, an inquest was conducted at Penge Council offices. Harry Colaluca, a tired figure, speaking in a weary, monotonous voice, told the coroner that he was Josephine's father and described how he had gone to work shortly before the murder took place. He had identified the body as that of his daughter, who had been married for six months, and would have been 20 years old that month. He identified the hammer used in the assault as belonging to him, and went on to explain that his daughter and her husband had lived at his home since they had been married and how Rayner was a very jealous individual. He used to take Josephine's army allowances from her when she was paid and would assault her on occasions, the last time being on Christmas Day 1942. Rayner told Harry that if Josephine ever left home, he would kill him and Alice. It was partly on Harry's advice, and that of her sister and probation officer, Miss Mayling, that Josephine joined the ATS.

The Trial

Dudley Rayner appeared at Penge Petty Sessional Court on Tuesday 23 February 1943, his wife's 20th birthday, where the case was referred to the Central Criminal Court at the Old Bailey, London, and on Friday, 12 March 1943 the trial commenced before Mr Justice Oliver. Amongst the trials of the Brookwood Killers, Rayner's rates as one of the shortest, lasting a total of only 9 minutes, seven of which were occupied by the appeal made by counsel for the defence, Mr A.L. Stevenson. When Rayner was asked to plead, he replied, 'Guilty, Sir', in a loud, clear voice.

The grave of Josephine Rayner in Beckenham, Kent. She had been in the ATS for just two weeks and the service demanded the return of her recently issued uniform.

Stevenson claimed that when he saw a hammer lying on the bedroom floor, Rayner picked it up and hit his wife hard in a moment of aberration. 'If that hammer had not been there this might not have happened. The evidence was that she died quickly.' Evidence was provided regarding the soldier's violent behaviour towards his wife in the form of two handwritten notes from Josephine. The first, on the back of a religious photograph, read, 'To my hubby to ask God to make you learn to trust your wife. She don't ask for your bashings and she don't do wrong. Josie.' The second read, 'Dudley. A woman can't stay with any man if he is everlasting taking her pay books. I will go to work to keep myself. I don't know yet, but I'll get a job somewhere. Good-bye.'

Rayner did not appeal against his sentence and was executed in Wandsworth Prison on Wednesday, 31 March 1943 by Albert Pierrepoint and his assistant, Steve Wade. His body was buried on the same day within the confines of the prison. Josephine lays buried in the war graves plot at Beckenham Cemetery, Kent. The case papers for her murder make distressing reading but there is something cold and disturbing in the official notifications from the ATS demanding that her uniform, which undoubtedly was blood-soaked, be returned to them with immediate effect.

Chapter 16

Private Arthur Thompson –
Death at the Nags Head Inn

Panel 20. Column 3
Service Number: 2940127
Unit: General Service Corps
Executed: Wednesday, 31 January 1945, aged 34

The Victim

Jane Coulton had been in the innkeeping business almost all her life, and it was to be one filled with heartache. Born Jane Smith on Tuesday, 30 March 1875, the daughter of James and Elizabeth Smith, her father, having worked in a local woollen mill, became the licensee of the Royal Oak in Keighley, Yorkshire. As soon as she could, she worked as a barmaid in the public house until Tuesday, 1 January 1895, when she married a local farmer, Joseph Heaton. Sadly, her married life was to be short-lived when Jane witnessed the death of her husband on Saturday, 16 November 1895, at the age of 23, as a result of enteric fever. Her life in tatters, she returned to the Royal Oak, where further tragedy was

Jane Coulton, brutally murdered in her own bed at the Nags Head Inn, Clayton Heights.

to strike when her father passed away on Thursday, 9 September 1897 at the age of 48. Her brother, Arthur, took over as the licensed publican and Jane continued to help run the business as best she could.

Another man was then to enter her life, Andrew Coulton. He had also suffered tragedy in his life. He had married Julia Holmes in 1905 but she sadly passed away in 1915 at the age of 34, leaving him to raise their only daughter, Edith, who was then aged 8. Andrew and Jane ran the Royal Oak together and were eventually married on Tuesday, 3 December 1918. They ran the pub for a further twelve years, until February 1930, when Andrew was fined £3 for selling intoxicating liquor during non-permitted hours. It seems that this impacted upon his licence, and they had to leave the Royal Oak, after more than thirty years. However, on Wednesday, 1 July 1931, they took over the Hope & Anchor at Horton, but this was to only last for a short period until, on Wednesday, 4 January 1933, the couple took over the Nags Head in Clayton Heights. Unfortunately, although they had settled again, Andrew passed away in February 1936. Jane then took over the Nags Head on 11 March 1936 as the publican, and continued to run it until 21 September 1944, when her life came to a lonely and murderous end.

The Assailant

Arthur Thompson was born in Lancaster in 1910, the son of Frederick Michael and Margaret Ellen Thompson (née Stewardson). His father was a well-known antiques dealer who eventually settled in Grange-over-Sands, Cumbria, and whose own turbulent life is described at the foot of this chapter. Arthur had nine siblings: Eva (b. 1901), Frederick (b. 1904), Alice (b. 1906), Ellen (b. 1908), Henry (b. 1911), Marjorie (b. 1913), twins Dorothy and Ivy (b. 1915) and Nora (b. 1916). Just four weeks after her last child was born, Margaret was to die from the effects of stomach cancer on Boxing Day 1916, at the age of 38, leaving her husband with nine children under working age.

Arthur attended school until 1927 at which point the 15-year-old joined the army, serving with the Royal Sussex Regiment. However, he was discharged from the service four years later following a conviction for larceny. In fact, during his thirty-four years of existence, Arthur Thompson would spend almost a third of it behind bars. Following his discharge from the army he began to work for a jeweller in Kendal, Cumbria, and for eight years travelled all around the country buying old gold. But the combination of the type of business he was in, his character and his family life were to see him appear in court on no less than fourteen occasions.

An example of his behaviour can be found in his case papers. In 1934, in Belfast, he went into a man's shop to buy some articles alleged to be gold. Upon finding that they were not gold, Thompson picked up a hammer and struck the man with it. In 1935 he broke into a house and, when challenged by the owner, he said, 'Your money or your life', and put his hands inside his coat as if to produce a weapon. In 1940 he entered a dimly lit shop and said to the shopkeeper, 'I want the till, there are two men on the other side with a gun.' During the early part of the Second World War, he was living in Bootle, Lancashire, where he worked as a labourer in the Liverpool Docks. It was not until August 1944, that he was called up for military service, joining the General Service Corps at Bradford. Described as being 'reckless and violent throughout the whole of his life', Thompson had no intention of meeting with the nation's demands and was soon in trouble. On the night of Friday, 1 September 1944, he was admitted to the Westwood Military Hospital near the Nags Head Inn at Clayton Heights after he had been attacked by three soldiers. They were also recruits, and Thompson used these words to describe the incident, 'I had a fight and got the worst of it. I was kicked in the eye, on the body, and the knee and had to have stitches in my head. There was a great deal of blood, and I was confined to bed for eight days.' Whilst at the hospital, he, along with other soldiers, visited the Nags Head Inn on several occasions, but claimed he did not know the licensee, Jane Coulton.

The Crime

On Thursday, 21 September 1944, just three days after Thompson was discharged from hospital, and as the men of the British 1st Airborne Division fought a bitter battle in the Dutch town of Arnhem, the barking of a white fox terrier named 'Judy' was to be the first indication that something was wrong at the Nags Head Inn. A concerned neighbour, knowing the pub had been closed due to a shortage of beer, thought it was unusual to hear the dog. They approached the inn and, upon gaining access, found Jane Coulton, who was now aged 69 and living alone, with one of her own stockings tied tightly around her neck and an empty purse under her head. The premises had been broken into at the back and it was found that certain items of jewellery, three valuable rings and some brooches were missing together with two pairs of scissors and an electric torch. Jane's purse had been rifled and everything, except for a sovereign, a half sovereign and some small change, was taken. The discarded cash bag was also found, but it was completely empty.

Detectives found blood spots on the outside window frame, through which it appears entry to the premises had been gained. More blood was found in the bedroom, on the wallpaper and on the counterpane of Jane's bed, and there was blood on her left ear. All of this was found to be from blood group A, whilst she was group B. There were also marks on a doorjamb in the bar, which were found to have been made by a pair of scissors, most likely one of the missing pair. Her stepdaughter, Edith Scarborough, explained that every night Jane would take the cash bag to bed with her, and hide it under her bolster. However, it only ever contained silver and copper coins, the notes she hid in a separate drawer which she kept locked, and which the thief had not found. She would keep just a few notes in her purse. A post-mortem revealed that death had been due to asphyxia, whilst a bruise on her face indicated that Jane had been struck a severe blow before death, possibly after being woken up.

Following police inquiries at the nearby Westwood Military Hospital, it was quickly established they were looking for an army deserter, Arthur Thompson, a member of the General Service Corps stationed at the New Grammar School in Bradford, who had been absent since the afternoon prior to the murder and who had been seen distributing silver coins to two patients, Private William Lilycroft and Trooper Laurence Hayes, at 2.00 a.m. on the morning of 21 September. Thompson had then made his way to the local YMCA at Moss House to find somewhere to sleep. Here, he exchanged silver coins for notes, explaining that he had been out drinking and had changed a lot of pound notes during the evening. During this stay, he wrote a letter to his commanding officer telling him that he was fully responsible for the street fight that occurred on 1 September, stating, 'I was drunk and fully determined to kill them for no reason other than I'm just a fighting man. I got the worst of it and I'm just leaving.' This referred to the fact that he was not returning to his unit and was leaving the army for good.

Thompson left Bradford later that the morning, having first attempted to get a taxi to Halifax, without success. Instead, it seems he boarded a bus and made his way to Burnley where he purchased a civilian suit and an overcoat. That afternoon, he was seen in a public house in the town, where he offered a lady's diamond ring to the landlord, who declined the opportunity to purchase it. The following day he exchanged the ring with a watchmaker in Lancaster for a gold wristwatch which, in turn, he sold to a jeweller in the seaside town of Morecambe, where he was staying in a boarding house. On the afternoon of Sunday, 24 September, he went to the Globe Hotel at Overton, 3 miles from Heysham, where he told the licensee he was having a holiday after winning a £60 prize. However, a barmaid recognised him as the man who had been reported in the newspapers, and whom the police wished to interview in connection with the Nags Head Inn murder. The police were informed and interviewed Thompson at the Globe Hotel, where he produced identification papers in the name of Reid. Having failed to satisfy the police as to his identity, he was taken to Heysham by police car. On the way he asked for the window to be opened, and he also asked for the car to stop in order that he could relieve himself. During this journey he managed to hide two brooches and two rings, the property of Jane Coulton, under the carpet in the rear of the car. Once at the police station he was unable to give a satisfactory account of his movements and was cautioned. He was informed that he answered the description of a man who had, at Burnley a few days before, shown the licensee of a public house a diamond ring, 'It was not me that offered the ring for sale,' he claimed. Thompson was then told that he would be taken into custody and transported to Bradford where he would be charged with the wilful murder of Jane Coulton, to which he replied, 'Not guilty'.

The Trial

On Tuesday, 5 December 1944, Thompson was brought before Mr Justice Oliver at York Assizes, held in the town hall, Leeds, for a trial that would last three days, and would see large queues of men and women forming for a seat in the public gallery. Geoffrey Hugh Benbow Streatfeild, who had served with the Durham Light Infantry and the Royal Flying Corps during the First World War, was the prosecuting counsel, aided by Myles Archibald. Their task appeared to be a relatively easy one, but all the evidence was circumstantial. Thompson was represented by Joseph Stanley Snowden, assisted by Eric Greenwood. Unbelievably, as the jury were being selected, Thompson said, 'I would prefer not to have any ladies on the jury, in case they are prejudice.' The jury was subsequently changed and contained twelve males. His defence was that the murder was committed at a time when he was in the Westwood Military Hospital and, therefore, he could not have possibly been responsible for the crime. It must have been perpetrated by somebody else.

Now, for the first time, Thompson introduced a new character, named 'Buck', into the proceedings who, he claimed, he had first met in Chichester in 1927. He said he had seen this man once for a few minutes when he was in Wormwood Scrubs in 1931, and claimed that he had seen him again

Geoffrey Hugh Benbow Streatfeild, who prosecuted Private Arthur Thompson.

at the Dolphin Hotel in Bradford on Thursday, 14 September 1944, and spent the evening with him, even though he had not seen him for thirteen years. There was no indication that he was going to introduce Buck into the case until he was at trial and when he was asked why he had not told the police anything about this man when they were investigating this matter, Thompson stated that he had stayed silent because he was 'unwilling to help the police, wanted to throw them off the scent and to protect Buck because of an unwritten law amongst criminals in the country, honour amongst thieves'. Allegedly, Buck had said he would come forward if Thompson was convicted and he had never mentioned Buck to anyone except his solicitor until he went into the witness box.

Thompson, who was seen to give very plausible, if not a little evasive, responses concerning all the questions put to him by the prosecution, gave a long and detailed explanation about meeting Buck on several occasions, when he would be given jewellery to sell on his behalf. Although he had only ever seen this man on two brief occasions until recently, he did not know his name or where lived, Thompson was asked how he proposed to get in touch with Buck after being given Jane Coulton's jewellery. He replied that it was worth Buck's while to please him, because if Buck committed robberies, he would ask Thompson to sell stuff for him and make 'some very easy money'. Thompson maintained that Jane Coulton had been killed by Buck and not him.

As nobody had seen Thompson entering or leaving the Nags Head Inn, the evidence against him was deemed to be purely circumstantial. However, the points that the prosecution raised were as follows:

- Blood spots found at the scene were from group A whereas the blood of Jane was group B. Thompson was group A.
- Articles belonging to Jane were found in his possession.
- He knew the pub quite well and had visited it on four or five occasions whilst in hospital.
- At the time of the murder he was seen near the Nags Head Inn.
- He attempted to prove his alibi by claiming he was at the Westwood Hospital about midnight when in fact he did not arrive there until 2.00 a.m. according to two witnesses.
- He distributed silver coins to the patients at Westwood Hospital and subsequently exchanged more silver for notes at the YMCA. Before the crime he had been short of money and had only received £2 in pay that week.
- Shortly after the death of Jane he wrote a letter to his commanding officer with a view to excusing his intended disappearance.
- He took pains to change into civilian clothes which might, however, be consistent with the desire to desert from the army.
- He attempted to dispose of the proceeds including rings and jewellery belonging to Jane.
- When arrested he attempted to hide the proceeds of the robbery in the police car.
- At the time of his arrest a pair of scissors, which could have made the marks in the bar of Nags Head Inn, were found on his person. These were similar to those owned by Jane Coulton.
- Thompson told lies to account for his movements between midnight and 2.00 a.m.
- He told an incredible story about a mythical figure named Buck.
- When he was asked to account for the jewellery found in the car, he had not said a word about Buck but clearly said, 'Just say I don't know anything about them.'

The prosecution described Thompson as a man of very bad character who had had no less than fourteen convictions dating from 1927, mostly for stealing. In 1931, he is alleged to have said when arrested on the charge of larceny at Kendall, he would have 'done the woman but he thought he could not get away with it'.

A report by the prison doctor, Dr Francis Brisby, formed the opinion that Thompson was mentally unstable but found nothing to suggest insanity, even though his father had died in a mental hospital. Whilst awaiting trial Thompson had been examined by an electroencephalograph at Sutton Hospital, in the same way that Terence Casey had, to ascertain if he was indeed epileptic. The only positive finding was confirmation that he had, at some time, suffered a head injury of some gravity and there was a suggestion of traumatic damage to the left hemisphere of the brain. On the night of the murder, he had had a lot to drink, somewhere in the region of fourteen to fifteen pints of beer. The high level of liquid consumption is something that was raised in the Terence Casey murder trial, as doctors believed it acted as a trigger for epilepsy, and violent outbursts related to the condition. Thompson claimed that the quantity of beer was not an undue amount for him, since when working as a dock labourer he was accustomed to consuming large quantities of drink. At the end of 1936 he had sustained an injury to his head and was in hospital long enough to suggest this was a serious matter. He had been in hospital again at Bradford at the beginning of September 1944 for the injuries he sustained in the street fight. Brisby reported there was a scar on the top of his head from the 1936 injury and, shortly after this, he was admitted to Manchester Prison where he had an epileptic seizure, which was believed to be genuine. Thompson told Brisby that he had another seizure about three months later, after his discharge, but he had not had any since. The doctor indicated there was no evidence that Thompson suffered from epilepsy or had any suggestive seizures or attacks. In the witness box, Thompson made a very able appearance and explained several apparent anomalies by saying he was a 'peculiar chap'. This apt piece of lay parlance does describe him and indeed is the opinion of most people who had anything to do with him.

After three days, the jury found Thompson guilty of murder and made no recommendation to mercy. Mr Justice Oliver, addressing the murderer, asked him if he had anything to say before sentence was passed. Thompson said, 'I have this to say: I am not guilty. Better men and braver men than me have gone to their deaths every day through civilisation and justice. What does it matter one more?' Justice Oliver continued, 'The jury have found you guilty of murder, and I entirely agree with that verdict.' The black cap was then placed on the judge's head, and as the dreaded words of the death sentence were uttered in the tense stillness of the crowded court, Thompson stood stiffly to attention, with his head thrown back and a grim look upon his swarthy face. When the judge had finished, Thompson turned smartly to the left, and, unassisted by the two officers in the dock, walked firmly down the steps leading to the cells.

Following the trial, the police made extensive efforts to ascertain who Buck might be, but they were unable to find evidence of anyone in existence who could be identified as the alleged criminal. At Manchester Assizes on Thursday, 11 July 1935, Thompson received a sentence of twenty months' hard labour for burglary with intent. It was assumed he served his sentence in Strangeways Prison. On 14 October 1935, Dr Buck Ruxton, a double murderer, was in Strangeways Prison awaiting trial. He was there until 13 March 1936 and the police believed that, as the pair were imprisoned at the same time, this is where he invented the name of 'Buck' from. However, the town of Buxton, Derbyshire, featured heavily in his life and that of his father. Equally, on several occasions he found himself appearing before Buckinghamshire magistrates. It may well have been that one of these locations was the inspiration for Buck.

The Appeal

Thompson appealed to the Court of Criminal Appeal where his counsel made a great deal of the point that two police officers had given incorrect evidence on oath to the effect that the electric torch belonging to Jane Coulton had been found on his person at the time of his arrest. In fact, the torch was not found on his person but subsequently at his lodgings. Thompson, at his trial, denied that the torch was found on him at the time of his arrest, and it was argued that his defence was prejudiced because the jury, no doubt, felt that he was lying when he denied the torch was in his possession. The judges did not attach much importance to this point and said that they were satisfied that in this case the jury could not be swayed one way or the other by their decision as to where the torch was in fact found, it was in the possession of the prisoner. His appeal was dismissed on 15 January 1945.

Arthur Thompson was duly hung at Armley Prison, Leeds, on Wednesday, 31 January 1945 by Thomas Pierrepoint, assisted by Herbert Morris. His body was buried on the same day within the prison grounds. Jane Coulton had been buried on 27 September 1944 at Oakworth, Christ Church, Yorkshire. Remember her.

Like Father, Like Son?

Whilst Thompson's crime was a tragic one, he had grown up in an environment of criminality. His father, Frederick Michael Thompson, also spent a considerable amount of time travelling the country, as an antiques trader. Having first declared himself a furniture dealer in 1901, he spent the next forty years in the antiques business and was not averse to regular court appearances for a variety of reasons, some of them a blueprint for his son's future behaviour.

In June 1918, after being called for military service, he attended a County Appeal Tribunal at Ulverston, Lancashire, where he described himself as a widower with nine children and no female relatives. His appeal was dismissed even though he was performing agricultural work two days per week, which he felt was contributing to the war effort. Frederick was the subject of a House of Commons question concerning his appeal against National Conscription for the drafting of eligible men under the National Service Act. He re-appeared in court on 1 July 1918 and was granted a stay until 31 October 1918, if he did four days of work per week of national importance. He never performed military service.

Following the death of his wife, Margaret Ellen, he advertised for a housekeeper and a spinster nurse, Hannah Jane Wilson, responded. They arranged to meet in Skipton where he suggested that, being a widower, it might be better to be married, and so on Tuesday, 18 December 1923, they tied the knot. However, after just two weeks of marriage, she left him on the grounds he struck her on New Year's Day. Thompson claimed he found her in an hysterical state, and that she had told his children things she ought not to have done. Hannah returned to her family in Colne, Lancashire, and subsequently discovered her husband had been living with a woman in Norwich, and immediately demanded a divorce.

In August 1922, Frederick appeared in court at Bradford where he was sued for selling fake Chippendale furniture. He lost the case and was told that he 'should have been embarrassed by the so-called antique'. Then, in August 1924, he claimed to have found the painting *Our Saviour* by Van Dyck, in a woodshed at Furness Abbey, and valued the masterpiece at £12,000. The painting, apparently, was taken on an exhibition tour during which time, he inspected another painting at Buxton, Derbyshire, and declared it to be *Madonna and Child* by Rubens, valued at £15,000. It seems he had planned to sell the paintings to an American collector but, in January 1925, the paintings were deemed not to be genuine and this resulted in another court appearance. Equally, in the same year, Thompson is said to have married Emily Isabel Lamb, but nothing to verify this can be found. This maybe because his divorce had still not been finalised.

In May 1927, in what was to be a highly reported event, Thompson was being held in Worthing Prison awaiting trial for having obtained an oil painting by false pretences. It seems that just a few hours before he was due to appear in court he prayed, 'God please get me out of here', and the cell door magically opened and he escaped. He was found on the Sussex Downs 5 hours later and taken back to court. Following his trial, he was re-arrested for a more serious charge of an attempt to defraud an elderly Sussex woman of thirty paintings and of stealing money from her. He was sentenced to six months' imprisonment. On 3 December 1928, five years after she married him, Hannah Jane Wilson's decree nisi was finally granted and she was rid of a man who had not only treated her badly, but had made every effort to stop her from divorcing him, even though he was living with another women, by whom he is believed to have had his eleventh and final child. Eventually, by 1939, Frederick would find himself a resident in the Cumberland and Westmoreland Mental Hospital, Garlands, Carlisle. He passed away there on Monday, 29 April 1940.

Whilst there is no documentary evidence to suggest that any of the crimes committed by Arthur Thompson had anything to do with his father, it can be demonstrated that father and son were in the same location when particular offences occurred. Therefore, it is reasonable to believe that two men, who are related, engaged in the same business during the same period and in the same location, may have collaborated in some way.

Chapter 17

Bombardier Joseph Howard Grossley – It was the Germans!

Panel 23. Column 2
Service Number: D/106883
Unit: Royal Canadian Artillery
Executed: Wednesday, 5 September 1945, aged 37

One of the most unfortunate factors when investigating the crimes of the Brookwood Killers is often the distinct lack of information regarding the victim. The vast resources currently available must be extensively trawled to establish even the most basic of information. Such is the case with Lily Griffiths, whose details are scant but what is known is that her life ended tragically, and most likely very painfully.

Aberdare, Glamorgan, the birthplace of Lily Griffiths. Her only son was to perish here following her murder by her common-law husband, Bombardier Joseph Howard Grossley.

The Victim

Lily Griffiths was born in the Welsh mining town of Aberdare, Glamorgan, on 28 October 1916, the daughter of Anthony and Averina Griffiths (née Davies). Her father worked as a coal hewer in a local mine, whilst her mother raised their nine children. Her siblings were: William Thomas (b. 1897), Griffith (b. 1899), Anthony (b. 1901), Mary Elizabeth, Ann, Averina, David Charles and Vivian (b. 1923). She lived with her parents, helping to run the family home, at a time when there was a great deal of industrial upheaval in the mining industry, at which Aberdare was at the centre. In 1940 Lily moved to London to help her sister, Averina, look after her home in First Avenue, Acton, where she lived with her husband, a prison officer, William Gardiner. The documents contained within the service files for the Canadian War Dead provide a great deal of detail about the man who would end Lily's life, but very little about her. The case records, held by The National Archives, contain a document provided by Averina, which offers the greatest insight into her life, and the man who would eventually end it.

The Assailant

From the outset life was set to be difficult for Joseph Howard Grossley. Records of his early life are filled with inaccuracies and controversy. It is known that he was born on the Wednesday, 25 September 1907 in Verdun, Quebec, Canada, an illegitimate child, whose father was believed to have been an officer in the United States army during the First World War. His mother, Florence Hamel, placed him in the care of her cousins, Frank and Clara Viens of East Spring Street, Winooski, Vermont, US, at the age of 5 weeks. The couple legally adopted him and raised him as their own son. There were no other known siblings.

During the early part of his life, he was deemed to be quick-tempered and not amenable to discipline. He attended school rather irregularly from the age of 6 and claimed he had reached Grade 8 by the age of 15. He played truant on many occasions and his uncle, who was the chief of police in Winooski, received reports on many occasions regarding his minor breaches of the peace. He left school to assist his guardians with their grocery store but quickly found himself embroiled in petty crime

154 The Brookwood Killers

and spent time in and out of various correctional facilities. He became involved with a local girl, Marie Goulet, aged 15, and this resulted in her becoming pregnant and, on 16 February 1925, the two were married at the Church of St Joseph, Burlington, Vermont. It was claimed that the marriage took place without the consent of their respective parents. However, a marriage certificate produced on 25 September 1945 indicates that the witnesses were Frank Viens, his adoptive father, and Francois Goulet, Marie's father. The marriage did not last more than a year and there was one child, Francis Lawrence Grossley, who was born on 15 November 1926, by which time Grossley was serving a sentence of two to ten years in the State Prison at Windsor, Vermont, for burglary.

Evidence suggests that, after his release from prison, he led a rather nomadic existence wandering across the US and Mexico for almost seven years taking on various jobs, none of which lasted very long, mainly on account of his becoming restless and wanting to move on. During this period of his life, he was picked up on many occasions by numerous law-enforcement authorities for vagrancy and acts of petty crime. He was deported from the US to Canada in 1930 following a conviction for petty larceny, after serving six months in a house of correction. It was around this time that he discovered he was not actually an American citizen, but a Canadian, a fact he was very resentful of, so much so, that he returned to the US illegally and is known to have been deported back to Canada on at least five separate occasions.

With the outbreak of the Second World War, he enlisted in the Canadian army on Monday, 22 July 1940, and arrived in the United Kingdom on Wednesday, 4 September. He was almost immediately placed before a medical board at Borden, Hampshire, with the diagnosis of 'cicatrix of the back', an old burn scar, resulting in a medical re-categorisation which was to see him marked unsuitable for combat duties and so he was given a clerical role. Just a few weeks later, he was admitted to the Connaught Military Hospital near Hindhead, Surrey, having been diagnosed with gonorrhoea, for which he underwent anti-bacterial treatment. However, this would not be the only occasion he would be treated for this condition, as well as syphilis.

From the day of his enlistment, Grossley had claimed dependants' allowance for his wife and child, even though he had not seen them for many years. In April 1941, one of the cheques was returned marked 'address of dependant unknown'. He wrote to his unit paymaster asking about the boy's welfare, but his letter would open a review of his file, and questions were then asked as to where and to whom the money was going. Further investigations not only revealed that he had been deceiving the Canadian army but also showed that the boy had been living with his grandparents and had not seen either his father or mother for many years. Grossley was now required to repay the allowances, a total of $889, and money began to be taken from his pay at the rate of $20 a month. This was the beginning of many financial issues for the Canadian.

He was employed as a clerk at the Canadian Military Records Office in London, and at Easter 1941 he met Lily Griffiths, a 25-year-old Welsh girl from Cwmaman, Aberdare, Glamorgan. They soon began a relationship and later rented an apartment in Stanlake Road, Shepherds Bush, where they lived as man and wife. The owner of the property, Lily Shattock, employed Grossley as a caretaker for the premises and recalled that there had been several complaints from other tenants about 'Mrs Grossley', as she was referred to, screaming at night. She also claimed that Lily had once confided in her that Grossley used to hit her when he was drunk. There was, apparently, an occasion when Lily believed he was seeing another woman, so she confronted him. Grossley produced his revolver and began to threaten her with it. When Lily told him that she thought it was not loaded, he shot a hole in a sideboard. Lily Shattock also recalled a situation at the house where she was attempting to evict a tenant, and Grossley offered to assist in removing the man. An argument ensued and the two men grappled with each other, the Canadian suddenly producing the revolver from his hip pocket, which Lily Shattock grabbed and threw behind a wardrobe. Although the tenant then left the premises quietly, she became very aware that Grossley could be a violent individual, even though he was very polite and cordial when he was sober.

The couple were beset with further difficulties when, on Wednesday, 12 February 1943, a son, Anthony Howard Grossley, was born at Hammersmith Hospital, London. This contributed to Grossley's monetary burden, as he was unable to claim dependants' allowance for a common-law-wife and child, and Lily was unable to work. Added to this, there were now complaints from the tenants where they lived about the baby crying at night. In a desperate effort to improve the situation, he endeavoured to obtain a discharge from the Canadian army on Friday, 12

March 1943, so that he might obtain gainful civil employment in England, but this application was refused. It would not be until 1 March 1944 that the army would agree to make an allowance payment to Lily, but this was just $8.50 a month. On 26 January 1945, Grossley absented himself from his unit and was never to return. He travelled with Lily to Porthcawl, on the Welsh coast, where they rented a room in a boarding house in New Road, which was where Lily's life would come to a murderous end.

The Great Island Farm Escape

At its peak, the Royal Ordnance Factory at Bridgend, Wales, known locally as The Arsenal, employed some 40,000 people, mainly women, to meet with the demands of the armed forces for munitions. Many of their employees travelled a considerable distance to reach the factory and, concerned that the travelling might be too much for their workers, especially in the blackout, they commandeered land at Island Farm next to the A48 and built several single-storey huts for the staff to stay in. However, their employees made it quite clear that these premises were unsuitable, and they preferred the comfort of their own homes, despite the drudgery of commuting.

The huts lay unused until October 1943, when the men of the US 28th Infantry Division were placed there whilst preparing for the D-Day offensive. Following the invasion of Normandy, the facility was used to house German officers, many whom were members of the SS. Designated Camp 198, it was commanded by Lieutenant Colonel Edwin Darling and was to see an escape that rivalled that of the Great Escape.

After the evening roll call at 10.00 p.m. on Saturday, 10 March 1945, eighty-four German prisoners of war began to break out of Camp 198 and disperse across the Welsh countryside. Almost immediately, fourteen of the escapees were recaptured but the others remained dangerously at large. The BBC made a radio announcement, which may have given Joseph Grossley a cause for thought. He, Lily and Anthony were staying in a house in New Road, Porthcawl, the seaside home of Jennie and Ernest Atkinson. On Monday, 12 March, Lily took Anthony with her on the bus to Aberdare, where she planned to leave him in the care of her sister. On hearing the news, a conversation with the Atkinsons revealed that Grossley had a gun in his possession. He showed it to them and when he was asked if he was going to take it out with him, Grossley stated, 'Yes, I always carry it and I may come across some German prisoners myself.'

The Crime

That night, Lily returned from her trip to Aberdare. She was described by Jennie Atkinson as looking tired and was sitting by the kitchen fire, knitting socks for Anthony. Grossley had gone out drinking at the Esplanade Hotel, after which he went with several other men to the Victoria Hotel, where more alcohol was consumed. At about 10.00 p.m. he returned to the guest house and Lily asked him where he had been. Grossley, clearly the worse for drink, snapped, 'Out'. He then beckoned Lily to go upstairs with him, where an argument took place. A short while later the couple came downstairs and went out.

Not long after they had left the house, several witnesses heard a scream, followed by a shot. Arthur James Speck and George Isaac Lewis were

Lily Griffiths was shot in this alleyway in Porthcawl. Her murderer, Bombardier Grossley, claimed it was carried out by escaped German prisoners of war.

visiting a friend in New Road when they heard the sound of a gun. On rushing outside they saw a soldier at the end of the lane, he said, 'Fetch a doctor, I have shot my dear wife.' They could see a woman lying on the ground, in great pain. The soldier told them he was a Canadian, and then fell on one knee and said, 'My darling, what have I done.' The woman responded, 'Don't worry dear, you couldn't help it.' They both claimed that they had been attacked by a man and pointed in the direction he had gone. Grossley then told Speck that whilst walking down the lane near to the guest house, they had been threatened by a German prisoner who tried to steal Lily's handbag and clothes. The German then attempted to attack Lily and during a scuffle his pistol had gone off, the bullet striking Lily.

With the arrival of PC Thomas Lewis, PC Thomas Nickolas and Dr Robert Hodkinson, the pistol was taken away from Grossley. He now made a slightly different statement and claimed they were out for a late-night walk and had been threatened by two German prisoners. He had used his pistol, which he was carrying, to frighten the Germans away. However, as they had made their escape down the lane, he had fired a shot and in so doing had inadvertently wounded his wife.

Lily was carried into the kitchen of a house in New Road, from where she was later taken to Bridgend Hospital and underwent a thorough examination. Dr Hodkinson noticed bruises on her face at the scene of the shooting, which were now more apparent and covered her arms, legs and abdomen. He observed that those on her face and body were consistent with blows, whilst the ones on her arms were likely to be the result of tight gripping. She had a serious gunshot wound that required an urgent operation, and he warned Lily she might not survive. During the operation he drained two pints of blood from the left side of her chest. Most shockingly of all, later that day, Dr Hodkinson had to perform an abortion on Lily. A foetus, about three to four months old, was removed.

Following her ordeal, Lily, made a statement to Detective Inspector Lancelot Bailey, who was investigating the case. In an effort to prevent Grossley from being sent to prison, Lily claimed that on the night of the shooting, Grossley was drunk, and they had gone for a walk down the lane. Here, Grossley threatened to kill himself and had produced a pistol. There had been a struggle as she tried to wrestle the weapon from him, and it went off. This was to be the statement that was submitted in court. However, as the realisation that her injuries were more serious and she was going to die, she changed her statement and made a dying declaration. She told Detective Inspector Bailey that on the night of the shooting Grossley was drunk and had beat her up, as he had done on many occasions when he had been drinking. He then took her outside at the point of his pistol, where he beat her up some more and then kicked her in the lower abdomen and shot her. He told her that she was to tell the story of the German prisoners. During this interview, just before she died, she made all the necessary arrangements for her sister to have custody of Anthony. At 5.30 a.m. on Friday, 16 March 1945, Lily Griffiths died at Bridgend & District Hospital from the wounds she had received on 12 March. Grossley was now a murderer.

Averina Gardiner – A Sister's Tale

In her statement to Bridgend police on 16 March 1945, Averina makes it clear that the relationship between the couple was a tempestuous and violent one, and that Grossley would regularly make intimidating threats to both Lily and her, some of which he would actually carry out. She had first met the Canadian in August 1941, when Lily had been looking after her home since October 1940 and had met him in March of that year. She claimed he had been billeted at the house, but Averina did not believe this and told Lily she could continue to live with her, but Grossley had to go. The couple left together, and it was the beginning of a tense relationship with a man who would spend years tormenting and abusing her sister and would eventually end her life.

In December 1941, Grossley arrived at the house and informed Averina that Lily was in the Park Royal Hospital, having suffered an accident at work. In fact, she had gone through an illegal abortion and had become seriously ill. She was released two days before Christmas and arrived at Averina's house on Christmas Eve sporting a black eye and swollen lip. When she was asked what had happened, Lily claimed she had fallen down the stairs at home, but later told her sister that Grossley had thrown a can at her when he was 'in one of his moods'.

In April 1942, Lily tried to leave the relationship and went to her sister's home, but Grossley arrived at the address and took her away. The following day, she was wearing a bandage on her leg, and when she was asked what had happened, she told her sister that Grossley had stabbed her in the leg with his army jackknife. Despite telling her to go back to Wales and escape the relationship, Lily refused to return to her parent's home saying she was 'afraid' to leave. Some months later, in a drunken rage, Grossley came to Averina's home and threatened the sisters, claiming they were trying to break up the relationship. He produced a knife and attempted to stab Lily, who fainted. Averina got into a struggle with him but, fortunately, his appendix burst at that very point, and he had to be taken to hospital.

Following the birth of Anthony, Averina felt that there was a slight improvement in the relationship, but it was not to last for long. Further incidents occurred in which her sister was knocked about by the Canadian. In September 1943, Averina was informed that Lily was in bed at home unwell. When she went to the address, she found her sister almost dying, having suffered yet another illegal abortion. After being admitted to hospital, where she remained for three weeks, Lily made a slow recovery and was very weak. Averina had taken Anthony into her care but the moment her sister was released from hospital, Grossley demanded that the child be returned. When Averina told Grossley that she was going to report him to his commanding officer for the way he was treating her sister, he threatened to blow up her house, kill her and her children. 'No one will part me from Lily and my baby.'

Averina saw Lily almost every day between Christmas 1943 and summer 1944, and she complained bitterly about the way Grossley treated her and how she was fed up being alone all the time. On 12 July 1944, as V-weapons rained down upon London, Averina and her daughter moved to Scotland to stay with her in-laws, whilst her husband was serving overseas as a sergeant in the Scots Guards. Although she returned to the capital in December 1944, she would not see Lily again.

The Trial

On Wednesday, 14 March 1945, Grossley had appeared before the magistrates court at Bridgend, Glamorgan, charged with the attempted murder of Lily Griffiths. He was remanded in custody until Thursday, 29 March. By this time, Lily had died from a septic infection of the left chest, and when he reappeared in court the charge had become one of murder. He was remanded for a second time and, at 10.30 a.m. on Wednesday, 11 July 1945, appeared at the Glamorgan Assizes, Guildhall, Swansea, before Sir John Singleton and a jury comprising twelve men. It was concluded by 2.10 p.m. the following day. Grossley pleaded not guilty and was represented by Mr Glyn Jones KC, Mr Dapho Powell and Mr Sibbering Jones. The prosecutors were Mr Ralph Sutton KC and Mr Godfrey Parsons. The representatives from the Canadian Military Headquarters were Major William Southward Coolin, unit commander, and Captain J.H. Ready on behalf of the Judge Advocate General's Office.

The prosecution produced several witnesses who would allege that Grossley was a violent, womanising deserter. Rose Stegmann, who lived in Jubilee Road, Perry Vale, claimed that one weekend Grossley stayed at her home, as he was seeing her daughter whose husband was a prisoner of war in Germany. She stated that as she picked his greatcoat up off the sofa, a revolver fell out onto the floor.

One of the most damming witnesses, however, was Jethroe Gough, the pathologist. He was to reveal not only the circumstances of Lily's death but the fact that she was expecting another child whom he had to abort. This may have been the final straw for Grossley who, already under considerable financial pressure, could not face the prospect of yet another mouth to feed. Lily had just secured a job at the Arsenal, the Royal Ordnance Factory in Bridgend, and he knew that a pregnancy would, most likely, see her thrown out of employment, particularly in an era when a woman living bigamously with a soldier and caring for an illegitimate child would be seen as a socially unacceptable liability for the employer. Gough also highlighted the fact that prior to being shot she had been kicked and punched by Grossley, with a particularly heavy blow to the stomach.

Sentence was to be executed by hanging and the body to be buried in the precincts of HM Prison, Cardiff.

The Appeal

On Tuesday, 21 August 1945, Grossley made an appearance before Mr Justice Wrottesley, Mr Justice Croom-Johnson and Mr Justice Stable at the Court of Criminal Appeal. He claimed the prosecution had not discharged the burden of proof, the trial judge had misdirected the jury and the verdict was unreasonable. Wrottesley, in response, stated that Grossley was a Canadian soldier, had a wife in Canada, that Lily Griffiths was his common-law wife and that they had one child, approximately 2 years old. He emphasised the point that Grossley was either a deserter or absent without leave from the Canadian army and that his financial circumstances did not appear to be good at the time of the murder. He referred to the dying deposition of Lily Griffiths wherein she stated that she and Grossley had struggled and he had told her he was going to commit suicide. Further reference was made to his statement in which he claimed he intended to commit suicide, and reference was made to the fact that Grossley had not given evidence. In a final judgement, Wrottesley said, 'It is clear, and was clear to the jury, that the pistol used in the shooting would not go off unless the trigger was pressed.' He further stated that in his opinion, and that of his brother justices, the jury was fully advised, properly directed and that there was ample evidence on which they could find Grossley guilty of murder. Finally, he stated that the court believed the trial was properly conducted in every respect and that the appeal must be dismissed.

The Last Letter

On 4 September 1945, Grossley, who had written prolifically whilst in prison, mainly protesting his innocence and informing the recipients that God will be his judge, wrote his final letter, to his step-parents. It reads:

Dearest Mother and Dad,
Just these last few lines, that I will ever be able to send you my dear.

For tomorrow at 9:00am I will be no more, everyone has been kind to me, and the Catholic priest spent much time with me, he was most kind like you or Dad would have been to me, I have made a general confession of all my life, I feel quite at ease in leaving for the great beyond.

Believe me mother and dad, I am not guilty of this crime, before earthly judge, yes. But not before God, the supreme judge of us all. I feel quite calm now I received the last sacraments this afternoon, in the chapel when I asked God in his great mercy to be compassionate to me.

I am happy to go mother and dad even though I would have liked to have seen you once more, well we will meet on the other side, God bless you both for all you have done for me always. You know what my life has been on earth so I am glad to leave now maybe I will find peace in the next world.

I'm sending you my effects, and you will receive all my money from the Canadian government, Ottawa, Canada. If you do not receive it soon write and ask about it. It comes to $1000, do what you wish with it. I wrote to Marie told her all about it, remember Misha Rose and children.

I can't say any more, the hour is drawing near so my little composition you will know how I feel and have always felt towards you both I never wanted to hurt you anymore.

Goodbye darling, your ever loving son.

Howard

xxx

On Wednesday, 5 September 1945, Joseph Howard Grossley was executed at Cardiff Prison by Thomas Pierrepoint, assisted by Steve Wade. His body was buried within the grounds of the prison later that day.

A Tragic Postscript

In the final moments of her life Lily Griffiths had requested that custody of her son be given to her sister, Catherine Davies of Glynhafod Street, Cwmaman, Aberdare. On Thursday, 23 August 1945, Grossley made a request that his son be sent to Canada, where he hoped he would be raised by a 'good roman catholic family' and receive a beneficial education, unaware that his son was, in fact, dead. On the evening of 15 August 1945, as many communities celebrated VJ Day, two children went to the Glynhafod recreation ground where they saw what they thought was a doll at the bottom of the bathing pool. When the water cleared, they realised it was a child, 2-year-old Anthony Howard Grossley. During an inquest held at Cwmaman, Aberdare, on 24 August 1945, Granville Davies of Glynhafod Street said he got the child out and tried artificial respiration without result. When people were bathing, he said, club members kept an eye on the pool, but that day no one was bathing, and no one noticed the child fall in. A verdict of accidental drowning was recorded by the deputy coroner. In a letter, dated 2 September 1945, Grossley noted the death of his son and went to the gallows fully aware that he had lost both Lily and Anthony. Whilst his name is recorded on the Brookwood Memorial, their last resting place is unknown. Remember them.

Chapter 18

Private August Sangret –
The Wigwam Murder

Panel 23. Column 3
Service Number: L/27572
Unit: Royal Canadian Infantry Corps
Executed: Thursday, 29 April 1943, aged 29

The story of the 'Wigwam Murder' is perhaps one of the more well-known crime stories of the Second World War, an event that was to see, for the first time in British legal history, the victim's skull being introduced as evidence in a murder trial. A great deal has been written about how a teenage girl met her death on a cold and damp Surrey common in autumn 1942, and there has been much conjecture around the man who was ultimately charged and executed for her murder. The story begins at 10.20 a.m. on Wednesday, 7 October 1942 when Marine William Moore, squirming through the scrub

Joan Pearl Wolfe, murdered by Canadian soldier Private August Sangret in what would become known as the 'Wigwam Murder'.

of Hankley Common, Surrey, touched something ghastly. Like a signpost to murder, an outstretched arm pierced the ground, and Marine Moore had crawled right on to it. The relics of a partly mummified female skeleton. Army bulldozers had pushed earth into huge mounds to create a training ground for tanks and half-track trucks. At the base of one of these somebody had scooped out the soil to make a grave. But who was the victim, and why were they buried there?

The Victim

Joan Pearl Wolfe was born in Tonbridge, Kent, on Sunday, 11 March 1923, the youngest daughter of Charles Frederick and Edith Mary Wolfe (née Groombridge). She had two siblings, Allan Edward Charles (b. 1920) and Yvonne Diamond (b. 1922). On 21 April 1930, when Joan was just 7 years old, her father died at the age of 34 from tuberculosis. Following her husband's death, Edith married Lesley John Wood in 1931, and a daughter, Enid, was born to the couple in the same year. Sadly, Lesley passed away in 1939 at the age of 31, and Edith went on to marry a third man, Charles Wells in 1942.

There is a great deal of information in the public environment that suggests Joan lived modestly with her parents in a strict Catholic household, but it appears there was also a significant amount of devastating disruption in her formative years. The death of her father, the remarriage of her mother within a year, the birth of a stepsister at the same time, the death of her stepfather when she was 16 years old and her mother's ultimate re-marriage to Charles Wells. It is perhaps hardly surprising that Joan, having been raised in a highly pious environment, was starting to question her religious beliefs and, without knowing the infinite details of her teenage years, what other catastrophic events had impacted upon her life? The rift between mother and daughter, however, was sufficiently deep enough for Joan to tell a police officer in July 1942 that both her parents were dead. Of course, this does not mean that Joan was without fault and may simply have been a recalcitrant teenager, determined to act under her own initiative. The evidence, however, does not really support this and it would seem that she was a gullible, extremely naïve individual yearning for stability, despite her somewhat wayward lifestyle.

Her mother's courtroom testimony indicates that, by the time she was 16, Joan was engaged to a young man in Tunbridge Wells, and, at around the same time, she ran away from home for the first time. She took herself first to London and then to Aldershot, where she began to associate with soldiers, particularly Canadians, and developed what is described as a 'somewhat nomadic lifestyle'. The relationship between mother and daughter is evidenced in a letter dated 4 May 1942 from Edith, which was produced in court, and indicates that she was gradually being driven to despair by her eldest daughter's increasingly unpredictable and irresponsible behaviour. She talks about Joan getting 'cured', a reference to venereal disease, which she believed her daughter was suffering from. The letter reads:

Dear Joan,

I have received your letter and also your other letter from the Quadrant, and you forget that I am here alone, and also, I had to fetch your clothing from the Swan Hotel, and then wash them and then I was going to send them, but once more you broke your word to me, Joan.

I cannot put any more faith in you unless you return to that hotel at once. I am finished with you. I have been more than fair to you, forgiven you for things that no other mother would have done. Joan, if you have any respect for me and yourself for God's sake go and get cured and make an effort to be a good girl. I will do anything for you if you will help yourself. I cannot help you if you do not help yourself.

I am not sending your ration book there because I do not want you to stay there. You said something about repaying me for all I have done for you. Joan, nothing can repay me for that, I do not want repaying for anything I have ever done for you, my child. I shall be paid in full the day you come and truthfully say, Mum, I have been cured and I am going to be a good girl. Joan, that will be the happiest day of my life. If you cannot do it for me, think about Allan. He looks up to his sister, and of course thinks you are a good girl. Joan, are you going to let him down as well as me? Joan, please think before it is too late and remember remorse is the worst thing in the world to bear. When I am dead you will think about all this and wish that you had been a better girl to me, so before it is too late, Joan, try hard to alter, won't you, and whatever you decide to do think well before you do it.

Love Mum.

P.S. – I am still praying every night for you, Joan.

By spring 1942, having met a young Canadian soldier, Francis Hearn, Joan travelled to Godalming, Surrey, where the pair had, apparently, planned to get married. At the time, she was working in the canteen at the RFD Company where they were manufacturing barrage balloons.

The wedding was arranged to take place in the local Methodist church on the basis that she was Roman Catholic, and he was not. However, it seems that Hearn was posted back to Canada on 15 July 1942 and would never return. Devastated and distraught, Joan spent that night at the home of an elderly spinster she had befriended, 68-year-old Kate Hayter, who lived at Kettlebury Hill, Thursley. Although she was apparently saddened by the loss of Hearn, just two days later, on Friday, 17 July 1942, Joan met August Sangret, an illiterate French-Canadian Cree Indian, in a pub in Godalming, where he was drinking along with some other Canadian soldiers. According to the statement of Sangret, they had drinks, went for a walk in Godalming Park, had sex and parted company. They subsequently met again on numerous occasions and a passionate affair began, with Sangret apparently telling his friends he was going to marry Joan.

On 23 July, after having collapsed in a Godalming street, Joan wrote her first letter to Sangret, even though he could not read, from her bed in the Emergency Ward at Warren Road Hospital, Guildford. Her words, whilst a little naïve, are filled with desperation and berate the authorities for not assisting her, even though they did so, on several occasions:

My Dear August,

Well, my dear, I hope I am forgiven for not turning up to see you last night, but I was in the police station five hours, and then they did not help me. I was walking along the road and suddenly came over queer. I fainted for the first time in my whole life. They brought me to hospital here. Where they are going to examine me. I shall know whether I am all right or not then.

I hope you will come and see me, as I really want to see you very much and being in bed all day is awful. You can come any night between 6 and 7pm and Sunday afternoon. Please try and come. I have your picture on the locker beside me. The nurses know you are my boyfriend, they told me to tell you to come see me. You have to tell them my name and ask for emergency ward. Well, hoping to see you soon, I will say au revoir.

God bless you.

Love Joan

On the 26 July 1942, Joan wrote again to August Sangret, but on this occasion to bring him news that she was expecting. There is no evidence to corroborate that she was ever pregnant, but it is possible she was and, if so, it is more likely to have been Hearn's child than Sangret's. Joan was believed to have been suffering from a sexually transmitted disease, which she may have contracted from Sangret, or one of the other soldiers she is alleged to have had sex with. Her letter to Sangret reads:

Dear August
Well, I hope that you are well as I have not seen or heard from you. Did you receive my last letter, as I was not sure of the name of the camp? I wish with all my heart that I could see you, it is so very lonely here without anyone to speak to, and there is so much I want to tell you. They are going to try and get me somewhere to stay in Godalming, or if this is not possible in Guildford. That will be nice because we will be able to see each other.

Just one week has passed since I have known you, dear. It seems such a long time. I shall be in here for about a fortnight and if you want to see me the visiting hours are from 7 to 8pm every night, and Sunday afternoon 2pm–4pm. I hope you will try and come to see me, as I want to tell you when I can come out because someone will have to meet me, and you are all I have in the world. Of course, if you do not want to come, I shall understand, August, but I am sure I shall never understand men. I do not know enough about them, but I can live and learn.

Anyway, I am pretty sure we are going to have a tiny wee one, maybe that is why you do not want to come and see me because you think that. I hope not anyway, but, dear, I would not blame you one little bit if you did not want to marry me, because I am really too young, and too old-fashioned to be married. I regret what we did now it is too late, for I should still say it is wicked. I hope God forgives me, for I am truly sorry, and do not want to do anything wrong really.

I guess you think I am silly, and I suppose I am but remember that I was brought up in a very strict Catholic school for 13 years, and that is why I am so old-fashioned. We were taught to have a baby before you were married was a sin. I cannot yet believe it of me, what would my priest at home say and my people would not have anything to do with me. Oh, dear August, why did we do it. You will not want to marry me anyway, because we hardly know one another and I do not know anything about babies. I suppose I should have to close this letter now, if I want to get it posted, so au revoir (daddy).

God bless you always dear.

Joan

Upon her leaving hospital, and with nowhere to stay, Sangret used his native skills to build a shelter that he shared with Joan when he could. Some weeks later, on Wednesday, 19 August 1942, the Canadian Military Police discovered a 'wigwam' outside Jasper Camp where Joan Wolfe was sleeping. Sangret was with her, and they were told that they could not camp there and had to move. Joan, it was alleged, begged Sangret to build her another shelter, to which he agreed, this time behind the Sergeant's Mess at Witley, but it was not too long before it was also discovered. On 23 August, Canadian Military Police found the second shelter and Sangret was placed under close arrest. Joan Wolfe was handed to the civilian police and sent to a hostel.

Just over a week later, on 1 September, Joan left the hostel and moved into an abandoned cricket pavilion at Thursley. Throughout the time she was there, Sangret visited her with increasing frequency, regularly bringing food for them to eat together as they discussed their future plans, including marriage. She continued to send letters to Sangret that were typically naïve, yet optimistic, regarding her hopes for marriage, her general loneliness and her desire to be in his company. Joan did, evidently, dislike Sangret's repeated accusations of infidelity with other soldiers, and he is known to have lost his temper on several occasions, particularly with American troops she spoke to. She was, however, soon ejected from this hovel and on the evening of 10 September a witness reported seeing her in the village of Witley looking for accommodation. Joan was seen alive for the last time on Sunday, 13 September 1942.

The Assailant

August Sangret was born Thursday 28 August 1913 in Battleford, Saskatchewan, Canada, the son of Napoleon Sangret. He was of mixed race, part French Canadian and part Cree Indian. Having received no formal education, he was unable to read or write, but could sign his name. From an early age he worked as a farm labourer in the Canadian town of Maidstone and the long hours and hard work would see him develop a supple and muscular physique. The poverty of the region, combined with the hardships of the Depression era, meant that he would regularly find himself unemployed, leading to numerous scrapes with the law for both vagrancy and theft. There were some instances of more serious crimes as he grew older, including an occasion where he served six months in gaol for a violent assault in 1932, and a three-month sentence in 1938 for threatening to shoot a woman. His sexual promiscuity would see him diagnosed with venereal disease for the first time at the age of 17 but it would not be the only occasion. He would be infected on no less than five occasions between 1938 and 1942, before he met Joan Wolfe. He had unsuccessfully attempted to cure himself using a potassium permanganate solution, but eventually had to be admitted to hospital where he underwent extensive treatment for a bladder obstruction.

Sangret enlisted in the Canadian army on Wednesday, 19 June 1940, serving with the Regina Rifles Regiment. Like many of his comrades, his career as a soldier was to see a series of both minor and major violations of military discipline, including several occasions when he was reported as being absent without leave. He arrived in the United Kingdom on Monday, 23 March 1942, and within a few weeks found himself at Camp 103 on the outskirts of Godalming, Surrey, known as Jasper Camp, where he was to undergo an army education to help him improve his illiteracy.

The Investigation

Veteran Scotland Yard investigator Detective Inspector Edward 'Ted' Greeno was a renowned policeman whose manhunting skills would lead to the arrest, conviction and execution of several soldiers listed upon the Brookwood Memorial. After the body had been discovered near Godalming, he was asked to spearhead the investigation and was soon on the scene, along with his assistant Detective Sergeant Fred Hodge.

The corpse was that of a girl wearing a green-and-white summer frock with a lace collar and woollen ankle-socks, now dank and rotten, first with her own spilled blood and then with the earth's clamminess. Her underclothes had not been removed but her shoes were missing. She was lying face down, or would have, if there had been a face, in a shallow, makeshift grave. The earth had been disturbed by a passing military vehicle, possibly a half-track, which had loosened the soil and exposed her arm and foot. The left arm was folded beneath her chest, with the exposed right arm notably outstretched, indicating the victim had likely been dragged to the location where she lay, although there was no suggestion that she had been subjected to a sexual assault prior to her murder.

Private August Sangret, described by Detective Inspector Edward Greeno as 'a handsome brute, stocky, 5' 4" with a deep chest and massive shoulders tapering on to a ballet dancer's waist. His hair was oily black and his face lean and swarthy.'

The badly decomposed head, chest and abdominal cavity were described by Home Office Pathologist Dr Keith Simpson as being a 'seething mass of maggots'. They had eaten much of the soft body tissue, including the face and neck, save for a small section of scalp and hair. Field rats had gnawed some of the carcass and the skull had disintegrated into twenty pieces leaving a tuft of short, cropped, bleached hair and some scraps of shrivelled scalp. Greeno immediately organised sixty policemen into a dragnet, strung out at 2yd gaps across the countryside. Marching slowly with each man only looking at the ground straight ahead of him. They started that day and went on for weeks. The earth was shaved, and the soil sifted. Slowly, bits of bone and teeth were found. The body was taken to Guy's Hospital where, on the evening of Thursday, 8 October 1942, Keith Simpson conducted an autopsy, in conjunction with Dr Eric Gardner. It was established, having carefully reconstructed the skull by wiring all the fragments together, that there was a large impact site at the rear of the skull measuring 5in in length and 1¾in breadth. This led to the conclusion that the victim had died as a result of a single, heavy blow to the back of the head, inflicted whilst they were lying face down. The weapon which had delivered this fatal blow was probably a pole or bough of wood, and the blow from this weapon had caved in the skull. The injury would have induced rapid unconsciousness, and death would have resulted within minutes.

Ted Greeno knew he had to trace who the girl was. The area was swarming with transient soldiers, English, American and Canadian. There was Jasper Camp where non-readers from Canada's prairies and backwoods studied for three months, and then left. There was another camp where Americans, switching from the Canadian army to their own now that the US was in the war, were sent for clearance. This was often just for a couple of days or weeks, and then they moved on. Then there was the British camp, where Marines were sent to train and be hardened, and then returned to their units. The murderer had to be found, and any one of 100,000 men could have done it, and then moved away. The long patient trail of questioning began. They quizzed soldiers by the dozen and by the hundred, as well as their officers, and civilians too. Amongst the illiterate men taking the education course at Jasper Camp Greeno noticed what he described as 'some swarthy, half-breed French-Canadians'. A Canadian brigadier told him about them saying, 'Good men. Great fighters. Sometimes a bit sullen, and sometimes with a streak of the real savage.'

Personal belongings in the form of a crucifix, an elephant pendant and a green purse found during the search on Hankley Common were identified by Edith Watts as belonging to her daughter. Superintendent Richard Webb, of the Surrey Constabulary, recognised Joan's name, having interviewed her in both July and August 1942, after she had been taken into custody due to concerns over her welfare. She had been found living on the common in makeshift shelters. On both occasions, she had worn a distinctive green-and-white dress like that discovered upon the body, and at Webb's own instigation, Joan had been sent to hospital. Furthermore, Webb was able to recall her companion had been the Canadian soldier mentioned in the letter discovered close to her body, August Sangret. Greeno arranged for an interview with the Canadian and, on first meeting him, described him as 'a handsome brute, stocky, 5' 4", with a deep chest and massive shoulders tapering on to a ballet dancer's waist. His hair was oily black and his face lean and swarthy.'

On 27 November 1942, a distinctive knife with a hooked point resembling a parrot's beak was discovered by a Private Albert Brown, hidden in a waste pipe within the washhouse at Jasper Camp when he was clearing a blocked drain. The knife had been found by Private Samuel Crowle, embedded in a tree close to one of the wigwams Sangret had earlier constructed in mid-August. Although Crowle had intended to keep the knife due to its unique blade, he had been advised by a colleague to give it to Corporal Thomas Harding, who had in turn handed it to Sangret on 26 August, suspecting the knife had belonged to him. An eyewitness testimony would reveal that Sangret had excused himself to wash his hands in this very washhouse on 12 October, immediately prior to his initial informal questioning by Inspector Greeno.

Now armed with the evidence of the knife, Greeno took Sangret to the location where Joan's body had been found. He described how Sangret:

> … stormed up hills and pointed out the whole panorama of the plain, pitted with tank traps and pimpled with manmade mounds. He showed me where he built the wigwams in which the two of them had lived, first behind the officers' lines at Jasper Camp and then behind the sergeants' lines. He took me to the burned-out shell of a cricket pavilion at Thursley into which they had moved after they were warned off the wigwams. Suddenly, I said: 'Look over there', pointing to where we had found the body. He became sullen and answered: 'No, I don't want to go there.' I pointed to the woods where the stick had been found a few hours earlier and he repeated: 'I don't want to no more.'

Greeno believed that, as a Cree Indian, this demonstrated his fear of the dead and that the murderer had been revealed.

The Trial

The trial commenced at the Surrey Winter Assizes on Wednesday, 24 February 1943, in the County Hall, Kingston upon Thames before Mr Justice Macnaghten. The prosecution was headed by Mr Eric Neve KC, assisted by Geoffrey Lawrence. The counsel for the defence was Mr Linton Thorp KC, assisted by Laurence Vine.

One of the outstanding parts of the five-day trial was the ghastly picture painted of her final moments by Keith Simpson. At some point between 13 September and 7 October Joan had suffered a devastating assault which he outlined as follows:

> I thought it had begun in the dell where Joan's papers were found, probably with the stabbing attack on her head. She must have run downhill, screaming with pain and fear, inviting pursuit to silence

her. Her crucifix ornament must have been torn or pulled away and the contents of her handbag spilled out as she ran, dizzy and faint because of her head wounds and with blood running from her head wound into her eyes. She was already stumbling at the rivulet, where a tripwire had been laid by exercising troops. She fell heavily, knocking out her front teeth and further dazing herself, but was almost certainly still able to cry out for help, still inviting a silencing injury. Lying prone, with her right cheek on the ground she was struck the final blow with the birchwood.

The jury was absent for 2 hours before finally finding Sangret guilty of murder. They accompanied their verdict with a strong recommendation to mercy. Mr Justice Macnaghten told Sangret, 'The jury have found that it was you who murdered Joan Wolfe, and none who heard the evidence can doubt the justice of their verdict.' The judge then passed sentence of death.

The Appeal

Sangret appeared at the Court of Criminal Appeal on Tuesday, 13 April 1943, before the Lord Chief Justice, Viscount Caldecote, Mr Justice Humphries and Mr Justice Lewis, having submitted his own notice of appeal. His counsel, Mr Linton Thorp KC, was unable to provide any grounds for a complaint, and felt the trial had been conducted correctly. The court, having established that no point of law had arisen and no objection could be taken to the summing up, rejected the appeal. A further appeal to the Home Secretary, Herbert Morrison, was also rejected. August Sangret was hung at Wandsworth Prison on Thursday, 29 April 1943 by Albert Pierrepoint and his assistant Henry 'Harry' William Critchell, his body being buried in the prison grounds immediately after execution. Joan Pearl Wolfe had been buried in the St Michael and All Angels churchyard, Thursley, on Friday, 8 January 1943, she was 19 years old.

Postscript

Ted Greeno in his memoirs had this to say about the case:

> One small doubt remained. Sangret murdered the girl because she was expecting his child – but was she? The doctors did not think so on the occasion that the police sent her to hospital, and when her body was found it was too late to tell. But this is certain: Sangret did murder her. He confessed before he died, and this is where I quarrel with the rules. It is never announced when a murderer confesses. But why not? There are always cranks and crackpots to argue that some wicked policeman has framed some poor fellow. So why make an official secret of the fact that the policemen did his job?

Remember Them

There were more than fifty witnesses at the trial of August Sangret, of which twenty-one were members of his regiment, all called to give evidence for the prosecution. Amongst them was Sangret's best friend, a man who also came from Maidstone, Saskatchewan Private Joseph John Wells. Four of them would lose their lives on the battlefields of Western Europe:

- Fusilier Edmund Peter Joseph Martineau
  Killed in Action, 22 May 1944, aged 33
  Buried at Cassino War Cemetery, Italy

- Fusilier Lawrence St Clair Naugler
  Died of Wounds, 29 August 1944 aged 24
  Buried at Montecchio War Cemetery, Italy

- Private Alexander Marshall Shearer
  Killed in Action, 12 October 1944, aged 27
  Buried at Adegem Canadian War Cemetery, Belgium

- Private Joseph John Wells
  Killed in Action at Ortona, 20 December 1943, aged 31
  Buried at Moro River Canadian War Cemetery, Italy

Chapter 19

Private Charles Eugene Gauthier – A Light of Love

Panel 24. Column 2
Service Number: E/10248
Unit: Le Régiment De La Chaudière, RCIC
Executed: Friday, 24 September 1943, aged 24

The passage of millions of servicemen and women across Britain throughout the Second World War was to see many relationships bloom, grow and, eventually, withstand the test of time. But there were also many tales of tears, bitterness and unrequited love, a small percentage of which were to end in tragic circumstances. Perhaps, amongst the executed men listed upon the Brookwood Memorial, the story of Private Charles Eugene Gauthier is one of the most touching in that it is a tale both of lost love and an example of British dogma of the time.

Annette Elizabeth Frederica Christina Pepper, described by Mr Justice Oliver as 'a light of love'.

The Victim

Annette Elizabeth Frederica Christina Willard was born on Christmas Eve 1912, the daughter of Frederick Arthur Ernest and Rose Lillian Willard (née Russell). Her father had served in the First World War as a company sergeant major with the 7th Battalion, Royal Sussex Regiment and following his discharge worked as a local chimney sweep. Her mother worked in the local cinema. In 1934, at the age of 21, Annette was to marry Philip Leonard Pepper, a 22-year-old electrical engineer.

A daughter, their only child, Valerie Annette Pepper, was born to the couple on Thursday, 24 January 1935 and by 1939, the family were living in Beechers Road, Portslade-by-Sea, Sussex.

With the outbreak of the Second World War, Leonard was called up for active service and, with his engineering background, served with the 127th Electrical and Mechanical Company, Royal Engineers, eventually achieving the rank of lance corporal. He was to be taken prisoner on Monday, 2 June 1941 on the island of Crete, on the day that German paratroopers committed a brutal massacre of civilians in the village of Kondomari, just west of the city of Hania. By March 1943, Philip had been transferred to a British prisoner of war camp in Germany. In August 1942, Annette, who had been working as a cinema usherette, moved with her daughter to a house in Mile Oak Road, Portslade, the home of Ronald Hill Webb, a Canadian soldier, and his wife, Margaret Edith. This was soon to be the location of a tragic event.

The Assailant

Charles Eugene Gauthier, a French Canadian, was born on New Year's Eve 1918, the son of Eugene and Clara Gauthier, of St Henri Taillon, a small rural village on the edge of Lake Saint-Jean, Quebec. He was one of eleven children and his upbringing, like so many of his compatriots who came from similar communities, was difficult. His family were described as 'god fearing people of the labouring class, poor but honest'. Invariably, the only employment available was farming or lumberjacking, so money was often sparse and the work hard. Not unsurprisingly, he had been in trouble with the law and eventually was imprisoned for six months following a car theft. However, Gauthier managed to get himself a job as a taxi driver and in 1935 married Georgette Tremblay. There were no children from the marriage. Instead, it seems that the couple chose to adopt a child, Julien, who was 10 months old when Gauthier enlisted in the Canadian army on Saturday, 9 November 1940, being attached to the Le Regiment de Quebec. He arrived in UK on Wednesday 30 July 1941 and, like many of the other soldiers featured in the book, Gauthier had a fair service record but was occasionally in trouble, overstaying his leave and committing the odd misdemeanour.

The Crime

He first met Annette Pepper on Saturday, 16 January 1943 outside the cafe at the Old Brewery, in Portslade, when his unit was stationed at Lancing. They were instantly attracted to each other, and Annette invited him to her home later that evening. She told him all about her life, how she was married and that she did not love her husband anymore. When Gauthier asked her if Philip knew this, she told him, 'Oh yes, I told him so often, but he is crazy about me.' Over the coming weeks, he would visit her home on most evenings, or she would take a trip into Lancing, where they would spend time together. However, Gauthier was to get an insight into the true nature of Annette when he made arrangements to meet her one evening and she failed to turn up. It

Canadian soldier Private Charles Eugene Gauthier, found guilty of the murder of Annette Pepper.

would seem that she had met with another Canadian soldier on that occasion, and had opted to spend the night with him. Although he was upset by this incident, he chose to forgive Annette and continued to see her. A poor decision that would eventually lead to both her death, and his.

On Friday, 12 March 1943, Annette, Valerie and the Webbs travelled to London for the weekend, whilst Gauthier planned to take himself to Brighton and await her return. The following morning Sergeant William Rendall arrived in the town and a set of events began which would lead to a deadly conclusion. Rendall was serving with the Edmonton Regiment and had been in an intimate relationship with Annette between November 1941 and March 1942, when he returned home to Canada, and his wife and child. The couple continued to correspond whilst he was away and when he was posted back to Aldershot, in December 1942, he took the first opportunity he had to seek her out. Rendall approached Gauthier in the street and asked him if he was 'Charlie', and if he was seeing Annette. The conversation was not a friendly one and Rendall made his feelings clear, as did Gauthier. Upon asking him what Mrs Pepper meant to him, Gauthier responded by saying, 'Nan loves Charles'. The two men agreed to meet at Annette's home upon her return in order that matters could be sorted out.

On the afternoon of Monday, 15 March 1943, Annette returned to Portslade with Valerie and the Webbs. It was not a welcome homecoming. Once she discovered that Rendall was in town, she asked Gauthier not to see her that night so that she could talk things over with her former lover. Gauthier refused her constant pleas, and eventually Annette told him that if he did not allow her to see Rendall alone, she would never see him again. At around 7.00 p.m., Gauthier went to the roof of the Old Brewery, where a single Bren machine gun was stationed. Checking that the magazine was loaded, he picked up the gun and carried it downstairs and then walked to Mile Oak Road, where he placed it in a field, opposite Annette's home. He went to the front door, the key was in it, and entered the hallway. As he walked into the living room, he saw Sergeant Rendall sitting there. Gauthier said nothing and walked into the kitchen at the rear of the house. Annette followed him and demanded that he leave. A row then ensued and Annette announced that she loved Rendall, and had never loved Gauthier. He slapped her around the face, she slapped him back and, after an altercation with Rendall and further demands from Annette that he should leave, he stormed out of the house. But this was not the end of the matter.

Annette now went back to Rendall but before she could say anything, it seems she fainted. He picked her up and placed her on the sofa. The Webbs, who had been out of the house for a short while, returned home and took Annette upstairs. In the meantime, Gauthier had picked up the Bren gun from its hiding place and returned to the front door of the house, which was now locked. He hammered on the door, which Margaret Webb opened, but on seeing the gun, she slammed it shut again. Enraged, Gauthier shouted, 'Llook out or I'll fire.' He then sent several rounds slamming into the door, one of which struck Sergeant Rendall in the ankle. Rendall then made a quick exit out of the rear door and went for assistance. In terror, Annette had run upstairs into her bedroom with Valerie, whilst Margaret and Ronald Webb and their 14-month-old baby were in another bedroom, with the doors closed.

Gauthier, calmly walked to the rear of the house and entered through the back door. As he did so he shouted, 'Annette, come down here.' There was no response, so he repeated his demand. A terrified Annette said,

'You will kill me if come downstairs.' Gauthier demanded that she come downstairs and, eventually, encouraged by Ronald Webb that there was no danger, Annette answered, 'If I come down, will you say on your honour you will not shoot?' Gauthier said, 'Oh yes.' Just as she stepped onto the landing, Gauthier fired a single shot from the Bren gun. The bullet struck Annette in the throat and passed out of her neck. As she stumbled forward down the stairs, he fired another three shots, all of which struck her in the stomach, passing out through her back. She collapsed onto the floor, dead. The killer now calmly placed the Bren gun in the corner of the room, removed the magazine and ensured there were no rounds in the chamber, and then laid the magazine on Annette's stomach.

Home Guard member Roy Hotston, on hearing the sound of shots, took his rifle and rushed to the scene. On seeing Gauthier, he pointed his bayonet at the soldier's back and marched him to the middle of the road. Gauthier, who appeared very calm said, 'Take it easy, I have done what I wanted to do.' The police also arrived at the scene and, as he was cautioned and arrested by 37-year-old Police Sergeant Cyril Gabbitas, the Canadian seemed almost resigned to his fate, saying, 'I shall not run away.' He claimed that he did not know what he was doing and that he did not realise that he had the Bren machine gun. (A Bren weighs around 25lb, so it would be difficult not to know you were carrying one.)

The Trials

Charles Gauthier was first tried on Monday, 12 July 1943 at Lewes Assizes, presided over by Mr Justice Travers Humphreys. He was defended by Mr Eric Neve KC and Mr Dutton Bryant under the provisions of the United Kingdom Poor Persons Defence Act. On this occasion the jury were unable to agree a verdict and, as such, the case was referred to the Central Criminal Court at the Old Bailey, London.

On Monday, 26 July 1943, as the men of the 1st Canadian Division continued to advance towards Adrano on the south-western slopes of Mount Etna, Sicily, Gauthier was brought before Mr Justice Oliver and was again defended by Eric Neve and Dutton Bryant. It was argued that the Canadian had been provoked into this sad and terrible action by a woman he had fallen violently in love with, and who seemed to be in

A Bren gun similar to that used by Private Charles Gauthier to murder Annette Pepper. Despite weighing 25lb, Gauthier claimed he did not realise that he had the gun.

love with him. The trial centred around two letters she had written, but he was not to receive until after her death, when they were handed to him whilst he was in Lewes Prison. In the first one, dated Wednesday, 3 March, Annette wrote a message which expresses both intimacy, her desire and her love for a man she had only known for a few weeks, yet it also seems a little naïve and shallow. It reads:

Charles Dearest,
I said I would write to you didn't I, so here I am to keep my promise. I don't quite know what to say honey, but I will have a real good try. Well darling first of all I must tell you this I do love you Charles and I sure am missing you dear.

You know darling I couldn't sleep Sunday night for a long time I just lay there with my eyes closed and I could feel you there beside me I could hear your voice telling me you loved me I could almost feel you pleasing me. You were so near me in my heart. Remember dearest all those things I whispered in your ear, how you belong to me, and I belong always to you. Remember too darling I said I want to belong to you.

Do you think of that now you are away from me? Do you miss me darling? It seems so strange not to have you coming over in the evenings. I expect to hear you come up the step every time the bus stops outside the house. Valerie sends all her love to you sweetheart and says with me, take care of yourself sweetheart. Be very careful won't you. I am being careful too Charles dear and I am also being very good.

Got a darn cold though darling, good thing that you weren't around dear you would get it too. You know dear I keep hearing your voice saying I love no one but you and I want to be able to turn around and put my arms round you. I do wish you so much darling believe me.

Well Charles dear I must go to bed now so guess I have to say good night darling and I do love you. See you in my dreams tonight darling so please be there won't you.

Good night darling God Bless you dearest.

All my love dear
Annette
Xxxxxxxxxxxxxxxxxxxxxxxxxxxxx

The second, undated letter, reads:

Charles Dearest,

Thanks a lot for your charming letter I received this morning. That's what I call quick work, honey. The postmark I noticed was Liss, that is in Hampshire. I know it fairly well.

Well Charles dear I am glad you are taking good care of yourself. I am being very careful honey. I expect you have got my letter by now, at least I hope so. Valerie sends her love to you darling, and she still thinks you are grand. So do I, honey. Gee darling, I feel so funny not having you come over evenings. Do you still dream of me, darling?

When I go to bed darling, I hold my coat up to my face and the perfume from you is still on it and it makes you seem very close to me. I am sitting alone by a lovely fire Charles dear and every now and again I look into the fire, and I can see pictures of you there, then somehow, I don't feel so lonely. I hope your scheme will soon be over darling.

There isn't much else I can tell you darling, so I'll stop now, just one more thing Charles, I love you darling and I am always thinking of you.

Cheerio for a little while dearest. God bless you. Always yours, Annette.

Gauthier testified that Annette claimed she was pregnant and had told him he was the child's father. The defence counsel asked for a manslaughter verdict on the grounds of provocation. Mr Justice Oliver instructed the jury to retire to consider their decision but directed them that there was no other outcome than that of murder, as the circumstances of the case did not allow a verdict of manslaughter. This shocking revelation devastated the defence counsel and instantly removed their argument for provocation. When the jury returned and the judge asked for their verdict, they stated that they had found Gauhtier guilty of murder but gave a strong and unanimous recommendation for mercy. The judge turned to Gauthier and said: 'Prisoner at the bar, you stand convicted of murder. Have you anything to say why the court should not give you judgement of death according to law?' Gauthier responded by saying, 'Just one thing I have to say, my lord. I joined the Army and came over to this country to fight for my country, and I never thought such a thing would happen to me. I'm very sorry for all that has happened. That is all.' A formal sentence of death was then passed.

The Appeal

The Court of Criminal Appeal sat on Thursday, 26 August 1943 before Mr Justice Humphries, Mr Justice Atkinson and Mr Justice Cassells. It was claimed by the defence, Mr Eric Neve KC and Mr Dutton Briant, that it was wrong of Mr Justice Oliver to withdraw the issue of manslaughter from the jury, that he ought to have directed the jury to consider there was such provocation to deprive a reasonable man of his self-control, and that if there was reasonable doubt Gauthier had been provoked a verdict of manslaughter should be returned. The woman he killed was the wife of a British soldier who was a prisoner of war in Germany, who had an intimate association with Gauthier and two other men and was described by Mr Justice Oliver in his summing up as 'a light of love'.

The judgement of the court, being delivered by Mr Justice Cassells, stated that there was:

> No evidence on which they could possibly find a verdict of manslaughter on the grounds of provocation, and that the circumstances in the case could not amount to that which in law was provocation. The court found that the treatment by Gauthier of Annette Pepper was not provocative, and in any event, there was on the part of Gauthier time for cooling, there was deliberation and preparation, and in the result, they found that Mr Justice Oliver was

right at the close of the evidence to say what he did and that he should direct the jury the way he did.

Gauthier's appeal was therefore, dismissed as was leave to appeal to the House of Lords.

Now, in a desperate effort to save Gauthier from the clutches of the hangman, the Canadians made a plea to the Home Office, not dissimilar to that of Private Charles Arthur Raymond who had been put to death a few weeks earlier, on the basis that the trial jury had made a strong recommendation for mercy, he was a young man, a country boy who was not used to being outside of his home environment with a clean civil and military record and had been provoked into a jealous reaction by a woman who had 'light morals'. The plea was to fall upon deaf ears. Major Maurice Forget, a member of the Canadian Judge Advocate General's Office and a leading proponent for the treatment of Canadian soldiers under the British legal system, was now pressing the Canadian government to pay for the legal cost of the condemned soldier, to which they agreed. There was a great deal of support for Gauthier and in one telephone call, Quarter Master Sergeant John Nolan of the Brighton Home Guard informed Major Forget that he believed Gauthier had not had a fair trial and had attempted to make his point to the Home Secretary but had been refused an interview and had, in fact, been ordered out of the Home Office.

A final letter dated Thursday, 23 September 1943 to Major General Percival 'Price' John Montague, Judge Advocate General Canadian Army Overseas, explained that the case had been reviewed by the Home Secretary, Herbert Morrison, who felt he was 'unable to reverse his decision'. Gauthier was finally hanged in Wandsworth Prison on Friday, 24 September 1943 by Albert Pierrepoint and his assistant, Alex Riley, having spent a record sixty days in the condemned cell. His body was buried on the same day within the prison grounds.

In 1952, at the age of 17, Annette's only daughter, Valerie Pepper, married John Hayward in Portslade. They remained together until her death on Tuesday, 10 May 1994 at the age of 59.

Chapter 20

Private Horace Beresford Gordon –
Got Any Gum Chum?

Panel 25. Column 1
Service Number: G/45066
Unit: Royal Canadian Ordnance Corps
Executed: Tuesday, 9 January 1945, aged 29

The victim of any murder can often pass into history having left nothing but a faint ripple in the passage of time. What is perhaps more cruel, is where there is a second, unnamed, victim. A human being who was denied the opportunity of a long and happy life, had it not been for the actions of the assailant. So, it was for Dorothy May Hillman, whose simple errand on a summer evening in 1944 was to end in the death of not one but two innocent people, one of whom was unborn.

The Victim

Dorothy May Streeter was born into a Sussex farming community, her life was short and uneventful, and, with the outbreak of war, there was little opportunity for excitement. Farmers were confronted with a potential labour crisis with many younger workers joining the armed services and others, attracted by higher wages and better working conditions, left their employment to join the thousands of labourers engaged in the building of the camps, aerodromes and other military institutions being constructed up and down the country. Life was hard on the farm and there was barely time for excitement, but the influx of service personnel from around the world provided the occasional opportunity for a small piece of fun and occasional delight.

On Saturday, 4 March 1944, the teenaged Dorothy married Ronald Hillman, a 21-year-old farm worker, and they began to share a home

A police detective stands close to where Dorothy May Hillman was brutally attacked. (*The National Archives – HO144/22221*)

at Palmer's Cross Cottages, Bramley, Surrey, with his parents. As a farmer, classed as a reserved occupation, her husband was a man who was susceptible to having his masculinity called into question by those who were in military service, or civilians who thought he should be 'doing his bit'. Nevertheless, he pressed on with agricultural work that was so vital to the country and now, within a short time of their marriage, Dorothy had fallen pregnant. By September 1944, with the course of the war looking more positive, and the air filled with the anticipation of victory, the young couple looked forward to raising a family and a brighter future.

The Assailant

Horace Beresford Gordon was born on Friday, 22 October 1915 in Kingston, Jamaica. His father, Cleveland Gordon, was a foreman in the local gas works and their home life was described as comfortable. There was always plenty of food and clothes and it was a very religious home, his mother being a committed Anglican. A choirboy for ten years, he attended a good elementary school where he was an average scholar, though he suffered with a stammer for some years. As a child he was good at sports including cricket, football and swimming, and he also ran for his school. At the age of 15 he left school and gained a position as an apprentice, working under the umbrella of the Jamaican Government Railway until 1937. Horace married Elma Hyde in Kingston, Jamaica, on Thursday, 31 March 1936 and the couple left the island the following year for British Honduras where they opened a restaurant that, apparently, did well. However, just a year later, in November 1938, Horace began working for the Chavvannes Steamship Line, his weekly wage dropping from $150 to just $40, and it seems that Elma returned to Jamaica, taking up residence in Victoria Avenue.

Following the outbreak of the Second World War Horace answered the call for volunteers to man a Canadian munitions factory, but left within six months, enlisting in the Canadian army on 1 February 1941 at Saint John, New Brunswick. He was initially classified as a cook and posted to the 1st Army Tank Ordnance Workshop at Westmount, Quebec. Here, it seems, his engineering skills outshone his cooking abilities, and he was reclassified as a fitter. Finally, he was posted to the United Kingdom on Saturday, 4 October 1941, making the perilous week-long journey by troopship. On arrival, he was attached to No. 1 VRD (Vehicle Repair Depot), part of No. 1 CCOD (Canadian Central Ordnance Depot) based at Priorswood, a large mansion near Godalming, Surrey. Horace was to remain stationed here until Tuesday, 15 June 1943, when he passed his driver training, and was then capable of manoeuvring huge 40-ton tank transporters.

Because of his perpetual grin, Horace Gordon was known to his fellow soldiers as 'Happy'. A nickname he gained because he always had a positive, upbeat attitude and a smile. Allegedly, he had a quick temper, though he was also quick to forgive, and had a habit of biting his nails. Gordon's nickname was probably also gained from his love of socialising. He was always friendly and curious about strangers, enjoyed going to the cinema with his comrades, but particularly loved going out dancing. He had a reputation for being particularly generous with his time, rations and money and, along with many other Canadian soldiers, was a popular dance partner with English women. With a reputation for being better dancers, it was also known that Canadian soldiers received higher pay than their British comrades and always had chewing gum and chocolate to share.

There was little in his service record to demonstrate that Happy Gordon was anything other than an exemplary soldier, so it is not surprising to read that on Tuesday, 2 February 1943 he was awarded a Good Conduct Badge. On D-Day, Tuesday, 6 June 1944, Horace was awarded his Overseas Chevrons and his Canadian Volunteer Service Medal, with Clasp. Truly an occasion to celebrate. The only remark that gives a small insight to his nature is found in the comments section drawn up by his commanding officer which reads, 'Big, easy going negro. His trip to the hospital was for a bad cold but he received treatment for syphilis while there.'

It appears that sometime after he arrived in the United Kingdom, his wife stopped writing to him. By September 1944 they had been out of touch for about five months. Horace had fostered a deep and affectionate friendship with a local white woman named Helen Manning and her family who lived in Station Road, Horsham, West Sussex. He had been welcomed into their home by Helen's husband, who was often away working, and was close with their adult daughter, and even allowed to stay. When he was not taking Helen and her daughters dancing, Horace liked to spend his evenings or days off cycling to Horsham on a bike he borrowed from the family. One September evening in 1944 he took a pound of pears in his backpack and set off on an unfamiliar route to Horsham, enjoying the Surrey and Sussex countryside. He was never to return.

The Crime

At about 5.45 p.m. on Thursday, 7 September 1944, following their supper, Horace Gordon and his chum, Private Harold Walter Deck, set off on their bicycles from their base at Priorswood. Horace had agreed to cycle with his pal as far as the village of Farncombe, saying he was going to Horsham for the evening to return the cycle he had borrowed from the family a few days before. It seems that he instead of taking the road to Horsham, he mistakenly took the road to Hascombe. He decided to cycle to the Royal Oak public house in Hascombe, as he visited it regularly and knew the landlady, Elsie Wiggett. As he was riding along, he saw a young woman who was walking towards Horsham, and he stopped to ask if he was on the right road for Horsham. She told him that he was, and he rode off.

Shortly after 6.15 p.m., the heavily pregnant Dorothy Hillman had set out with her dog to make the walk along the A281 to the Leathern Bottle Inn, to buy some cigarettes and tobacco for her father-in-law. As she was walking along, a black soldier pulled up next to her on a lady's bicycle to ask her for directions. She recognised him as a Canadian and asked, 'Have you got any gum, chum?', so it seems he took off his backpack to oblige.

It is from this point that the versions of events differ. Happy Gordon claimed that the straps of his backpack became twisted, and he wanted some help in removing it. He had asked Dorothy if she could 'do him a favour', meaning help him to remove the backpack. He believed that she misunderstood his innocent request, shouting at him, 'Go away, you dirty black nigger!' and slapped his face. He asked her what she meant, at which point she allegedly grabbed his tunic. There was then a confused scuffle where he tried to stop her screaming for her husband who was working in a nearby field. An apple knife had fallen from his pocket, they both tried to grab it and she then fell forward onto the blade, cutting her neck. Seeing blood streaming down her neck, he panicked and cycled off towards Horsham. He had seen Dorothy walking up the road and did not think she was mortally wounded.

Two members of the RAF, Leading Aircraftsman Arthur Cecil Sadler and Leading Aircraftsman Meadway, happened to be cycling towards Guildford when they saw two children crossing the road some distance ahead. At the same time, they claimed to have seen a black Canadian soldier coming towards them on a lady's pushbike cycling very fast. Then they witnessed a woman crawling along the side of the road, her face was covered in blood and there was blood on her dress. It was Dorothy Hillman, and she cried out to them, 'Help me'. It was obvious to Sadler that she needed more than first aid, so he cycled to the Leathern Bottle Inn and called the police. His colleague went to a nearby house to fetch some blankets and left Dorothy in the hands of Sam Pelling, a 61-year-old local gardener. On the return of the airmen, a passing motorist was flagged down and asked to fetch Ronald Hillman. By the time he reached his wife the emergency services were on the scene and the couple were transported to hospital.

On arrival at hospital, it was quickly established that Dorothy had been stabbed four times in the stomach, three times in the breast, twice in the thighs and once in the back and neck. The most serious wounds were those beneath her breasts and a punctured lung. Dorothy claimed that the soldier had stabbed her repeatedly, aiming for her heart as she tried to ward off his blows. He had tried to rape her and get her to perform oral sex, then given up the attempt and ridden off on his bicycle. Despite her injuries she had tried to drag herself back home, aided by her dog, which began pulling her along by its lead, which was wrapped around her right wrist.

Now alerted about the incident, and by sheer chance, two policemen, Detective Constable Brian Gunning and Detective Sergeant Edward Storr, were at the foot of Winkworth Hill, near the village of Hascombe, when they spotted a black Canadian soldier on a lady's bicycle. They stopped him and asked for an account of his movements and wanted to know why he had blood on his clothes and handkerchief and one of his knees was covered in mud. As they searched his belongings, they were shocked to find a bloodstained knife. He was now told that he was suspected of attempted murder, attempted rape and indecent assault and, it seems, just 2 hours after she had left her home, Dorothy's attacker was being held at Godalming police station, making a statement.

In a first statement, made at the time of his arrest, Gordon claimed he had decided to go to Guildford for an evening's entertainment but on the way, changed his mind and decided to visit his girlfriend in Horsham. He explained that the battledress he was wearing was an old one, and he wiped blood on it when he cut himself fixing a radiator on his vehicle, and when he accidentally struck his hand with a hammer, a few weeks earlier. The wound subsequently reopened and although it bled profusely, he had not sought medical attention. He had ridden through a mist patch, which explained why the blood was wet, he asserted. He apologised for lying, saying that he had been confused and frightened. His statement concluded, 'If I am to die, that is the truth, so help me God.' Analysis of the blood found on his clothes, knife and handkerchief established that it was of the same group as Dorothy's.

On Friday, 8 September, the police searched the copse described by Dorothy, and found a branch had been pushed back, the ground disturbed and signs indicating a struggle. They also discovered Dentyne chewing gum wrappers, an army service cap and bloodstains on the ground. After being made aware that he would have to attend an identification parade, Gordon decided he wanted to make a new statement. This time, he claimed, he wanted to 'tell the truth and nothing else but the truth'. He maintained that he had been lost and had asked a young woman for directions. He then claimed that as he was cycling along, he was flagged down by a woman who was covered in blood. He asked her what had happened, and she claimed she had been attacked. He then gave her a piece of chocolate and some Dentyne gum, thinking it would 'revive her as she was in pain'. After wiping blood from her face with some grass and his handkerchief, he decided to ride to Cranleigh to fetch the police but took a wrong turning. Realising that he had his apple knife with him he was worried he would be accused of a crime but before he could act, he was stopped by police and arrested for the attack. He added that he had an old service cap with him under his left shoulder strap and this must have dropped out when he took his pack off.

The following day, Saturday, 9 September 1944, Dorothy was confronted with her alleged attacker after detectives brought Horace Gordon to Guildford Hospital in order that a dying declaration could be taken. As she lay in her hospital bed, she whispered to detectives that as she approached the Leathern Bottle Inn, she saw a black man on a lady's cycle. He had smiled at her and offered her some chocolate and chewing gum, quite a luxury at a time of widespread rationing. She also told detectives that he told her she could have some more if she climbed over a fence with him and did him a sexual favour.

During the discussion, Gordon asked Dorothy several questions, and one of the responses is quite revealing. 'Did I ask you if your husband would like to buy some cigarettes? How many packs of cigarettes did I have in my haversack?' Dorothy responded by saying, 'How could I know. You said you had two. I said it all depends how much you want for them.' Clearly, a conversation had gone on about the sale of cigarettes and, most likely, chocolate. Sadly, immediately following this traumatic interview, the first tragedy struck when Dorothy, suffering excruciating labour pains, gave birth to a stillborn foetus which, it was estimated, had been dead for about 36 to 48 hours, indicating that the baby had died at the time of the attack. Now, the young mother was in a fight for her own life after suffering significant blood loss during the birth of the baby, coupled with her infected stab wounds. Over the next two weeks, Dorothy appeared to improve but, despite the strict hygiene observed in the hospital, and the use of medication such as penicillin, Dorothy suffered from the effects of septicaemia and died on Friday, 22 September 1944. This was now a case of murder.

The Trials

Gordon appeared before the Guildford County Petty Sessions on Friday, 29 September 1944 and was remanded to appear at the Surrey Assizes held in Kingston upon Thames, on Friday, 1 December 1944 before Mr Justice Humphries. Witnesses described what they had seen that summer evening, and there was some contradiction.

Doreen Mary Hanbrooke, a nursery nurse, who was working at Graphon Grange, described how she had returned from a trip to Guildford and, after getting off the bus at the Cranleigh turning, had walked down the Horsham–Guildford Road and, having stopped and spoken to the matron of the facility, heard a bicycle bell ringing. She had seen a black soldier cycling towards the Leathern Bottle Inn, who raised his hand and gave a whistle. He was apparently wearing a forage cap. A second witness, Ralph Pelling, a British soldier serving with the Queen's Royal Regiment, and the son of Sam Pelling who had been the first civilian to discover Dorothy, was on leave and cycling to the Royal Oak at Hascombe to meet a friend on embarkation leave. He explained how, at the time of the attack he was near Palmer's Cross, and had seen a woman with a dog who he knew from the area and whom he rather disparagingly described as 'looking old from a distance' and 'stoutish, short, stubby and fat'. Oddly, he described the black soldier he saw as being hatless, contrary to Doreen Hanbrooke's observation.

Henry James Walls and James Davidson, of the Metropolitan Police Forensics Laboratory, described how the mud found on Gordon's trouser knee was consistent with that found in the copse. However, the mud on his boots was not the same. There were numerous blood stains on the battledress blouse and trousers as well as on Dorothy's clothes which was identified as human but could not be individually grouped. A small single-edged knife was covered in human blood and the shape of the blade was consistent with the bloodstains found on Gordon's handkerchief.

A post-mortem was carried out on Dorothy by renowned Home Office pathologist Keith Simpson, and in a five-page report he detailed the severe wounds she had suffered at the hands of her attacker. Describing her as a healthy young woman, 5ft 3in in height, he found a total of sixteen wounds on her body, including five defensive injuries she suffered in an attempt to grab the weapon. In summary, she had been the victim of a savage and determined assault, and her death had been caused by septicaemia as a consequence of the major wounds being infected. The prosecutor claimed that Dorothy's wounds were so serious it was a miracle that she had not died at the roadside. In his concluding speech for the Crown, Mr Thorp said it was impossible to believe that Mrs Hillman had gone into the copse to perform some form of consensual sex. Gordon had committed murder because his unwonted lust was rejected, and because of his victim's condition his attack had been one of the most bestial nature.

In his defence, the jury were told that on seeing Dorothy Hillman standing at the side of the road Gordon had asked her for directions to Horsham and, in return, she had asked him for some chewing gum. After this conversation she suggested they should get off the road in case they got knocked down and they went into the copse. He took his pack off his shoulders to give her some chocolate and gum. When he put his pack on again the straps were twisted, so he said, 'Would you do me a favour? It won't hurt you and won't take long.' Dorothy mistook this as a request for sexual favours and her racist rant had provoked Gordon into an unnatural response. He was one of several black soldiers in the area asked to account for their whereabouts that night but, despite close scrutiny of Dorothy's alleged sexual and criminal past by police, court and the Home Office, it was her dying statement that was prioritised over Gordon's version of events. Gordon had no previous criminal record, and an apple knife was not usually an instrument of violence. The prosecutor responded by stating that it was significant Gordon had not mentioned Dorothy Hillman's alleged racist abuse until he made his full statement to the police.

Summing up, Mr Justice Humphries told the jury they must not allow their revulsion at the death of the stillborn child to affect their verdict.

They must decide whether Gordon had intended to kill or cause serious harm to Dorothy. Furthermore, they must be satisfied that her death was directly linked to the attack made upon her a fortnight earlier. If they believed this was not the case, Gordon was entitled to a verdict of manslaughter.

After retiring for 1½ hours, the jury found Horace Beresford Gordon guilty of murder. Sentencing him to death, the judge told him, 'The jury have convicted you of murder upon evidence which in my opinion left them no alternative.' It seems that Gordon showed no emotion at his sentence.

The Appeal

On Tuesday, 19 December 1944, Gordon's appeal was heard at the Criminal Appeal Court, London, by the Lord Chief Justice, Lord Caldecott, Mr Justice Singleton and Mr Justice Cassels. It was stressed that he had no previous criminal convictions, no reputation for violence and that Dorothy's comment was highly provocative considering that the word 'nigger' was not used in Jamaica or Canada because it was insulting. British justice, however, did not seem to agree on this point. His appeal was dismissed, but his execution date was postponed allowing a petition for clemency from the Canadian government and to consider a petition received from Jamaica. Hundreds of his fellow servicemen petitioned the Home Office for mercy, and further petitions with an equally impressive number of signatures were received from Jamaica. Helen Manning wrote numerous letters to the Home Secretary in an effort to save Horace Gordon from the gallows. None of these persuaded the Home Secretary to recommend a reprieve. It later emerged that the police had interviewed several women in the area who Gordon had been seeing. All of them had spoken of his cheery, non-violent nature, which was reflected in his fellow soldiers' opinion of him. But he had never expressed remorse for Dorothy Hillman's death and the loss of her stillborn child and despite his happy demeanour doctors who examined him concluded that he was a psychopath.

Horace Gordon was hung in Wandsworth Prison on the morning of Tuesday, 9 January 1945 by Albert Pierrepoint and his assistant, Steve Wade. He was buried within the prison grounds. There is no known record to indicate where Dorothy May Hillman, or her child, are buried.

A Question of Murder?

It is interesting to note that as the Surrey Assizes began on 29 December 1944, there were two cases of murder involving Canadian soldiers. One was that of Horace Gordon, the other being Private John Francis Donovan, who had been accused of strangling 17-year-old Constance Sybil Curtis, a factory worker whose naked body had been found on waste ground in Camberley on 15 April 1944. Police Sergeant Daniel Hobbs found her dead body lying on a patch of trampled grass. Two parallel lines ran from the area where she had apparently been attacked, a distance of nearly 60ft. He found a pair of girl's shoes which appeared to have been pulled off near a hillock over which the body had been dragged. She was naked except for her stockings. Her clothing, which had been forcibly removed, had been thrown over her. A post-mortem showed that she had been strangled and beaten to death.

Connie had been seen the night before at a fairground in the company of a Canadian soldier. The prosecution case had rested on the confident identification of Donovan as the man who was with Connie only an hour or two before her death. He was indicated as the killer by Elizabeth Baigent, who Connie lodged with, after their dodgem car bumped into another one carrying two Canadian soldiers. One got out and they exchanged places. Later that evening, Connie came home and asked the time, telling her landlady, 'I won't be long' and went back out. She was never seen alive again. Although Baigent claimed it was Donovan, two witnesses failed to pick him out of an identity parade.

At his trial, his alibi broke down and he gave contradictory evidence after Police Sergeant Bignall went to the fair the week after the murder to support Police Constable Noakes in a quest to find the killer. Bignall stopped Donovan and asked him if he had been to the fair before and he agreed he had been at the last one, when Connie had been murdered. Even though he claimed he had not gone to the fair on the day of her murder, as his best trousers had been stolen and he could not go. His defence counsel claimed mistaken identity based on the celebrated fraud case of Adolf Beck from 1896, and Donovan was acquitted. Connie Curtis lays buried in the St Michael's cemetery, York Town, Camberley. No one was ever apprehended for her murder.

Chapter 21

Private Mervin Clare McEwan –
The Tattooed Killer

Panel 25. Column 1
Service Number: A/29600
Unit: No. 1 Army Field Workshop, Royal Canadian Ordnance
Corps
Executed: Thursday, 3 February 1944, aged 35

The Victim

The life of Mark Turner would, most likely, have passed by almost unnoticed, had it not been for the manner in which it ended. Born on Monday, 10 September 1860 in the Yorkshire town of Halifax, he was the son of George and Hannah Turner. His mother was widowed at an early age and by the time he was 10 years old, Mark found himself working in a local cotton mill alongside his brother, Addison, to help their mother supplement her meagre income. Perhaps wanting a little more for himself, he entered the Civil Service in 1882, being employed by the General Post Office as a letter carrier, more commonly referred to as a postman. On Saturday, 29 March 1884, Mark married the love of

Mark Turner, the 82-year-old retired postman victim of Canadian deserter Private Mervin Clare McEwan.

his life, Louisa Wilson. The couple were to have two daughters, Ruth and Gladys, but sadly neither of them survived childhood. Ruth died in 1888 at the age of 4 and Gladys would not survive her first year, passing away

in 1892. And so, the couple travelled through life together with only one another for company.

During the First World War, Mark would have been responsible for delivering and collecting the many letters and parcels that passed between the families of Halifax and their loved ones who were serving in the armed forces. No doubt, he had to deliver some of the worst news a family could expect from the front. In August 1921, he retired after forty years' service with the GPO and in March 1922 was awarded the Imperial Service Medal for his long service. He settled into a quiet retirement which was turned upside down in May 1933 with the death of Louisa at the age of 75. Now alone, Mark began to see out the remainder of his life as clouds began to form over the rapidly changing world. By the time the Second World War had broken out, Mark was living a somewhat isolated existence in his two-roomed cottage in Moorfield Street, Halifax, and had taken to sleeping on a sofa bed in his living room in the colder months. Although his general health was depicted as good, he was suffering badly with sciatica and had to make use of a walking stick but despite this was known as a cheerful and kindly man. In spring 1943, perhaps with reminiscences of his early life, it seems that Mark, who was getting by on a pension of 35s. a week, had taken pity on a young man, with a broad Scottish accent, who was sheltering in a disused hut on Savile Park, opposite his home. This, it came to light, was a Canadian soldier, Mervin Clare McEwen, a deserter.

The Assailant

The life of Mervin Clare McEwan was in very stark contrast to that of Mark Turner. He was born in Amherst, Manitoba, on Saturday, 9 October 1909, the son of George Eric and Olive May McEwan (née Black). On Wednesday, 22 January 1930, at the age of 47, his father died from the effects of a cerebral haemorrhage, and Mervin was left to help support his family. Records show that he was a known criminal, having spent two years in the Guelph Correctional Centre, also known as the Ontario Reformatory, and a further five years in Kingston Penitentiary for house-breaking and larceny.

On Thursday, 25 June 1931, 15-year-old Harriett Stephenson gave birth to a daughter, Margaret Beth, the child of Mervin McEwan. A few months later, on Saturday, 19 September, the couple married in the rural village of Thedford, Ontario, the marriage certificate stating that he was an 18-year-old truck driver. Their marital life was a tumultuous one and, in spring 1940, they were divorced. However, some form of reconciliation appears to have taken place, on the basis that he wanted to ensure his daughter had a roof over her head. Despite his criminal record, McEwan enlisted in the Canadian army on 9 September 1940, and he and Harriett remarried nine days later.

Private Mervin Clare McEwan, whose unique tattoos sealed his fate.

McEwan embarked for service overseas at the Canadian port of Halifax on Sunday, 15 December 1940, first setting foot in the United Kingdom from a troopship at Glasgow on Boxing Day. Within a fortnight of being stationed in Britain with No. 1 Army Field Workshop he began a career of absence and crime, being reported as AWL (Absent Without Leave) on numerous occasions. Matters began to get progressively worse and the Canadian eventually found himself in civil court on Thursday, 5 March 1942, at Darlington, Yorkshire, where he was sentenced to twelve months' imprisonment with hard labour for larceny and sent to Durham Prison to serve his time.

McEwan was released from prison on Thursday, 5 November 1942, and attached to the Canadian Ordnance Reinforcement Unit. No sooner had he left gaol than he was admitted to hospital with a minor ailment. Following his discharge from hospital he was sent to No. 1 Canadian Field Punishment Camp, for a short period, but planned to abscond. On Friday, 12 February 1943 McEwan walked out of camp, never to return. The bitter weather saw snow on the ground for most of the month and he took shelter wherever he could. By late March, McEwan had made his way to Halifax, Yorkshire, where he found himself living a somewhat hand-to-mouth existence in a hut on Savile Park, opposite the home of Mark Turner. The hut was cold, and empty of everything including food. So, he would raid the local YMCA for sustenance and cigarettes and was almost starving when he first met Mark Turner and his friend, 85-year-old William Crabtree, who were both members of the Spring Edge Old Men's Parliament, and who regularly sat on the benches in the park. The retired postman invited McEwan to his home for a hot oxo, laced with whiskey, and encouraged him to sit by the fire. He told McEwan that he would always find a cosy chair and a hot drink in his home.

The Crime

On the night of Friday, 2 April 1943, Mark Turner again invited his neighbour, William Crabtree, and McEwen to his home for a drink. Both men left about 9.00 p.m., with the Canadian returning to his cold and draughty hut. Sometime later, he went back to the old man's home, and entered through a back window. He crept into the tiny living room, where Mark was asleep on a bed-settee, and began to take some cold meat and a bottle of whiskey. As he did so, he knocked over some dishes, which crashed to the floor. Mark Turner, awoken by the noise, called out 'What's going on there?' McEwan, who claimed he was frightened by the old man's cries, grabbed a cobbler's hammer which was laying on a table and struck Turner on the head, but he continued to cry out. A merciless attack then ensued, and McEwan rained down blows on the old man's head. He then picked up a knife and attempted to stab him through the blankets, but it did not penetrate sufficiently far enough to cause any further injury. After battering his skull nine times with a hammer, he sat down in the tiny living room and wolfed the old man's rations of nine eggs. After this meal, he took the bottle of Scotch that the victim had so greatly prized and guzzled it until he was sick. He then rifled through the dead man's pockets, took his wallet containing £20 and every coin he could find. He then changed into the victim's suit, stole a suitcase, some more of his clothes and his identity card. He even took his spectacles and his much-loved rosary.

In the early hours of 3 April, Fred Hall, who lived next door, had heard some loud knocking coming from Mark Turner's house. The following morning, not having seen his neighbour, he looked through Mark's kitchen window, where he noticed several articles scattered about. He got a ladder and, on looking through the bedroom window, saw more items strewn about, and the whole place in disarray. He spoke to Tom Lomas who knew Turner and had a key to the back door. On entering, the pair saw that the house was in a considerable mess. In the kitchen was the bed-settee, which was partly closed, with bits of the bedding sticking out. Police Constable George Crisp was called and made a search of the premises and found some partially consumed food on the kitchen table. Matches, cigarette ends and eggshells littered the place, drawers had been ransacked and the floor was covered with things that McEwan could neither wear nor carry. Crisp returned to the living room and noticed the partly closed bed-settee in the kitchen and, on opening it, found the body of Mark Turner wrapped in the bedclothes. On examination, Turner was found to be dead, his body lying across the settee from corner to corner, with all the bedclothes pulled right up to the chin. He had several severe head injuries, blood covered the bed clothes and the surrounding wall, and it appeared that the attacker had attempted to close the bed-settee with the body inside it.

McEwen had committed the ultimate crime and was now on the run. He travelled to Manchester where he met widow Annie Elizabeth Perfect in a local cafe. Her husband, Arthur Basil Perfect, had died on Friday, 1 November 1940 in Withington Hospital, Manchester, as a consequence of a lung and bowel infection, leaving Annie alone to raise their eight children. McEwan was wearing the murdered man's clothes and, it was later alleged, told her his name was Jim Acton, a merchant sailor who had recently spent fourteen days adrift after his ship was torpedoed. In fact, Acton was Annie's maiden name and, as they lived together for a short while as husband and wife, it is more likely that she knew he was a deserter and aided him in his attempt to evade the authorities, as he was able to bring some cash into the home. It is not surprising, given her circumstances, that Annie may have chosen to ignore the fact that he was a deserter, but she may not have known at the time that he was also a murderer.

In the meantime, Scotland Yard's renowned detective Ted Greeno was hot on the trail of the vicious killer. In his memoirs, Greeno describes how it was quickly established that this was the work of a deserter. An army shirt was found stuck behind a picture, a battledress was stuffed behind the scullery boiler and army issue underpants were hidden in a gramophone. A Canadian army service number was found on the clothes, so it did not take long to determine who the clothing belonged to. Why he had been foolish enough to leave these obvious clues behind instead of throwing them in the river or setting them alight was unclear, but McEwan had been identified and a manhunt was now on.

McEwen's description was quickly transmitted around the country. He was aged 34, about 5ft 6in tall, of stocky build, with a red face, blue eyes, thick lips and brown hair brushed back. Tattooed with an aeroplane on his right arm and a scroll on his left arm featuring the word 'Mother', the police felt he would be easy to identify. Sightings of the wanted soldier were reported up and down the country, with each one proving to be a fruitless escapade. At one point Greeno had engaged the services of the British, American and Canadian provost marshals from the army and air forces, including the famous cricketing twins Eric and Alec Bedser. He had called in ten-thousand civilian police and a further thousand service police who, with no warning at all, would cordon off huge districts where every man would be stopped, and his identity card checked. Eventually, by a stroke of luck, two Military Policemen waiting in a YMCA canteen queue for a cup of tea overheard a conversation about a strange man living in a woman's lodgings, who never went out and seemed to get excited if anybody mentioned the police. On Wednesday, 23 June 1943, having established the address, Police Constable James Fynn made a visit to Annie Perfect's residence in Cecil Street and, on seeing a man with both wrists tattooed, asked for his identification. He produced an identity card in the name of Mark Turner. The police officer could see that the last letter had been changed. He asked the man to sign his name, which he did. The signature read Mervin Turney. McEwan had inadvertently given himself away and, realising he had been caught out, gave the police his real name and was promptly arrested.

The Trial

On Tuesday, 13 July 1943 Mervin Clare McEwan appeared at Halifax Borough Court wearing grey flannel trousers, a tennis shirt, brown pullover and a Macintosh raincoat. The place was crowded as Gerald Richard Paling KC, appearing on behalf of the Director of Public Prosecutions, detailed the despicable attack on an elderly man. As the nine scalp wounds found during the post-mortem examination were being graphically described by Professor Peter Lindsay Sutherland, the West Riding County Pathologist, Annie Perfect, who had travelled to Halifax for the hearing, collapsed and had to be carried from the courtroom. Bertha Bulmer, whose mother was a cousin of Mark Turner, performed household chores at his home and described him as 'a kindly old gentleman of hospitable nature'. The police evidence, and McEwan's own admission, would seal his fate.

McEwan was remanded in custody and re-appeared, smartly attired in a new battledress, at Leeds Assizes on Wednesday, 1 December 1943 before Mr Justice Stable, and made a plea of not guilty to the charge of murder. The jury needed just 40 minutes to reach a verdict. McEwan was found guilty of the crime and sentenced to death. His execution date was originally set for Thursday, 23 December. Just over a week after the sentence was passed, on 11 December 1943, William Crabtree passed away at his daughter's home in Kensington Road, Halifax. It was claimed that the stress of the court case, and having to give evidence, was too much for him.

The Appeal

McEwen launched an appeal against his sentence, and his execution date was duly postponed. On Monday, 17 January 1944, as the Battle of Monte Cassino commenced in Italy, the Canadian soldier appeared before Mr Justice Humphries, Mr Justice Cassels and Mr Justice Asquith at the Central Criminal Court of Appeal. His defence counsel, Mr Paley-Scott, attempted to claim that only the initial blow to Mark Turner's head was made with intent, and that McEwan's mind had 'gone blank' after the first strike. However, Mr Justice Asquith, who was well acquainted with the case, described this claim as 'fantastic' and the appeal was dismissed.

McEwan was hanged at Armley Prison, Leeds, on Thursday, 3 February 1944, by Thomas Pierrepoint, assisted by Steve Wade. His body was buried on the same day within the prison grounds. His name would be recorded on the Brookwood Memorial which is visited by many thousands of people every year. In contrast, Mark Turner, had been quietly buried on Thursday, 8 April 1943, and rests in grave No. 146 at Christ's Church graveyard, Halifax, and most likely receives no visitors. A year after her son's death, on Wednesday, 28 February 1945, Olive May McEwan passed away. Sadly, Annie Perfect passed away herself on 14 May 1951 aged just 43 from the effects of abdominal cancer, and is buried in Manchester's Southern Cemetery, close to her husband.

Chapter 22

Private Charles Arthur Raymond –
A Voluble and Incessant Talker

Panel 25. Column 1
Service Number: E/22936
Unit: 5th Infantry Brigade Company, Royal Canadian Army
Service Corps
Executed: Saturday, 10 July 1943, aged 23

In wartime Britain, the daily movement of military vehicles was nothing out of the ordinary but, by 1943, the passage of military traffic was unprecedented, bringing with it a high level of traffic accidents and tragic deaths. Equally, throughout the war, it was not unusual to see military personnel seeking a lift home, back to base or just on a short trip during some time off. So, it was for one WAAF, whose efforts to get a ride back to the airfield where she was stationed ended in tragedy, not through a road accident but because of a vicious and cowardly attack, for which the offender then attempted to frame a comrade.

The isolated grave of Aircraftswoman 1st Class Marguerite Burge at the Havant and Waterloo Cemetery, Hampshire.

The Victim

Marguerite Burge was born on Friday, 21 January 1921. Her mother's name was Le Roux, and, for some yet unexplained reason, she opted to give up her daughter, who was fostered by Thomas Wellman and Ada Mary Ann Wellman (née Hedger), of Bedhampton, Hampshire.

Thomas had served with the King's Royal Rifles during the First World War and the couple had four children of their own. Marguerite's early life appears to have been a relatively happy one for a foster child growing up in the Depression period. With the outbreak of the Second World War, Marguerite, described as slim and attractive, enlisted in the WAAF, with the rank of aircraftswoman 1st class. By the beginning of 1943, she found herself working in the Sergeant's Mess at RAF Tangmere. She made friends at the base, both male and female, but she was not in any form of intimate relationship with anyone, as would later be established. Like so many other WAAFs at the time, she had a job to do, and she got on with it, but still liked a bit of fun when she found the time.

The Crime

Events began on Saturday, 30 January 1943, when Marguerite departed from Tangmere at about 2.00 p.m. It was pouring with rain, but she was going to meet Sergeant Stanley Clarke, an instructor in the Army Physical Training Corps, for an afternoon by the sea at Bognor Regis. The couple had arranged to meet at Boxgrove Corner at 2.30 p.m. from where they would catch the bus to Bognor. Stanley arrived on time and waited for a quarter of an hour, but Marguerite was late and when she reached Boxgrove Corner he had gone. She was seen sitting on a fence at the couple's proposed meeting point, known as Flippance Cottage, by a soldier from the RAF Regiment, George Hardwick, who described the young WAAF as 'wearing a touch of lipstick'. They talked for a while until his bus arrived, by now it was 3.30 p.m., still raining and beginning to get dark. Marguerite was also seen by Aircraftswoman 1st Class Gladys Love and Aircraftsman 1st Class Horace Raymond Webber, both of whom knew her. Accepting the fact that she had missed her date, Marguerite began to walk back towards the airfield.

As she made her way along the Halnaker–Goodwood Road a Canadian army truck pulled up, and several witnesses saw her talking to the driver. Just a short time later she was savagely attacked, stabbed four times in the head and three times in the chest, then dumped in a field and left for dead.

At about 2.00 p.m. the following day, Sunday, 31 January, it was still raining heavily when two members of the local Home Guard were cycling along the road from Halnaker Cross towards Goodwood when one of them, Leonard George Bailey, spotted what he thought was an airman in uniform lying in a field. The two men cautiously approached the man and were horrified to discover that it was a very gravely injured member of the WAAF, she was unconscious, her stockings were torn, her clothes wet and her skull smashed in. One of the men immediately cycled back along the road to find two RAMC nurses they had recently passed. On their return, the police were telephoned and Captain Hugh Weir of the 11th Convalescent Depot at Goodwood arrived on the scene, followed shortly afterwards by a police officer, Constable Thomas Hughes.

It did not take long before St John Ambulance medics were on the scene and attended to Marguerite's head wound. Detective Constable Arthur Charles Lewis Evans, based at Chichester, helped to stretcher the unconscious WAAF to a waiting ambulance, from where she was then taken to the Royal West Sussex Hospital. On arrival, Dr Charles Kay Warwick, the House Surgeon, found that she was soaking wet, cold and suffering from exposure. Her uniform had to be cut off and it was quickly established that she had suffered significant head injuries and stab wounds above the left breast. There was also a lot of bruising, and insects were crawling all over her body. Her condition deteriorated and at 6.30 p.m. it was decided that an operation to relieve pressure on her brain was necessary. This commenced at 8 p.m. but, unfortunately, she died on the operating table without ever regaining consciousness. Her cause of death was recorded as an intra-cerebral haemorrhage. A post-mortem would show her skull had been punctured several times by a sharp instrument, and there were wounds on her body as well. This was now a murder case.

The initial investigation was conducted by Sussex Police officers, Superintendent Ernest Savage and Detective Inspector John Widdicombe, but they soon realised that this might prove to be a difficult case and they called in Scotland Yard. Detective Chief Inspector Tom Barratt and Detective Sergeant Charlie Morris travelled down to Sussex and the inquiries began. Forensic evidence was scant, but a search of the field uncovered a grey balaclava helmet, a diary and, about 75yd from the body, a blood-splattered screwdriver. The diary identified the deceased as 22-year-old Marguerite Beatrice Burge, who was stationed at nearby RAF Tangmere. The two Scotland Yard detectives now began the task of tracing Marguerite's known movements up until the time of her attack.

Witnesses in the vicinity of this quiet English country lane who had seen an army lorry, although were unaware of what was really happening, were very clear and precise in their recollections. One of these, James Glasspool, was a local shepherd. On the day of the assault, he was watching his flock from a hut in the field where the girl was later found.

> I saw a lorry stop in the road by Inkpen Furze. It was an Army lorry. It was then 4 p.m. It stayed there about a quarter of an hour, then it moved up a few yards and the driver got out and went down behind the lorry, then he got back in the lorry again and drove on again a few yards and then got out and came round behind the lorry again; then he moved on again and stopped by the gap in the hedge. The driver got out and came through the gap. He was dressed in khaki. He came into the field in which my sheep were. He was in the field only about a minute or two then got into the lorry and drove away towards Goodwood. The lorry went away very fast.

Leslie Boxall, who lived close to the scene of the murder, and his next-door neighbour Frank Goff confirmed Glasspool's statement. They were watching a local shoot and noticed an army lorry, which appeared to have Canadian markings, in the roadway coming from the direction of Halnaker. It was standing on the road near a hedge, and they witnessed a WAAF standing by the cab door who seemed to be talking to the driver of the lorry. Next thing it passed them with the WAAF inside, after which it stopped by the copse known as Inkpen Furze.

Inquiries now began in earnest to locate this man. There was, however, a noted lack of cooperation from the Canadian army, a reluctance to open up to the British police. Despite this, the Special Investigation Department (SIB) of the Canadian Military Police swung into action and began investigating all the army units in the area. This, however, was wartime Sussex, on England's invasion coast, and there were some 40,000 Canadians stationed in the area, but Chief Inspector Barratt, who had now been detailed to head the investigation, battered away at his task and his team questioned over 800 soldiers. But then came a lucky break.

Sergeant Joseph Carrier of the Canadian Provost Corps was interviewing 23-year-old Private Charles Arthur Raymond, a driver with 'B' Platoon, 2nd Divisional Transport Company, Royal Canadian Army Service Corps, when, out of the blue, he suddenly claimed that he knew who killed the WAAF. 'You had better make a close check up on Patry; he is a bad 'un, and he is always talking about the murder,' Raymond stated. This referred to Private Arthur Patry of the same unit and, it would seem, the search had now quickly narrowed down, and two prime suspects were focused upon.

The Assailant

In contrast to that of Marguerite, the life of Charles Arthur Raymond, a French Canadian, was deemed to be chaotic and disrupted. He was born on the Tuesday, 1 July 1919 at Rivière-du-Loup, Quebec, the son of Joseph Raymond. His mother had died when he was just 5 years old and his father, who was illiterate, soon remarried. His relationship with his stepmother, half-brothers and sisters was poor. Raymond himself was virtually illiterate, socially awkward but was a good mechanic and worked as a truck driver before the outbreak of war. He enlisted at the Enemy Alien Concentration Camp in the Citadelle of Québec on Tuesday, 5 September 1939, initially being placed into the Royal Rifles of Canada. Soon after his enlistment, most likely due to his mechanical skills, he found himself transferred to the Royal Canadian Army Service Corps as a driver and arrived in the United Kingdom on Christmas Day 1939. His service record shows one or two

Private Charles Arthur Raymond, who attacked Aircraftswoman 1st Class Marguerite Burge. He returned to the scene of his crime the following day with a comrade, Private Arthur Patry. On finding her still alive, he left her where she lay for a second time.

misdemeanours but nothing out of the ordinary for the time. However, in a statement made on Saturday, 1 May 1943, Sergeant H.G. Hanson gave the following overview of Raymond, which perhaps best describes his general behaviour as a soldier:

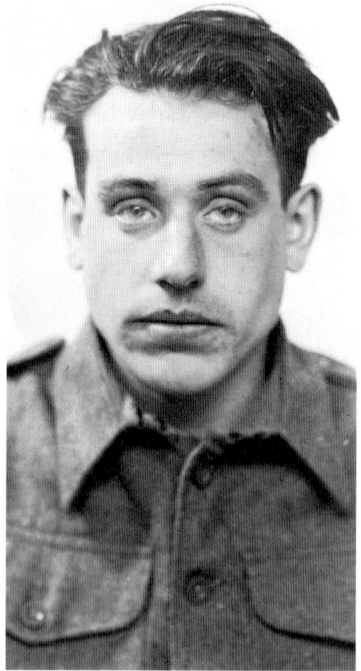

I herewith enclose a declaration upon the conduct and actions of Private C. Raymond E/22936 since he has been in my platoon. He has on one occasion been convicted on being charged with stealing and has been accused on several other charges of the same sort. He is very lazy regarding his personal appearance and seems to have an aversion to water. He seems to be very dull mentally and does things without regarding the consequences or results. He also seemed to be absent-minded and a liar. I have found him a willing worker, but only when there was someone in charge of him to supervise.

In the meantime, as the investigation continued, tyre marks on the verge of the road where the lorry had pulled over were examined, and meticulous checking of vehicle records and movement logs for Canadian army vehicles revealed the lorry in question, a 3-ton Chevrolet with the serial number CL4234779. The items collected from the field had been sent to the Metropolitan Police Laboratory at Hendon for detailed analysis. Blood, from the group A, matching that of Marguerite Burge, was found on the screwdriver and on the balaclava helmet. A single hair recovered from the balaclava was found not to belong to the victim.

Before interrogating Arthur Patry, the Military Police checked on his movements on the day of the murder. He had been on leave in Scotland and only arrived back in camp at 11.00 a.m. that day. At 1.45 p.m. he was given a lorry to service, which he worked on with two colleagues until after 3.15 p.m. After this time, he was observed in the vicinity of the workshop by another soldier, and at 4.30 p.m., the approximate time of the murder, he replaced the duty NCO in the orderly room who did not return to relieve Patry until 7.00 p.m. that evening. However, Patry had been at the scene of the crime and had seen Marguerite laying on the ground, almost an hour before she was found, and long before she died. Raymond, upon being re-interviewed, repeated his accusation against Patry and

Private Arthur Patry, who Private Raymond attempted to blame for the killing of Marguerite Burge.

then dropped this second bombshell. He and his comrade had seen Marguerite's body the day after the murder. Raymond said that they had been for a drink that morning and on the way back to camp they had spotted 'something blue in a field'. They investigated and found the body of a WAAF. They presumed that she was dead and decided to do nothing about their find in case they 'got into trouble'.

Chief Inspector George Hatherill, who spoke French, had helped to form the SIB of the Military Police and would later head Scotland Yard's Flying Squad, interviewed Raymond on Friday, 26 February, and then accompanied him as they retraced the route he claimed to have followed on the day of the murder. They drove to Butler's Garage in the village of Lavant, on the outskirts of Chichester, where Raymond had filled his truck with petrol. During the journey, the Canadian again claimed that Arthur Patry was a 'wise guy' and it was he who had murdered Marguerite. Raymond was then taken to Chichester police station where he made a written statement which included the new accusation that he had heard Patry talking in his sleep about 'WAAFs and detectives'. Raymond was now digging his own grave. The police felt it was time to interview Patry. He agreed that he and Raymond had seen the body but had not reported the incident because they did not want to get into trouble with the police. His explanation of that morning's events ran as follows:

> Raymond asked me to go to the pub with him. I told him I had no money and he said, 'Don't worry, I have got some.' We left the hut to go to the pub and passed through the fields to go to the Richmond Arms pub. When we got there Raymond said, 'Let's go to the other pub, where a woman told me it's open earlier Sundays.' I went with him, and we walked about halfway to the pub when he said: 'There is something behind that hedge.' I looked to the hedge but could see nothing. Raymond said: 'There is something, there is a girl behind the hedge.' I went to look and said, 'It's a man' and he said, 'No, it's a girl.' I saw some shoes which made me think it was a man. I went forward a bit and I saw it was the body of a girl. I could see through the hole in the hedge. The girl was wearing Air Force uniform. Raymond approached the body and I said 'Let's go' because I thought she was dead, and I didn't want to get into any trouble. Raymond said nothing. Neither of us touched the girl.

During his interview, Patry also went on to state that Raymond had asked him if he thought the police could trace fingerprints after it had been raining. Clearly one of these men was not telling the truth, and Patry could not have been involved in the murder as he had not left the base. This was good enough for Barratt. Raymond was arrested and charged with the killing of Marguerite Burge.

The Trial

Raymond appeared at Chichester County Police Court on Thursday, 4 March 1943 charged with murder and was remanded in custody. He appeared again on Wednesday, 24 March when the case was moved to the Old Bailey.

The trial opened on Monday, 10 May 1943 before Mr Justice Lawrence. All the proceedings were translated into French, with Lieutenant Desjardins, Raymond's platoon commander, acting as an interpreter for Raymond, who only spoke French. Keeping a watchful eye on proceedings was Major Maurice Forget of the Canadian Judge Advocate General's Office, a man who was to later make some damning statements regarding the British justice system and its treatment of Canadian soldiers who were charged with capital crimes.

During the trial, Sir Bernard Spillsbury, the Home Office pathologist, described Marguerite's injuries.

An extensive bruise on and around her chin indicated that she had been struck a 'violent blow with the fist', and a wound and bruising at the back of the head could have been due to a heavy fall backwards as a result of such a blow. In addition to the stab wounds through her lungs, her heart and her head, there was bruising on her thighs, abdomen and wrists. Lastly, some of the injuries occurred whilst her assailant was kneeling on her when she was on the ground. She was then left, seriously injured, in the field, where she lay all night in a heavy thunderstorm. It had been a savage, brutal assault. Dr James Davidson, director of the Metropolitan Police Laboratory at Hendon, stated that not only were the bloodstains found on Raymond's clothing the same type as Marguerite's but, just as importantly, lipstick found on his uniform matched that worn by the dead WAAF. Semen stains found on her uniform skirt were deemed to have belonged to Raymond. A screwdriver that he 'always carried in a pocket' matched with the puncture wounds to the WAAF's skull, and those on her breast. The hair found in the grey balaclava was similar to Raymond's but completely different to Patry's. But Raymond continued to protest his innocence.

Glasspool, the shepherd, and the other witness then followed into the witness box and in turn gave their accounts. Finally, came Raymond, the only witness called by the defence. He emphatically claimed that he had been at the scene at the time but had witnessed Arthur Patry commit the crime. However, the evidence was to wholly disprove this. It was demonstrated that he had been out in his lorry on the day

Lieutenant Colonel Thomas Walter Colby Carthew DSO, CdG, KC, who defended Raymond and described the Canadian as a very 'voluble and incessant talker'.

of the assault, a 3-ton Chevrolet with the serial number CL4234779. He had dropped Private Roger Dumas in Chichester at 3.10 p.m. and had told him that he needed to fill the lorry with fuel. He had then stopped at a garage near the scene of the murder. According to the garage register, Raymond had signed for the petrol at 3.30 p.m. Dumas also said that Raymond was wearing a grey balaclava similar to the one found near Marguerite's body. Lastly, it was stated that on Monday, 1 February, Raymond had handed his tool kit to another soldier, and it was noted that a screwdriver was missing from the set.

Raymond was represented in court by Lieutenant Colonel Thomas Walter Colby Carthew DSO, CdG, KC, a former soldier who had served with 4th Battalion, Bedfordshire Regiment, and the Royal Flying Corps during the First World War, and who was supported by Harold Brown and Reginald Bray. A lawyer of great standing and military experience, Carthew was of the opinion that Raymond believed he was telling the truth and the witnesses, all forty-three of them, were lying. He depicted the Canadian as a very 'voluble and incessant talker', so much so that he had, in many instances, contradicted himself in numerous ways. Despite what was described as an 'able and energetic defence' by Carthew, Mr Justice Lawrence, in his summing up, stated that 'there were too many coincidences' that pointed to Raymond as being the perpetrator of the crime.

The jury took just 20 minutes to reach a verdict and the Canadian was found guilty of the murder of Marguerite Burge. Mr Justice Lawrence, now wearing the traditional black cap, pronounced sentence of death against Raymond. The jury did not make a recommendation for mercy.

The Appeal

On Tuesday, 22 June 1943, an appeal against the sentence was launched at the Court of Criminal Appeal before Chief Justice Lord Caldecote, Mr Justice Wrottesley and Mr Justice Croom-Johnston, based on misdirection by the presiding judge in that he did not comment sufficiently on the points raised by the defence, which were;

- How did Raymond get Marguerite into the field?
- Why was Marguerite not seen by the witnesses who saw Raymond in the field?
- When Marguerite was found, her tunic was buttoned up with no holes in it, despite all her injuries.

It seems that the defence team then opted to go down the 'insanity' route, as well as trying to blacken the name of the murdered WAAF. They attempted to gain access to her personal diaries and made much of the fact that she often hitch-hiked with strange soldiers and accepted money from them too. Raymond tried to appear mentally disturbed, claiming the WAAF was appearing in his cell and haunting him.

The Chief Constable of Sussex, in a note to his deputy at the time, had the following observations to make:

Raymond puts forward a new story and for the first time admits killing the girl. This wicked man, as you know so well, put forward cunning deliberate lies to implicate another man and it is only through the tenacity and thoroughness displayed by Barratt that no suspicion fell upon the unfortunate man Patry. This cold-blooded murderer now seeks mercy by casting aspersions on the character of the girl, but I cannot see any reason why we should believe a word of them. In the Petition a Major of the Canadian Army Medical Corps, states that at the time of the offence Raymond was believed to understand the difference between right and wrong and the nature and quality of his act. This Major goes on to say that Raymond is an uneducated childish type of individual of sub-normal intelligence, but from the outset of this enquiry he displayed such animal cunning in endeavouring to throw police off the scent which forces me to the conclusion that he is not so very childish or backward. It is not a case for mercy.

On Raymond's 24th birthday his solicitor submitted a report outlining the case on the basis that, despite the fact he had been found guilty and lost his appeal, it would aid the Canadian military authorities in their continued efforts to save him from execution. An extract reads:

Although a strong circumstantial case was put up, I do feel that the position would have been vastly different had Raymond kept silent during the time of investigation by the Police. Had he done so, investigations by the prosecution would have had to have taken a totally different line and may have resulted in the prosecution never being able to prove he was there. As I have said, I very carefully pointed out to Raymond that the statements which he had made to the Police were very damaging to him, whereby he admitted being at the scene of the alleged murder at the appropriate date and time. He persistently maintained, however, that what he had said in his last statement to the Police was true and that it was Patry who committed the murder.

In a final statement, made in the presence of his solicitor and two senior Canadian army officers, Raymond claimed that he had known Marguerite for six months after meeting her at a dance. That two of his comrades would write to her on his behalf, due to his illiteracy. On the day she was attacked, she accepted a lift in his truck and, he suggested, she asked him for money, so he gave her 10s. At the same time, he had asked her not to see any other servicemen. She allegedly said, 'It's alright, I will go out no more with others.' During the journey he stopped by a field near Boxgrove, and the couple got out and sat by a haystack where they talked, and where, he claimed, they had been many times before. An argument ensued and he alleged that Marguerite slapped him across the face. He punched her and knocked her to the ground and, he claimed, she struck her head on a plough. Her final moments are described in his own words:

> She lost consciousness. There I killed her, I do not remember how, I had my screwdriver that is all I remember. I carried my screwdriver in my pockets, I do not remember I had completely lost my head. We had not always quarrelled, she 'jerked me off' as the truck was moving. She did it often; I told her that I was respectable that she was, that I did not want to seduce her; then she would 'jerk me off'. She hit me because I told her that I would not go out any more with her and that she could run around for dirt or rotten things with others.

The Canadian authorities continued to make strenuous efforts on behalf of Raymond but in a later report stated that it was difficult to prepare a case for clemency on the basis that:

- The murder was a particularly brutal one.
- The day after the assault Raymond, in company with Patry, saw Marguerite, who was then still alive, and left her there.
- Raymond gave several conflicting accounts of the occurrence, and little could be gained from him that might assist.
- There was nothing particular about his family circumstances, or his army service, which could not be said of a great many Canadian soldiers.

In his final letter, dated Monday, 5 July 1943, to Sir Frank Newsam, the Under Secretary of State at the Home Office, Raymond made one last plea for his life. Guided by Major Forget, Mr Bray and Lieutenant Desjardins, Raymond made much of the fact that he did not speak English, felt out of place as a result, and had been mistreated by this terrible woman. It reads:

> Sir,
>
> I have been told that it is you who must decide my fate, this is why I am begging you to read this letter before making a decision. I've made a statement to Major Forget, Mr. Bray and Lieutenant Desjardins and I am providing you with this letter.
>
> I have told them all about the circumstances that brought me to kill this girl. I had known her for a long time, and I loved her very much. I used to save my money before being able to give it to her

because I could not stand the idea of other men making love to her and she promised me more than once, several times that I was the only one she would go out with and that she would be faithful to me.

I had never attempted to do anything to her that she did not want me to do, and I was afraid that other men would touch her. Even that Saturday afternoon, as I have said to Major Forget, Mr. Bray and Lieutenant Desjardins I saw her meeting and speaking with the big man of the Royal Air Force just after she promised me to leave the other men that she didn't care about. I never wanted to hurt her, but I knew that I could not trust her since then and I made the decision to no longer see her.

When I told her of my decision, she gave me a violent slap around the face. And then my character changed, and I lost my temper and hit her on the chin with my fist, but I didn't intend to cause her serious injury and I didn't see that she was close to the plough, but her head hit it and she lost consciousness. After that everything went black inside me, and I don't remember stabbing her.

Sir, I am only 23 years old, and I was 19 when I joined up in Canada in 1939 and I came to England as a volunteer to fight in the war in Dec 1940. I don't speak much English and I've been unable to meet many English people and I feel out of place in this country. I have never done anything bad before and I suffer my punishment now whenever I see the face of this girl that I've always loved. My father and my own brothers and sisters are all in Canada and I know how they hope that you will hear my prayers and that you will grant me clemency.

(Sgd) C A Raymond

[Deepest gratitude to Suzanne Make for translating this letter into English]

Unimpressed, the Secretary of State, Herbert Morrison, upheld the original verdict of the court, and Private Charles Arthur Raymond was hung at Wandsworth Prison on Saturday, 10 July 1943 by Thomas Pierrepoint and Steve Wade. His body was buried later that day within the confines of the prison walls.

Marguerite Burge is buried in an isolated grave at the Havant and Waterloo Cemetery, Hampshire.

Although her clothing had been in disarray when she was found and her underwear torn, she had not been raped and was, in fact, still a virgin. The diary and some letters written by Marguerite, which had not been produced in court, were demanded by the defence from Sir Frank Newsam. These were produced, as requested, and showed that there was no connection between her and Raymond and were not relevant to the case at all. The contents of his final statement and letter remain unfounded.

Chapter 23

Gunner Kenneth Charles Sydney Prior – A Disgraceful Death

Panel 3. Column 3
Service Number: 1111690
Unit: 4th Reserve Anti-Tank Regiment, Royal Artillery
Date of Death: Sunday, 21 December 1941, aged 36

The investigation, capture and trial of some of those soldiers listed on the Brookwood Memorial who were accused of a civil crime has resulted in the availability of an extensive trail of documents and articles in both local and national archives, as well as some previous historical publications. These help to provide the details and circumstances of those involved with the case. However, there is one murder case in which the assailant was not tried by a civil court, and for whom there is very limited documentation. The reason for this is that the assailant chose to take his own life just moments after committing the crime. There were numerous cases of murder/suicide across the country throughout the Second World War, many committed by serving members of the armed forces, whose graves are maintained by the CWGC. Unfortunately, the graves of their victims are not given the same reverence, and this is particularly tragic in circumstances where the victim was a member of the civilian volunteer services, such as the Women's Land Army. The CWGC are responsible for the graves of those members of these services who were killed 'by enemy action', but not in cases of accident, disease or criminal acts.

December 1941 was an especially dark period in the United Kingdom. German forces had turned against Russia, the Japanese empire had launched an attack on the US naval base at Pearl Harbor on Sunday, 7 December and followed it, three days later, by sinking the British warships HMS *Repulse* and HMS *Prince of Wales* in the South China Sea.

British troops were fighting the Afrika Korps in the Western Desert, but operations were stuck in a gruelling stalemate. At sea, the merchant service continued to be attacked by lethal U-boats in their efforts to starve the inhabitants of the British Isles whilst in the air the full extent to which air crews were failing to find, or hit, their correct targets were only just becoming clear. There was certainly no sense of an Allied victory and little to celebrate. At home, Parliament had passed a second National Service Act, which widened the scope of conscription still further by making all unmarried women and all childless widows between the ages of 20 and 30 liable to call-up. Men were also now required to perform some form of national service up to the age of 60, which included military service for those under 51. This resulted in the call-up of Kenneth Charles Sydney Prior, a 38-year-old former soldier from South London.

On the evening of Sunday, 21 December 1941, in the small West Yorkshire village of Mytholmroyd, located halfway between Bradford and the Lancashire town of Rochdale, Gunner Prior, serving with the 4th Reserve Anti-Tank Regiment, Royal Artillery, entered a cottage in Sunny Bank and asked two of the occupants, Mrs Bird and her daughter, to leave the room in order that he could speak to his wife, Eileen, alone.

The Victim

Eileen Gagliano was born on Sunday, 28 September 1919 in Deptford, South London, one of triplets. Charles and Kathleen made up the trio, three of the eleven children born to Antonio and Emma Gagliano (née Cromarty). The others being: Philomena (b. 1907), Antonio (b. 1914), William (b. 1916), Francis (b. 1921), Barbara (b. 1924), Spiranza (b. 1927), Florence (b. 1929) and Audrey (b. 1932). Their father, born in Naples, had served with the 2nd/1st West Riding Heavy Battery, Royal Garrison Artillery, during the First World War and had been discharged in April 1918 on grounds of sickness. He started his own business, operating a chandler's store close to the South London docks, in Edward Street, Deptford. It was most likely the bombing of the docks in 1940, the memories of what life had been like for members of the German community in London during the First World War and the treatment of Italians under the Trattato di Londra (Treaty of London) that caused the family to change their name from Gagliano to Gallian.

By 1939 Eileen was living in Billington Road, Deptford, and had a job as a machine operator in the tin-box trade when she met Kenneth Prior, who was working in the biscuit trade at that time.

The Assailant

Kenneth Charles Sydney Prior was born on Tuesday, 20 February 1906, in Clements Road, Bermondsey, London, the son of Osborne Charles and Nellie Prior (née Freeman). At the time of his birth, his father was working as grocer's assistant and his mother raised their children in the family home. At the outset of the First World War Osborne enlisted as a rifleman in the King's Royal Rifle Corps, serving on the Western Front with the 7th and 16th Battalions. Sadly, he died on Monday, 15 November 1920 at the age of 38, from infective endocarditis, an infection of the heart lining, whilst still in service with the army and is remembered on the screen wall of the Brockley Cemetery, Lewisham.

In October 1923, Kenneth, aged 17, enlisted in the Territorial Army, becoming a part-time member of the Royal Artillery. In August 1924, he entered the Regular Army, becoming a professional soldier. Having completed six years' service with the Colours in January 1931, he was

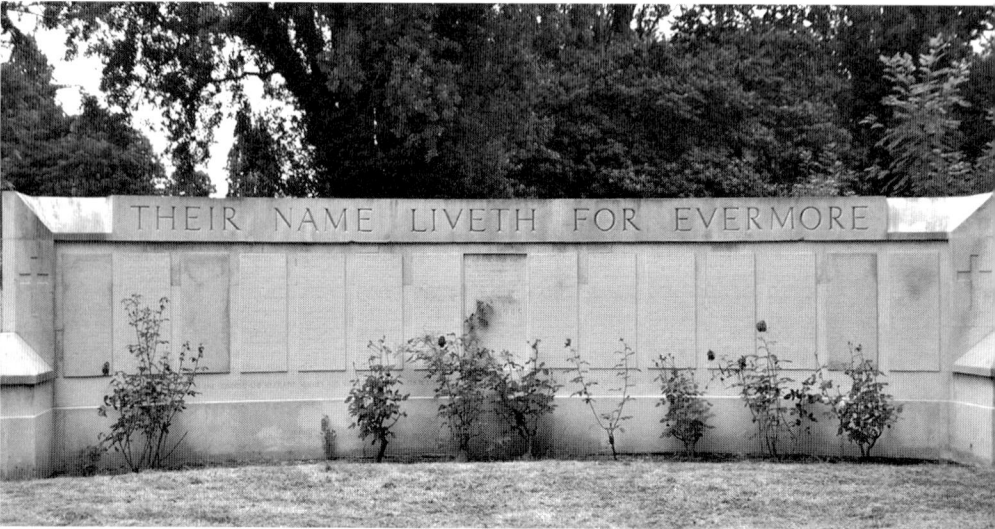

The screen wall at Brockley Cemetery, Lewisham, where the name of Rifleman Osborne Charles is inscribed. His son, Gunner Kenneth Charles Sydney Prior, is listed on the Brookwood Memorial, the only known murderer not to have been tried by a civil court.

discharged and became a member of the Army Reserve for a further six years, completing his total service by August 1936. He married Eileen Gallian in 1939 and a son, Colin, was born to the couple the following year. With the introduction of the parliamentary Act, and the increasing demands for manpower, he was called up for further service on Thursday, 15 May 1941, joining the 4th Reserve Anti-Tank Regiment, Royal Artillery. Like so many other servicemen in the early stages of the war, his wife and child moved away from the dangers of London and took up lodgings close to where he was stationed.

The Crime

There was, however, a dark secret in the life of Kenneth Prior, he was already married. It is uncertain if Eileen had known this at the outset of their relationship, but she certainly became aware of it when proceedings were started against her husband in a London court for bigamy, and she had been required to give evidence in the case. It appeared that, in 1931, Prior had married Grace Emily Marsh, who was born on Tuesday, 10 August 1909, the daughter of Henry Stanley and Lila Marsh. The couple had three sons, Charles (b. 1932), Kenneth Richard (b. 1933) and Stanley (b. 1934), and by 1935 the family home was in Ontario Street, Southwark. There is no indication as to the state of his relationship with either wife, but the fact that Eileen had given evidence against him set a course for a murderous end.

Now, on this dark December night, with socks covering his British army issue service boots in order that his approach was not heard, Prior entered the cottage where his wife and child were sheltering. He wasted no time, immediately after Mrs Bird and her daughter left the room they heard a scream. Prior had slashed Eileen across the throat with a razor. No sooner had she dropped to the floor, than he swiped the blade across his own throat. Mrs Bird opened the door to a horrific scene, a blood-soaked room and the couple both on the floor, dead. An inquest found that he had murdered Eileen, and then feloniously cut his own throat. The coroner commented that 'from the rapidity with which the tragedy occurred after Prior entered the house, it was evident that he had gone with the express intention of murdering the woman'. Given the nature of his death, the fact that his wife was taking him to court and the shame he had doubtless brought upon his family, there are no details as to what happened to his body. It is possible that he was cremated or, more likely, buried in an unmarked grave. Given he was a serving soldier at the time of his death he was entitled to commemoration under the charter of the CWGC and, therefore, his name is recorded on the Brookwood Memorial. The only documentation currently relating to this in the public domain is a short coroner's report and his Royal Artillery casualty card which is simply marked in red 'Disgraceful Death'. It appears that Eileen was also laid to rest in an unmarked grave and their son left an orphan. As for Grace Emily Marsh, she married George Arthur Penston in 1944, and passed away in 1956 at the age of 47. Remember them.

Chapter 24

The Third Man – Killer and Victim

Driver Mohamed Musallam Souleiman
Panel 17. Column 1
PAL/32094
Unit: 68 Reserve Transport Company, Royal Army Service Corps
Executed: Friday, 24 September 1943, aged 32

Private Abdel Ghaffar Mohamad Mansour
Panel 20. Column 3
Service Number: PAL/14129
Unit: 610 Smoke Company, Pioneer Corps
Murdered: Thursday, 10 June 1943

Amongst the cases of the Brookwood Killers is an unusual and disturbing incident, one which would ultimately see the names of both the victim and the assailant recorded on the memorial. The case is disconcerting by virtue of the fact circumstantial evidence would be the determining factor in defining a young man's fate, despite the fact that some significant doubt would be cast by the defence as to who was present, and who actually committed the murder.

The Facts

The story begins on the evening of Wednesday, 9 June 1943, when an African serviceman, Private Raphiadu, discovered the mutilated body of Private Abdel Ghaffar Mohamad Mansour, a Palestinian serving with No. 610 Smoke Company, Pioneer Corps, in a disused latrine at the Pioneer Corps Base Depot near Qassissin, Egypt. This huge, tented encampment was used to train and acclimatise pioneer labourers from all parts of the British Empire, before they were distributed across the Mediterranean theatre to undertake a variety of roles, such as road and rail building, the digging of defensive positions, guard duties and numerous arduous but necessary tasks. It was getting dark when members of the SIB arrived on the scene, but it was clear that the body had been dragged to the location where it was found, and the pockets turned out on his uniform shorts. Perhaps this was a simple robbery, or was there more to it?

A post-mortem, carried out by Major Raeburn at No. 6 General Hospital, indicated that death had occurred between 7 p.m. on 8 June and 1.00 a.m. on 9 June and the body, almost completely decapitated, had suffered ten savage wounds, all apparently caused by a knife which had been found a few yards from where the victim lay. A British army issue waterproof wallet was also found and, more significantly, a blood-stained detachable epaulette, with a brass RASC title fitted to it, was discovered close to the body, trodden into the sand.

Driver Mohamed Musallam Souleiman, serving with No. 68 Reserve Transport Company, RASC and, at the time, an absentee from his unit, had visited Qassassin on 8 June, apparently wanting to see his friend, Private Abdel Ghaffar Mohamad Mansour. The two men had spent the afternoon in the company of two other soldiers, Corporal Abdul Fattah and Corporal Salameh, and it would be the last time anyone would see Mansour alive again. Souleiman was seen in Cairo on 9 June, dressed as a civilian. Here he visited an Egyptian civilian doctor, Mohamed Fathi Naguib, whose surgery was in Khayrat Street, to have wounds dressed on both his hands, which he claimed he had suffered whilst in charge of labourers at El Arish. Dr Naguib stitched the wounds and Souleiman asked him for a medical certificate, requesting that it be backdated until 7 June, something the doctor declined to do. Souleiman was arrested by Egyptian police, still wearing civilian clothes, on 12 June 1943, outside a Cairo cafe after being pointed out by Corporal Salameh. He was returned to Qassassin, where he was held whilst the case was investigated by the SIB.

The Court Martial

On Tuesday, 3 August 1943, Major General Richard Augustin Marriott 'Ram' Basset MC, CdG, ordered proceedings for a General Court Martial, which took place at Qassassin on 10 August. Basset had recently committed another Palestinian soldier for trial, Corporal Hassan Naameh

Medlish, who was awaiting execution at Moascar, Egypt, for the murder of an Egyptian civilian after an apparent argument over a hashish deal. Officers were now selected to make up the court, in line with the terms laid down in the *Manual of Military Law*.

President: Lieutenant Colonel G. Pascoe, Royal Tank Regiment, Commandant of No. 305 POW Camp

Members: Major H.R.C. Bennett, Royal Army Service Corps, 24 Base Supply Depot, RASC

Major K.C. Netherton, Royal Army Service Corps, 683 Motor Ambulance Company, RASC

Captain C.M.P. Payne, Royal Scots Fusiliers, 1 Infantry Training Depot

Captain R.L.C. Scott, Royal Army Service Corps, RASC Base Depot

Prosecutor: Major G.A. Whiteley, Royal Artillery, LSO 18 Area

Defence: Captain S.K. Arnold, York & Lancaster Regiment, solicitor

Judge Advocate: Major G. Veale, JAG Branch, GHQ MEF, Barrister at Law

Interpreter: Sergeant S. Barbour, Pioneer Corps Base Depot

Much of the court records have not survived but it is evident that the case was heard over a period of four days, during which time a good deal of circumstantial evidence was provided to demonstrate that Souleiman had committed the murder. Equally, there was some very firm factual evidence indicating that whilst Souleiman was in the vicinity of the crime, he had not committed the murder and there was, in fact, another person involved.

The prosecution claimed that Souleiman, being the last man to see Private Mansour alive, had slaughtered the soldier in an argument over the sale of hashish. An absentee, he had donned civilian clothing in an effort to hide his identity, fled to Cairo in order to escape justice and had sought aid from a civilian doctor who he had purchased a sick certificate from. He had asked the doctor to backdate the note in order that he could demonstrate he had not been in Qassassin on the day of the murder.

When he was arrested by Egyptian police he was found to be carrying a watch and two rings which belonged to the dead man, as well as bank notes and some photographs that were stained with human blood. A medical officer from the RAMC, Major Raeburn, who had performed the post-mortem, indicated the wounds on Souleiman's hands may well have been caused by a knife blade and could have been obtained during a bitter struggle for possession of the weapon. Lastly, a blood-stained detachable epaulette with a brass RASC title affixed to it was a damning indication that Souleiman was at the crime scene and there was no doubt he was the killer.

In his defence, Private Souleiman claimed he had been absent from his unit for fifteen days due to sickness and, on attempting to return to it, found they were moving to Qassassin. He arrived at the camp on 6 June, two days before his unit arrived, and met up with Private Abdel Mansour, whom he knew from a time when he was himself part of No. 610 Smoke Company. Mansour shared a tent with Corporal Abdul Fattah and Corporal Salameh, and Souleiman had visited the shelter on two occasions. The first time, on 6 June, he had drunk tea with the three soldiers and played cards, winning the game and, it would seem, all their money. On the second occasion, the night of the murder, they again drank tea, played cards and discussed the price of hashish, which Souleiman claimed was cheap in Palestine and expensive in Egypt. This was borne out by the earlier court martial of Corporal Hassan Naameh Medlish, where it was also mentioned that the transporting of hashish from Palestine to Egypt could be financially lucrative. The group then decided to go to the NAAFI where they purchased a tin of fruit, which Mansour opened using a British army jackknife he had borrowed from Corporal Fattah. They then returned to the tent where Souleiman purchased a watch and two rings from Corporal Salameh.

Another game of cards commenced and an argument broke out concerning the money Souleiman had won previously from the others. He claimed that bottles were thrown inside the tent and when he attempted to leave, he grabbed his haversack and fell over, cutting himself on the broken glass that was scattered around. An old wound on his knuckle had also opened up when he struck an iron tent pole during the melee, and Corporal Salameh had given him a khaki shirt to wrap around it. Souleiman and Salameh then left the tent and walked to Qassassin station, where Salameh had provided the injured soldier with a *galabeya*, a loose-fitting, traditional Egyptian garment, which he had worn ever since. Souleiman also claimed that Salameh took him to a *dhobi*, where he left his haversack containing bloodstained clothing that needed to be washed. Salameh had suggested that, as Souleiman was an absentee, he should make his way to Cairo and Salameh would bring the uniform to him after it had been cleaned. Salameh had purchased a railway ticket for Souleiman and, as he attempted to catch the moving train, he had fallen over a piece of barbed wire, worsening the injury to his hand. After arriving in Cairo, Souleiman had visited a doctor to have his injuries treated and had asked for a backdated certificate, as he did not want to get into trouble for being absent. After having his wounds tended, he visited a cafe in Cairo where he met Corporal Salameh, who was also dressed in civilian clothing. The two men drank tea together and it was at this point that the Egyptian police arrived on the scene and, after being pointed out by Corporal Salameh, Souleiman was arrested for the murder of Private Mansour.

Corporal Abdul Fattah gave evidence that Souleiman had visited the tent in which he was billeted and, significantly, was wearing a khaki shirt and slacks at the time, along with brass titles, although he was unsure if these were either Palestine or RASC titles. He claimed that Souleiman and Private Mansour had been seen 'whispering' to one another. Fattah, a Palestinian who claimed he knew nothing about drugs, said he had seen the two soldiers passing something around that was black and green, which he believed was both sousse and hashish and that they were chewing on it. He stated that Mansour was in possession of a watch, which belonged to him and that he had asked Mansour to sell it for him. He has also seen a gold ring Mansour was wearing and the two men leave the tent together, but neither had returned. Corporal Salameh had arrived at the tent a short while after the two men had left, but he did not say anything and left after a couple of minutes. Fattah claimed he had remained in the tent for the rest of the evening.

For his part, Corporal Salameh claimed that he had only ever seen Souleiman on parade when he was serving with the unit, that he had never given him a shirt, never played cards with him and, in fact, had never played cards at all, never suggested that Souleiman should wear civilian clothes, never taken him to the *dhobi* or railway station at Qassassin, had not seen a fight in his tent on the night Mansour was murdered, and had gone to the NAAFI to buy cigarettes with a sergeant who was now stationed in Port Said. He added that he had never sold any watches or rings to Souleiman and had never seen, or owned, the photograph produced in court, although he did recognise the men in the picture as being from No. 610 Smoke Company.

The Defence

Although the circumstantial evidence put forward by the prosecution was strong, the defending officer, Captain Arnold, cast doubt and suspicion on the case regarding several issues. A pair of shorts found in a bucket of water outside the *dhobi*'s shop a few days after Souleiman was arrested were covered with human blood which, by the manner in which the spray pattern ran, was most likely caused by the cutting of an artery. Following his arrest, Souleiman had tried on the shorts, which were distinctive and not standard army issue, and it was found that they did not fit him. They were too tight and clearly made for a much smaller man. Had there been a third man at the crime scene, and had that man been Corporal Salameh? Two witnesses who saw Souleiman in the tent on the night of the murder gave different accounts of what he was wearing. One claimed he was in a pair of khaki slacks, as Souleiman had asserted, whilst another stated he was wearing shorts. Arnold also suggested that there had been some form of collusion between Corporal Salameh and the Egyptian police. Some of the money that had apparently been taken from Mansour was missing, the remainder being found to have some blood spots on it, as did some photographs found wrapped in the remaining money.

Captain Arnold argued that the uniform of Mansour was 'stiff with blood' and the knife found at the scene, a butcher's knife not a jackknife, was covered with blood clots. Yet the money, the photographs and the detachable epaulette were marked with just a few spots of blood. If they had been removed from Mansour's possession at the time of his death, why would they not be thick with blood? There were a great many inconsistencies in the case and Arnold branded Corporal Salameh a liar, saying:

There is another thing in deciding whether he was a liar. On the accused was found a photograph. Salameh says, 'that is not my photograph, I have never seen it'. Evidence is then brought by one of the persons on the photograph, a Corporal Dimour, who said 'yes that is my photograph. I had six copies, three went to my friend, two went home, some three months ago I gave the other one to Corporal Salameh and he gave me one of himself in exchange'. I think the court can say beyond all reasonable doubt that the story Dimour told is a true story and he did give that photograph to Corporal Salameh. There is no reason for him to lie, he barely knows the accused but he knows Salameh. When taxed with regard to this Salameh first of all said 'no I never had that photograph' and then a little later another one is produced and it shook Corporal Salameh and he began to think, perhaps I better give some explanation there as to how Dimour got my photograph, and he said 'yes I remember, I had several taken I put them on the table in my tent and a lot of soldiers came in and took them. The tent was always open perhaps Corporal Dimour came in then took it. I might've given it to him I don't know I can't remember.' Having said no I did not give the Corporal the photograph he later said perhaps I gave it to him I can't remember.

Souleiman may well have been present at the time of the killing, but there was no real proof he was the murderer. In his final summing up, Arnold had this to say:

What happened that is consistent with the evidence? Did the accused and the deceased have a violent fight together, a fight which was not the fault of the accused, did the accused have to protect himself when the fight became so violent and so bloody that it was necessary to kill the assailant in order to defend himself? Did some third person join and attack them both and the accused then ran away, with the third person then attacking and killing Mansour, whom it is known carried a considerable amount of money? All these propositions are reasonable propositions, but they do not show that the accused is guilty of murder. All that they show is this, that the accused was in a position where we could have committed the murder and also that the deceased was murdered. On the evidence of the prosecution alone I suggest that the accused is entitled to an acquittal.

It is at this point that the Judge Advocate representative, Major Veale, interjected and indicated that sufficient argument had been put forward, and so it was now time for the court to make a decision. His ten-page summing up outlined much of the circumstantial evidence but it is surprising to read how Veale, entrusted with ensuring that justice was done, advised the court to 'be very careful' of factual evidence put forward by the defence, particularly concerning the khaki shorts which were a clear indicator that a third person may well have been involved.

On Friday, 13 August 1943, Mohamed Musallam Souleiman was found guilty of the crime and sentenced to death. A submission to the Commander-in-Chief, General Henry Maitland 'Jumbo' Wilson, made by Revd Brigadier Hugh Scott-Barrett, clearly states that the sentence should be carried out. Driver Mohamed Musallam Souleiman was executed by firing squad at Qassassin on Friday, 24 September 1943. As with Corporal Hassan Naameh Medlish, there appears to be no explanation as to why their names are recorded on the Brookwood memorial, as opposed one in the North African theatre.

Was justice done?

Conclusion

For a number of reasons, some having to do with the subject matter and others with the circumstances, this has been an especially challenging and difficult book to write. The act of murder has always held a particular fascination for many of us, but the murderer is often portrayed as an isolated and exceptional outsider, rather than a member of a structured organisation such as the military, and is rarely celebrated upon a national memorial.

By disclosing the cases of the Brookwood Killers, I hope to have provided the reader with the opportunity to begin to explore the subject of civil murders perpetrated by members of the Commonwealth armed forces during the Second World War, and question the manner in which some of the assailants are commemorated. At a time in the United Kingdom's history, often portrayed as a period in which a strong air of togetherness existed, there was a significant rise in crime across the country, with a surprising amount committed by members of the armed forces, whose role was to defend the populace. In contrast to the murderer, whose name is today recorded in perpetuity, the victim often passes by almost unrecognised. Some lay in isolated graves, but many are buried in unmarked locations, or their bodies disposed of, and their names forgotten. I hope I have gone some little way to addressing this.

REMEMBER THEM

Sources and Bibliography

The National Archives

Lance Corporal Frederick James Austin, ASSI26/54/1, HO144/21647, PCOM9/916

Private Terence Casey, CRIM1/1538, MEPO3/2259

Lance Corporal Walter Clayton, ASSI52/580, ASSI86/4, HO144/22861, PCOM9/1137

Private John Gordon Davidson, ASSI52/559, MEPO3/2272, PCOM9/1034, HO144/22036

Sergeant Ernest Charles Digby, ASSI26/56/4, HO144/22034, MEPO3/2264, WO166/11320

Private Charles Eugene Gauthier, CRIM1/1524, HO144/21864, PCOM9/989

Private Horace Beresford Gordon, ASSI36/65, PCOM9/1063, HO144/22221

Bombardier Joseph Howard Grossley, ASSI84/35, DPP2/1345, DPP2/1399, HO144/22224

Private David Miller Jennings, ASSI26/53/2, HO144/21563, PCOM9/898

Private Cyril Johnson, CRIM1/1390, HO144/21653

Gunner Ernest James Harman Kemp, CRIM1/1582, MEPO3/2269, PCOM9/1029, HO144/22035

Private Mervin Clare McEwan, MEPO3/2251

Corporal Hassan Naameh Medlish, WO71/1083

Private Arthur Peach, ASSI6/72/8, HO144/21640, MEPO3/2189, PCOM9/911

Private Charles Arthur Raymond, CRIM1/1501, PCOM9/992, MEPO3/2247, HO144/21867

Corporal Dudley George Rayner, MEPO3/2248, CRIM1/1485, HO144/21863

Private August Sangret, MEPO3/2237, HO144/21861, PCOM 9/974, HO144/21860

Private Theodore John William Schurch, KV2/76, KV2/77, WO204/12796, WO204/13021

Driver Mohamed Musallam Souleiman, WO71/1087

Private Arthur Thompson, HO144/22174

Publications

After the Battle magazine
Britain at War magazine
Clark, Andrew, *A Keen Soldier*, 2002

Critchley, Macdonald (ed.), *The Trial of August Sangret*, 1959

Eddleston, John J., *Murderous Sussex: The Executed of the Twentieth Century*, 1997

Fielding, Steve, *The Executioner's Bible*, 2008

Fielding, Steve, *Pierrepoint: A Family of Executioners*, 2006

Greeno, Edward, *War on the Underworld*, 1960

Higgins, Robert, *In the Name of the Law*, 1958

Hylton, Stuart, *Their Darkest Hour*, 2001

Jones, Steve, *When the Lights Went Down*, 2000

Phillips, Peter, *The German Great Escape*, 2005

Read, Simon, *Dark City – Crime in Wartime London*, 2010

Smithies, Edward, *Crime in Wartime*, 1982

Stanley, Peter, *Bad Characters*, 2010

Trow, M.J., *War Crimes*, 2008

True Crimes magazine

Websites

www.ancestry.com

www.blackkalendar.nl

www.britishexecutions.co.uk

www.britishnewspaperarchive.com

www.canadabayconnections.com

www.capitalpunishmentuk.org

www.cwgc-archive.com

www.findagrave.com

www.findmypast.com

www.murderresearch.com

Index

British and Commonwealth Formations

1st Airborne Division 91, 143
1st Canadian Division 181
4th Division 70
7th Armoured Division 103
38th (Welsh) Infantry 14
46th Division 43
48th (South Midland) Division 79

5th Infantry Brigade, RCASC 204
12th Infantry Brigade 70
144th Brigade 79
201st Guards Brigade 103

1st Cameronians 63
1st South Lancashire Regiment 68, 70
2nd Essex Regiment 87
2nd/5th West Yorks Regiment 51–2
3rd Parachute Regiment 134
4th (R) Anti-Tank Regiment 218–21
4th Bedfordshire Regiment 212
7th King's Royal Rifle Corps 220
7th Royal Sussex Regiment 177
8th Wiltshire Regiment 97
9th Cameronians 60, 63
11th South Staffordshire Regiment 78,
   82
13th Black Watch 123
16th King's Royal Rifle Corps 220
17th Divisional Train 69
25th Mountain Regiment, RA 132
36th Northumberland Fusiliers 29
39th Signal Training Regiment 13
68 Reserve Transport Company, RASC
   223
70th Queen's Royal Regiment 31, 193
188th Field Regiment, RA 12, 15

610 Smoke Company, Pioneer Corps
   223, 226, 228
1038 Port Operating Company 40

Border Regiment 62
Edmonton Regiment 179
Essex Regiment 87, 88
Punjab Regiment 110
RAF Regiment 205
Régiment De La Chaudière 177
Régiment de Quebec 178
Regimental Training School 90
Regina Rifles Regiment 171
Royal Canadian Army Service Corps 207
Royal Sussex Regiment 42, 142
Royal Tank Regiment 225
York & Lancaster Regiment 225
Young Soldiers Battalion 62

Army Physical Training Corps 32
Royal Army Service Corps 69, 86, 99,
   100, 223, 225

Auxiliary Territorial Service (ATS) 95,
   133, 135–6, 139–40, 159
CWGC viii–xi, 7, 47, 75, 77, 110, 218, 222

Military Police 31, 49–50, 84, 102, 110,
   170, 202, 207, 209–10
NAFFI 69, 71–2, 76–7
Royal Air Force 8, 74, 216
Royal Artillery 12–13, 29, 42, 98, 132,
   218–20, 222, 225
Royal Marines 108, 112
Royal Navy 8, 47, 74, 88, 110
Women's Auxiliary Air Force (WAAF)
   8, 30–7, 60–3, 204–8, 210–14

Locations

Aberdare, Glams. 152–3, 155–7, 163

Aldershot, Hants. 100–1, 166, 179

Armley (Prison) 150, 203

Ashford, Kent 51–3, 56, 59

Auchanachie, Abs. 123–4

Bedhampton, Hants. 204

Bognor Regis, West Sussex 205

Bradford, Yorks. 143–51, 219

Brentwood, Essex 89

Bretton, Yorks. 13

Bridgend, Glams. 156, 158–61

Bristol, Avon 5, 25, 28, 86, 90, 93–6, 98

Brixton (Prison) 56, 72

Broadstairs, Kent 14–15, 28

Buxton, Derbys. 149

Cairo, Egypt 102, 224–5, 227

Camberley, Surrey 196

Cardiff (Prison) 161, 163

Chichester, West Sussex 146, 206, 210–12

Chopwell (Tyne & Wear) 70

Clayton Heights, Yorks. 142–3

Colchester, Essex 80–1

Dagenham, Essex 89

Dunkirk, France 10, 70, 73, 89

Eltham (S. London) 32–6

Enfield, Middx 13

Godalming, Surrey 90, 167–71, 188, 190

Great Island Farm, Glams. 156

Guildford, Surrey 135, 168–9, 190

Hankley Common, Surrey 165, 173

Hascombe, Surrey 189–91, 193

Horfield (Prison) 25, 28, 86, 98

Keighley, Yorks. 141

Kendal, Cumbria 142, 148

Kidbrooke (S. London) 30–2

Lewes, East Sussex 181–2

Manor Park (E. London) 38

Milborne Port, Som. 12

Moascar, Egypt 40–2, 47, 225

Morecambe, Lancs. 60–1, 64–5, 67, 145

Oakworth, Yorks. 150

Old Bailey (London) 35, 56, 139, 181, 211

Penge (S. London) 134–9

Pentonville (Prison) 110

Pontypool, Mons. 113

Porthcawl, Glams. 156–7

Portslade-by-Sea, Sussex 178–80, 185

Putney (S.E. London) 112, 114, 116–220

Qassassin, Egypt 224, 226–8, 230

St Helens, Lancs. 122, 125, 127

St Nicholas at Wade, Kent 14–15, 28

Scarborough, Yorks. 13, 144

Scotland Yard (London) 33, 83, 132, 171, 201, 206

Sittingbourne, Kent 14

Tiverton, Devon 82–3

Tunbridge Wells, Kent 166

Ulverston, Lancs. 150

Verona, Italy 106–7

Wakefield, Yorks. 13

Walsall, W. Mids. 78–83

Walton (Prison) 67, 131

Wandsworth (Prison) 5, 36, 38, 59, 110, 120, 140, 175, 185, 195, 216

Wanstead (E. London) 30–1

Wincanton, Som. 22

Winson Green (Prison) 85

Witney, Oxon. 23, 25

Wormwood Scrubs (Prison) 146

Judiciary

Justice Asquith 203
Justice Atkinson 184
Justice Cassells 35–6, 98, 184, 195, 203
Justice Charles 73, 76, 120
Justice Croom-Johnson 56, 161, 213
Justice Hallett 120
Justice Hilbery 129
Justice Humphreys 28, 85, 98, 129, 175, 181, 184, 193–4, 203

Justice Lawrence 211, 213
Justice Lewis 175
Justice MacNaughton 83, 174–5
Justice Oliver 98, 129, 139, 145, 148–9, 177, 181, 183–4
Justice Singleton 26, 119–20, 195
Justice Stable 66, 161, 203
Justice Wrottesley 161, 213
Lord Caldecote 95, 129, 175, 195, 213

Individuals

Abbas, Mahmoud Saleh (Pte.) 39
Allen, Henry (Harry) v, 67
Allen, Winifred (ACW2) 32
Anelay, Robert (Pte) 70, 76–7
Appleton, Gladys May 121–2, 126, 128, 132
Ashton, Norman Henry 55
Atkinson, Ernest 156
Atkinson, Jennie 156–7
Austin, Frederick James (L/Cpl) 11, 86–98
Austin, Lilian D.P. (née Hardman) 87–97
Austin, Ronald Bevan (later Furness) 89, 98
Austin, William Allen (War Res.) 137
Austin, William Thomas 89

Bailey, Lancelot (Det. Insp.) 158–9
Bailey, Leonard George (Home Guard) 206
Barker, George Leslie 122
Barratt, Tom (Det. Chief Insp.) 206–7, 211, 213
Basset, Richard A.M. (Maj. Gen.) 41–2, 46, 224
Belcher, Arthur (Spl Con.) 32
Beveridge, Peter (Chief Insp.) 25
Bidmead, Horace 93
Blackman, Betty (ACW2) 32
Bowker, Wilfred (Pte) 70
Brands, Alexander (Lt KC) 109
Brisby, Francis (Dr) 148
Bromage, John Henry (Lt) RN 108–9

Brown, Albert (Pte) 173
Bulmer, Bertha 203
Burge, Marguerite 204, 208–9, 211, 213, 216
Burnett, Edward (Dr) 138
Byrne, Laurence Austin 35, 119

Carthew, Thomas W.C. (Lt Col.) 212–13
Casey, Terence (Pte) 11, 111–20, 148
Clarke, Thomas Patrick (Cpl) 128
Clayton, Walter (L/Cpl) 11, 60–7
Claxton, John Francis 26
Clyne, James Wilson (Dr) 116–17
Colaluca, Angelo 134
Coolin, William Southward (Maj.) 161
Coulton, Jane 68, 141–50
Courtenay, Edward Foran (Col. Sgt) 83
Cowlishaw, Frank 84
Crabtree, William 200, 203
Critchell, Henry v, 59
Cross, Stanley William v
Crowle, Samuel (Pte) 173
Culver, Norman John (Maj.) 96
Cummins, Gordon 8
Curtis, Constance Sybil 196
Cust, Arthur (Chief Cons.) 132
Cussen, Edward J.P. (Maj.) 109

Dallow, Samuel (Det. Sgt) 80–1, 84
D'Archambaud, Charles 134
D'Archambaud, Juliette 135
Darling, Edwin (Lt Col.) 156
Davidson, James 56, 193, 211

Davidson, John Gordon (Pte) 11, 121–32
Davidson, Robert 123
Davis, Arthur (Chief Insp.) 83
Davis, Elizabeth Violet 115
Deeley, Iris Miriam (ACW1) 29
Delasalle, Sidney (LAC) 8
Digby, Dawn 12, 15, 20–8
Digby, Doreen 14, 15, 20, 26, 28
Digby, Ernest Charles (Gnr) 8, 11–28
Donovan, John Francis (Pte) 196
Dorchester (Prison) 75, 77
Dorchester, Dorset 68–70, 72–3
Downie, William 123
Drury, Harry James (Det. Sgt) 55
Dumas, Roger (Pte) 212
Dunn, James Stephen (Insp.) 24–5

Evans, Arthur C.L. (Det. Con.) 206

Farley, Albert Edward 68, 71–3, 76
Fattah, Abdul (Cpl) 224, 226–7
Firth, James Brierley 129
Forget, Maurice (Maj.) 4, 211
Freeman, Harry (Prebendary) 27
Fynn, James (PC) 202

Gabbitas, Cyril (Pol. Sgt) 181
Gagliano (Gallian), Eileen 219, 221
Galvin, Jeannie 125–8, 132
Gardner, Eric (Dr) 172
Gauthier, Charles Eugene (Pte) 11,
    177–85
Gharbawi, Abdulla El 40–5
Gibbons, Freda 115
Gibbs, Edith 19–20, 24
Gilmour, James Gordon (2/Lt) 123, 132
Gilmour, Madge Gordon (née Sim) 123
Gilmour, Williejohn Oberlin (2/Lt) 123
Glasspool, James 207, 212
Golding, Muriel Lilian 53
Gordon, Horace Beresford (Pte) 11,
    186–96
Gough, Jethroe 161
Green, James Thomas (L/Cpl) 125
Greeno, Edward 'Ted' (Det. Insp.) 33–5,
    171–4, 176, 201–2

Gregson, Harry 52
Grice, Winnie 83
Grierson, Hugh 56, 73
Griffiths, Averina 153, 159–60
Griffiths, Lily 152–3, 155, 157, 159–60,
    162–3
Grossley, Anthony Howard 155, 163
Grossley, Joseph Howard (Bdr) 11,
    152–64
Gunning, Brian (Det. Con.) 191

Hall, Fred 200
Hanbrooke, Doreen Mary 193
Haveron, Robert (Cpl) 83
Hayes, Laurence (Tpr) 144
Haynes, Alan Arthur (Tpr) 22
Helfferich, Otto (Col. – Abwehr) 105–6
Hendy, Marion Alice 90, 93, 98
Herd, Ruby 128
Heys, Arthur (LAC) 8
Hill, John Denis Nelson (Dr) 118
Hill, Harold (Pte) 8
Hill, Olga Davy 13–28
Hillard, Richard A.L. (Maj.) 108
Hillman, Dorothy May (née Streeter)
    186, 190, 194–5
Hillman, Ronald 186, 191
Hirsch, Werner Paul (Dr) 81
Hodge, Fred (Det. Sgt) 171
Hodkinson, Robert (Dr) 158
Hotston, Roy (Home Guard) 181
Howard, Stephen Gerald (KC) 119
Howatson, Andrew (Flt Lt) 37
Hughes, Hector (KC) 57
Hughes, Thomas (PC) 206
Hyde, James (PC) 116

Jacques, Joyce 60–1, 63–5, 67
Jenner, William 85
Jennings, David Miller (Pte) 11, 68,
    70–7
Johnson, Cyril (Pte) 11, 51–9
Jones, Elizabeth 15
Jones, Glyn (KC) 161
Jones, Reginald Hastings (Dr) 54
Jury, Ronald 33

Kemp, Ernest James H. (Gnr) 11, 29–38
Kewell, William Kimberley (PC) 116
Kirk, Henry (Harry) v, 98
Koopman, Charles 8

Leat, Marie Adele (née Picquet) 90,
    93–4, 97
Leith, Frank (Cpl) 70–1
Lett, Gordon (Maj.) 107
Lewis, George Isaac 157
Lewis, Thomas (PC) 158
Lill, Harry (Pol. Sgt) 72
Lilycroft, William (Pte) 144
Logan, Harold Bishop (Dr) 93
Love, Gladys (ACW1) 205
Lyon, Kitty 78–85

McEwan, Mervin Clare (Pte) 11,
    197–203
McGinn, Frank (Det. Sgt) 127–8
McGregor, Margaret 32–4
Mansour, Abdel (Pte) 223–9
Marsh, Edward (Det. Sgt) 137
Marsh, Grace Emily 221–2
Marshall, Dorothy 20
Martineau, Edmund P.J. (Fus.) 176
Medlish, Hassan Naameh (Cpl) 11,
    39–49
Memory, Charles (Pol. Sgt) 34
Miller, Gladys Jane 115
Milton, Bridget Nora 112, 114–20
Mitchell, Beatrice (WPC) 95–6
Montague, Percival John (Maj. Gen.) 185
Moore, William (Mne) 165
Morris, Albert Edward (PC) 117
Morris, Herbert 38
Morrison, Herbert 37, 75, 98, 131, 175,
    185, 216
Mullins, Claude 118
Murch, Walter (Sgt) 72
Murdoch, James Hunter (Dr) 66

Naugler, Lawrence St Clair (Fus.) 176
Nelson, Charles (PC) 116
Neve, Eric 174, 181, 184
Newsam, Frank (Sir) 28, 38, 97, 215, 217

Nickolas, Thomas (PC) 158
Nolan, John (QMS – Home Guard) 185

O'Sullivan, Andrew 32

Packe, Michael St John (Maj.) 91
Page, Irene 100, 110
Paling, Gerald Richard (KC) 202
Palmer, Joseph (Rflmn) 113
Parkes, Edward Burdon (Dr) 96
Patry, Arthur (Pte) 208–15
Peach, Arthur (Pte) 11, 77–85
Pelling, Ralph 193
Pelling, Sam 193
Pepper, Annette E.F.C. (née Willard)
    177–85
Pepper, Philip Leonard (L/Cpl) 177–8
Perfect, Annie 201–3
Perfect, Arthur Basil 201
Phillips, Thomas v
Philpott, Arthur (Chief Insp.) 127
Pickering, George (Insp.) 93–4
Pierrepoint, Albert v, 6, 38, 67, 110, 120,
    140, 175, 185, 195
Pierrepoint, Thomas v, 28, 59, 75, 85, 98,
    131, 150, 163, 203
Platt, Arthur William (Lt) 23
Prior, Kenneth Charles Sydney (Gnr) 11,
    218–21

Quill, William James (Plt Off.) 31

Raymond, Charles Arthur (Pte) 11, 185,
    204, 207
Rayner, Dudley George (Cpl) 11, 133–40
Rayner (née Colaluca), Josephine (Pte)
    133–40
Rendall, William (Sgt) 179–80
Richards, John (Capt. – ALIAS) 102,
    104, 108, 109
Richards, Violet 79, 82–3, 85
Riley, Alex v, 75, 110, 131, 185
Riley, Joseph Gerard (Pte) 70
Roberts, Geoffrey (KC) 95
Rutherford, John 74, 76
Ruxton, Buck (Dr) 149

Sadler, Arthur C. (LAC) 190
Sangret, August (Pte) 11, 83, 165–76
Savage, Ernest (Supt) 206
Scarisbrick, Martha 128
Schurch Theodore John William (Pte) 11, 99–110
Scott-Barrett, Hugh (Revd Brig.) 46, 230
Sells, Peter (Pte) 83
Shearer, Alexander Marshall (Pte) 176
Simpson, Keith (Dr) 118, 172, 174, 194
Smail, Daisy 51–9
Smail, Maggie 51–9
Smith, Charles (Pol. Sgt) 82
Souleiman, Mohamed M. (Pte) 11, 223–30
Speck, Arthur James 157
Spillsbury, Bernard (Sir) 211
Stegmann, Rose 161
Stevenson, Melford (Maj.) 108
Stones, Barbara 62
Storr, Edward (Det. Sgt) 191
Stranks, Charles James (Revd) 67
Streatfeild, Geoffrey H.B. 145–6
Sutherland, Peter Lindsay (Prof.) 202
Sutton, Ralph (KC) 161

Taylor, Gerald Osbrey (Dr) 73
Taylor, William 115
Thompson, Arthur (Pte) 11, 141–51

Thorne, Kathleen Maude 72
Thurley (Digby), Violet 13
Torkington, James (Pte) 70
Trabi, Hussein Mohamed Ali (Pte) 39
Trapnell, John (KC) 95
Turner, Mark 68, 197–203
Tyrrell, Phillip Watson 114

Wade, Stephen v, 6, 140, 163, 203, 216
Walton, John (ARP) 115
Ward, Vera 55
Wardrope, Annie 123–4
Warren, Dorothy 77
Warwick, Charles Kay (Dr) 206
Weaver, Lionel Hunter (ARP) 115
Webb, Margaret Edith 178
Webb, Ronald Hill 178
Webber, Horace Raymond (AC1) 205
Webster, James Mathewson (Prof.) 25, 28, 82, 96
Weir, Hugh (Capt) 206
Wells, Charles 166
Wells, Joseph John (Pte) 176
Widdicombe, John (Det. Insp.) 206
Wilson, Hannah Jane 150–1
Wilson, Henry Maitland (Gen.) 46, 230
Wolfe, Edith 166, 173
Wolfe, Joan Pearl 165–6, 170–1, 175
Wood, Lesley John 166